THE SCOURGING OF SHU-TORUN

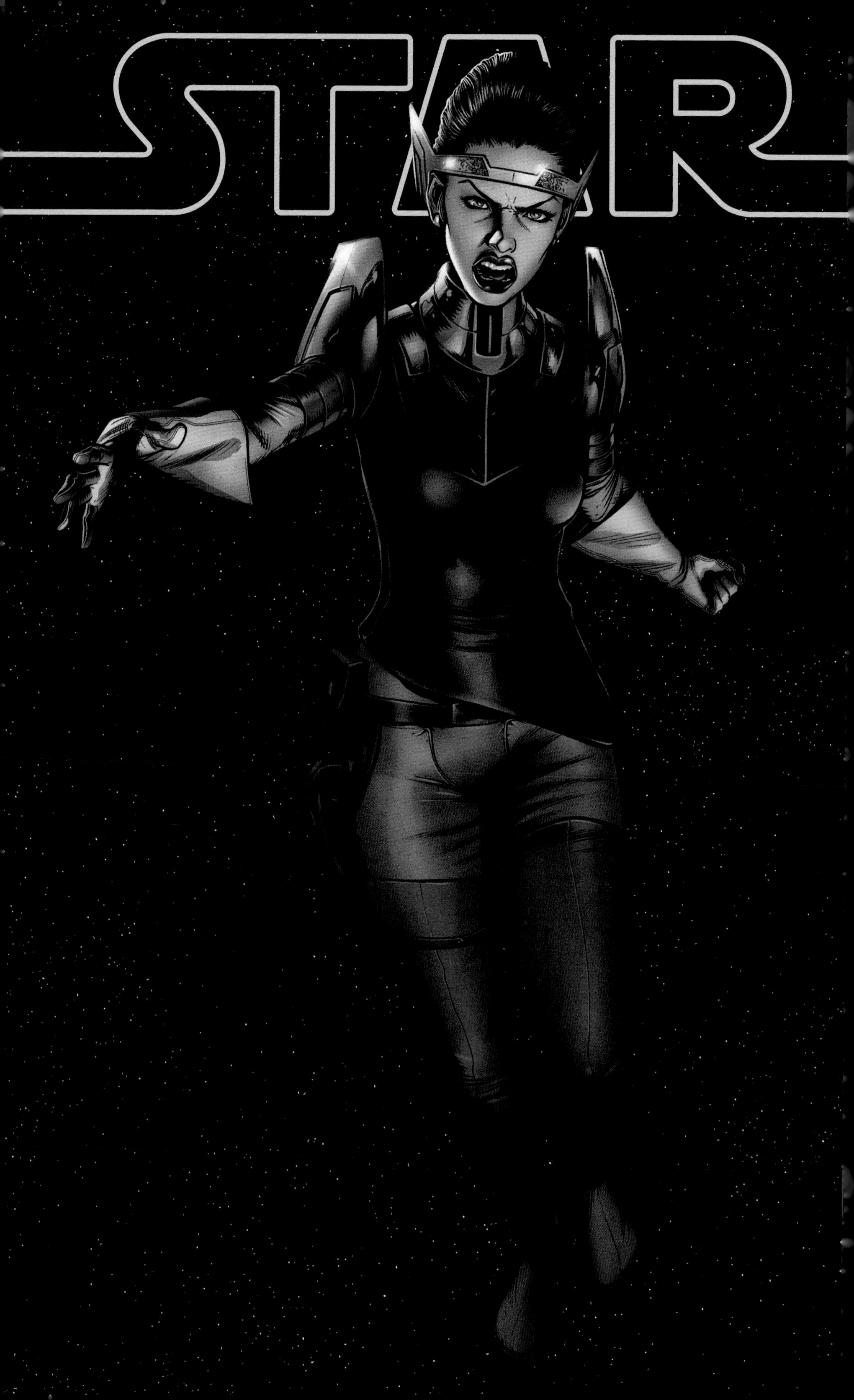
STAR

WARS ™

THE SCOURGING OF SHU-TORUN

Writer	**KIERON GILLEN**
Artists	**ANDREA BROCCARDO** (#62) &
	ANGEL UNZUETA (#63-67)
Color Artist	**GURU-eFX**
Letterer	**VC's CLAYTON COWLES**
Cover Art	**GERALD PAREL**
Assistant Editor	**TOM GRONEMAN**
Editor	**MARK PANICCIA**
Editor in Chief	**C.B. CEBULSKI**
Chief Creative Officer	**JOE QUESADA**
President	**DAN BUCKLEY**

For Lucasfilm:

Assistant Editor	**BEATRICE KILAT**
Senior Editor	**ROBERT SIMPSON**
Creative Director	**MICHAEL SIGLAIN**
Lucasfilm Story Group	**JAMES WAUGH, LELAND CHEE,**
	MATT MARTIN
Lucasfilm Art Department	**PHIL SZOSTAK**

Collection Editor	**JENNIFER GRÜNWALD**	VP Production & Special Projects	**JEFF YOUNGQUIST**
Assistant Editor	**CAITLIN O'CONNELL**	SVP Print, Sales & Marketing	**DAVID GABRIEL**
Associate Managing Editor	**KATERI WOODY**	Director, Licensed Publishing	**SVEN LARSEN**
Editor, Special Projects	**MARK D. BEAZLEY**	Book Designer	**ADAM DEL RE**

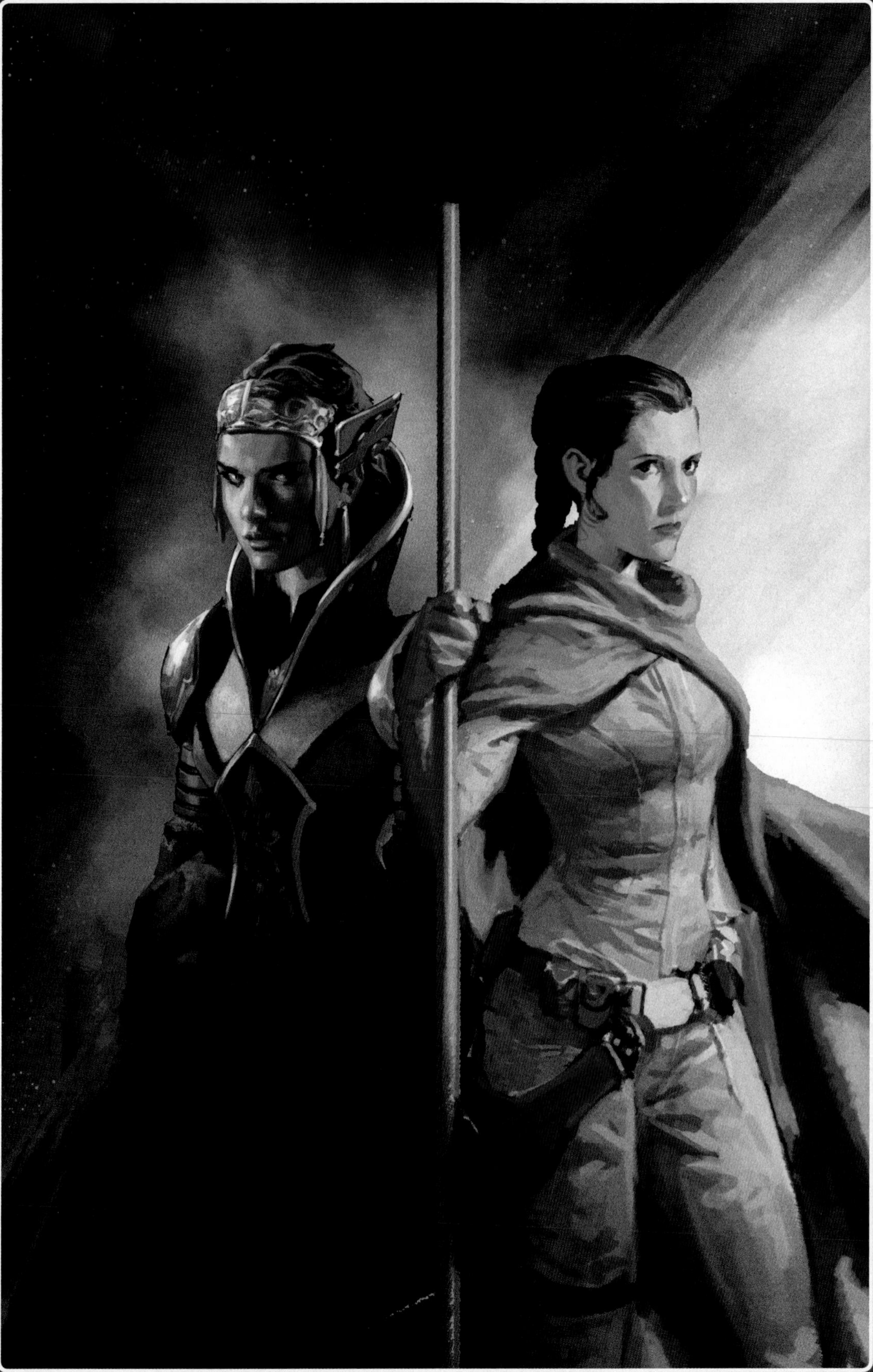

THE SCOURGING OF SHU-TORUN

Queen Trios of Shu-Torun's betrayal allowed the evil Galactic Empire to launch a surprise attack against the Rebel Alliance's fleet, scattering the rebels and nearly crushing their heroic cause once and for all.

Princess Leia Organa, Jedi-in-training Luke Skywalker and smuggler Han Solo narrowly escaped the assault and reunited with the Alliance thanks to the aid of new allies.

Now, Leia has a score to settle with the Empire—and with Queen Trios. . . .

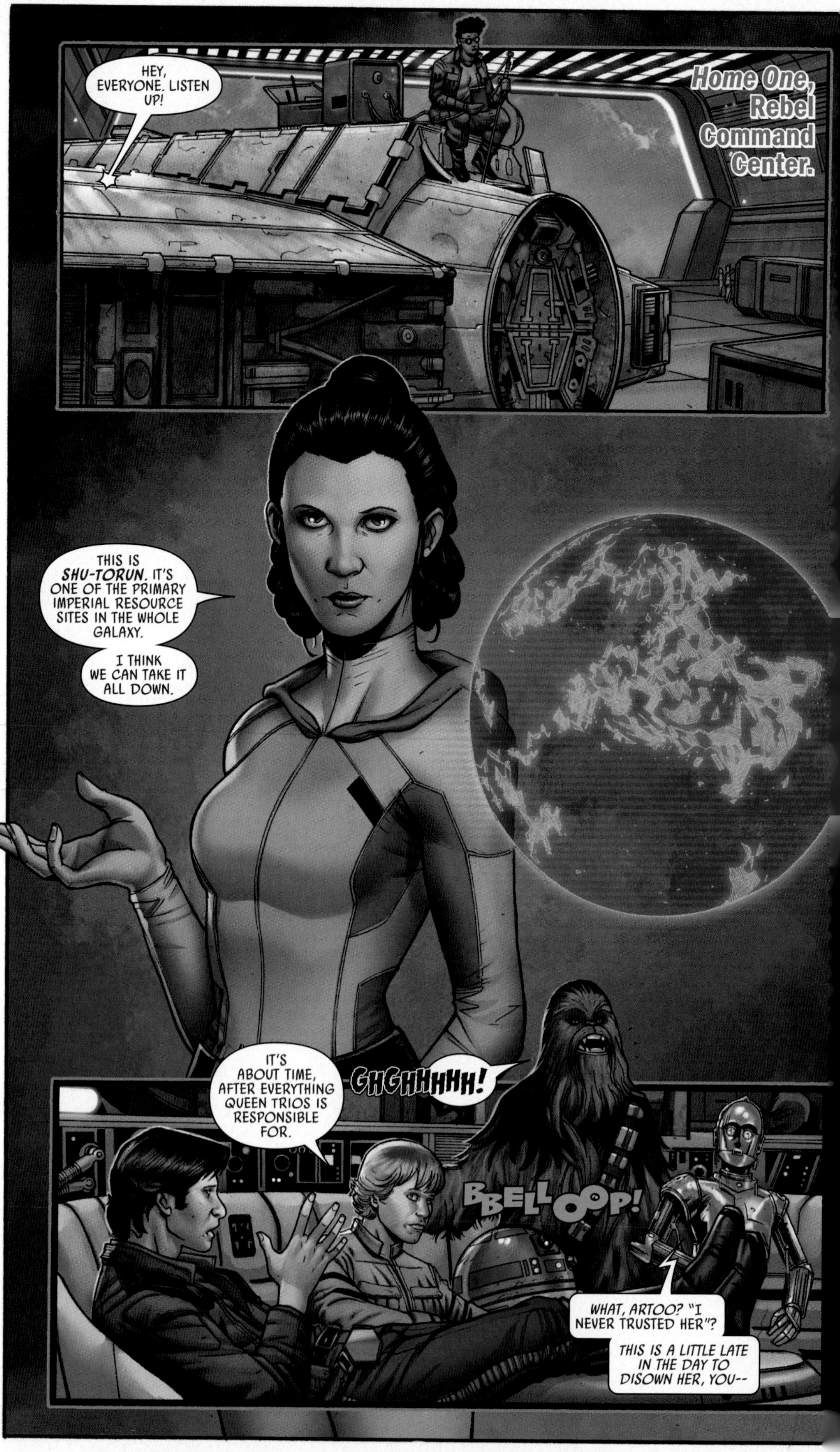
Home One, Rebel Command Center.
HEY, EVERYONE. LISTEN UP!
THIS IS SHU-TORUN. IT'S ONE OF THE PRIMARY IMPERIAL RESOURCE SITES IN THE WHOLE GALAXY.
I THINK WE CAN TAKE IT ALL DOWN.
IT'S ABOUT TIME, AFTER EVERYTHING QUEEN TRIOS IS RESPONSIBLE FOR.
GHGHHHHH!
BBELLOOP!
WHAT, ARTOO? "I NEVER TRUSTED HER"?
THIS IS A LITTLE LATE IN THE DAY TO DISOWN HER, YOU--

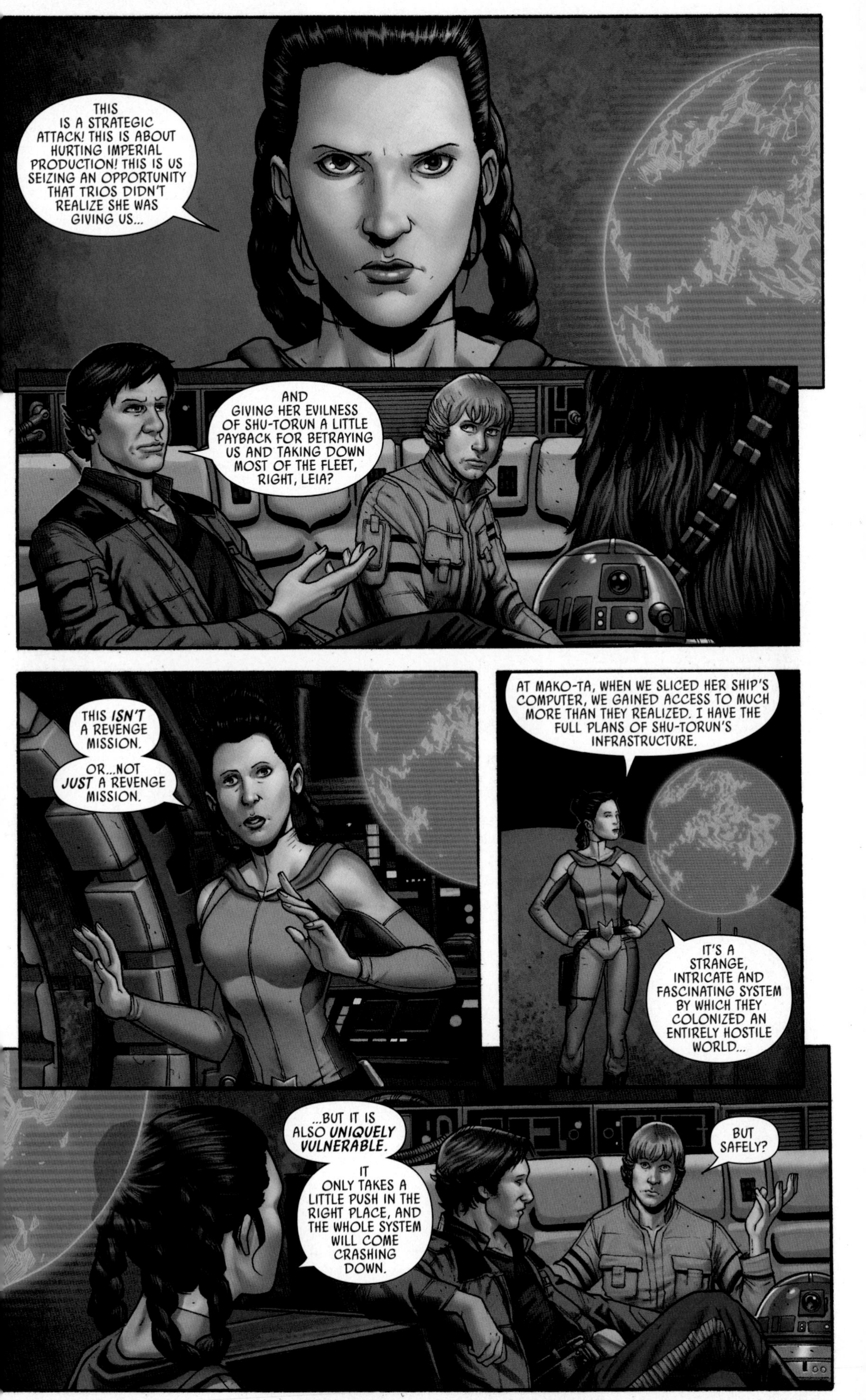
THIS IS A STRATEGIC ATTACK! THIS IS ABOUT HURTING IMPERIAL PRODUCTION! THIS IS US SEIZING AN OPPORTUNITY THAT TRIOS DIDN'T REALIZE SHE WAS GIVING US...
AND GIVING HER EVILNESS OF SHU-TORUN A LITTLE PAYBACK FOR BETRAYING US AND TAKING DOWN MOST OF THE FLEET, RIGHT, LEIA?
THIS *ISN'T* A REVENGE MISSION.
OR...NOT *JUST* A REVENGE MISSION.
AT MAKO-TA, WHEN WE SLICED HER SHIP'S COMPUTER, WE GAINED ACCESS TO MUCH MORE THAN THEY REALIZED. I HAVE THE FULL PLANS OF SHU-TORUN'S INFRASTRUCTURE.
IT'S A STRANGE, INTRICATE AND FASCINATING SYSTEM BY WHICH THEY COLONIZED AN ENTIRELY HOSTILE WORLD...
...BUT IT IS ALSO ***UNIQUELY VULNERABLE***.
IT ONLY TAKES A LITTLE PUSH IN THE RIGHT PLACE, AND THE WHOLE SYSTEM WILL COME CRASHING DOWN.
BUT SAFELY?

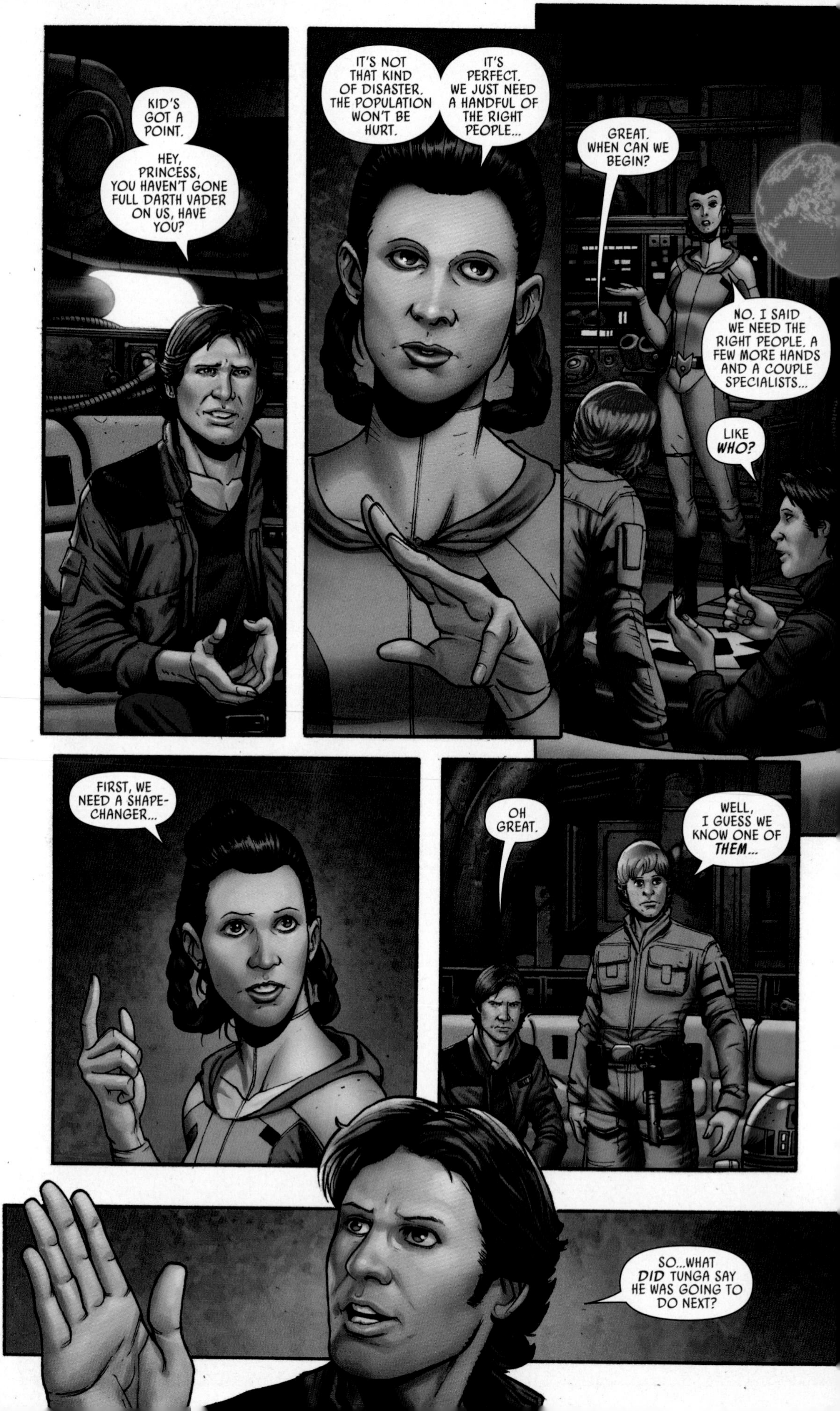
KID'S GOT A POINT.
HEY, PRINCESS, YOU HAVEN'T GONE FULL DARTH VADER ON US, HAVE YOU?
IT'S NOT THAT KIND OF DISASTER. THE POPULATION WON'T BE HURT.
IT'S PERFECT. WE JUST NEED A HANDFUL OF THE RIGHT PEOPLE...
GREAT. WHEN CAN WE BEGIN?
NO. I SAID WE NEED THE RIGHT PEOPLE. A FEW MORE HANDS AND A COUPLE SPECIALISTS...
LIKE WHO?
FIRST, WE NEED A SHAPE-CHANGER...
OH GREAT.
WELL, I GUESS WE KNOW ONE OF THEM...
SO...WHAT DID TUNGA SAY HE WAS GOING TO DO NEXT?

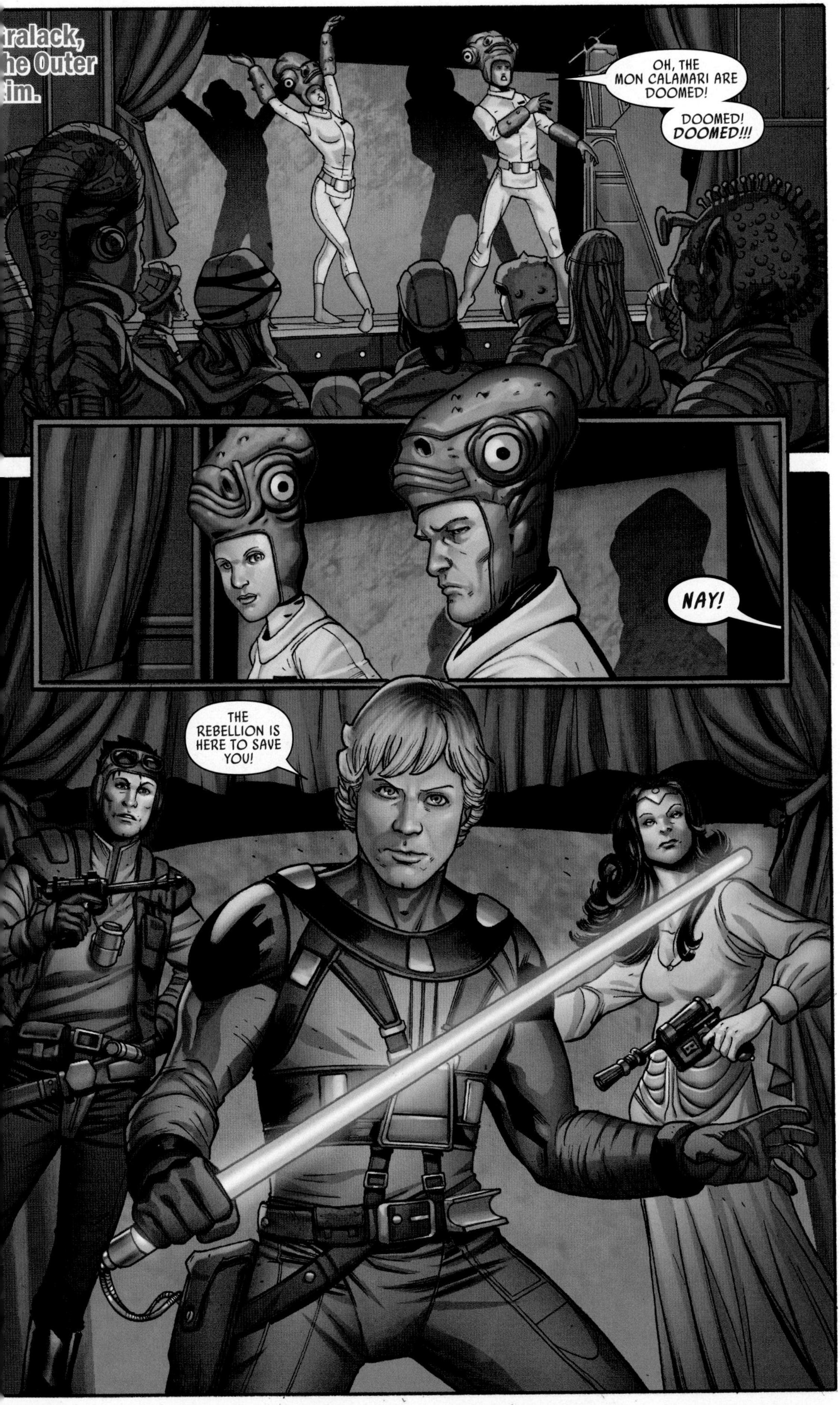

ralack,
he Outer
im.
OH, THE MON CALAMARI ARE DOOMED!
DOOMED! DOOMED!!!
NAY!
THE REBELLION IS HERE TO SAVE YOU!

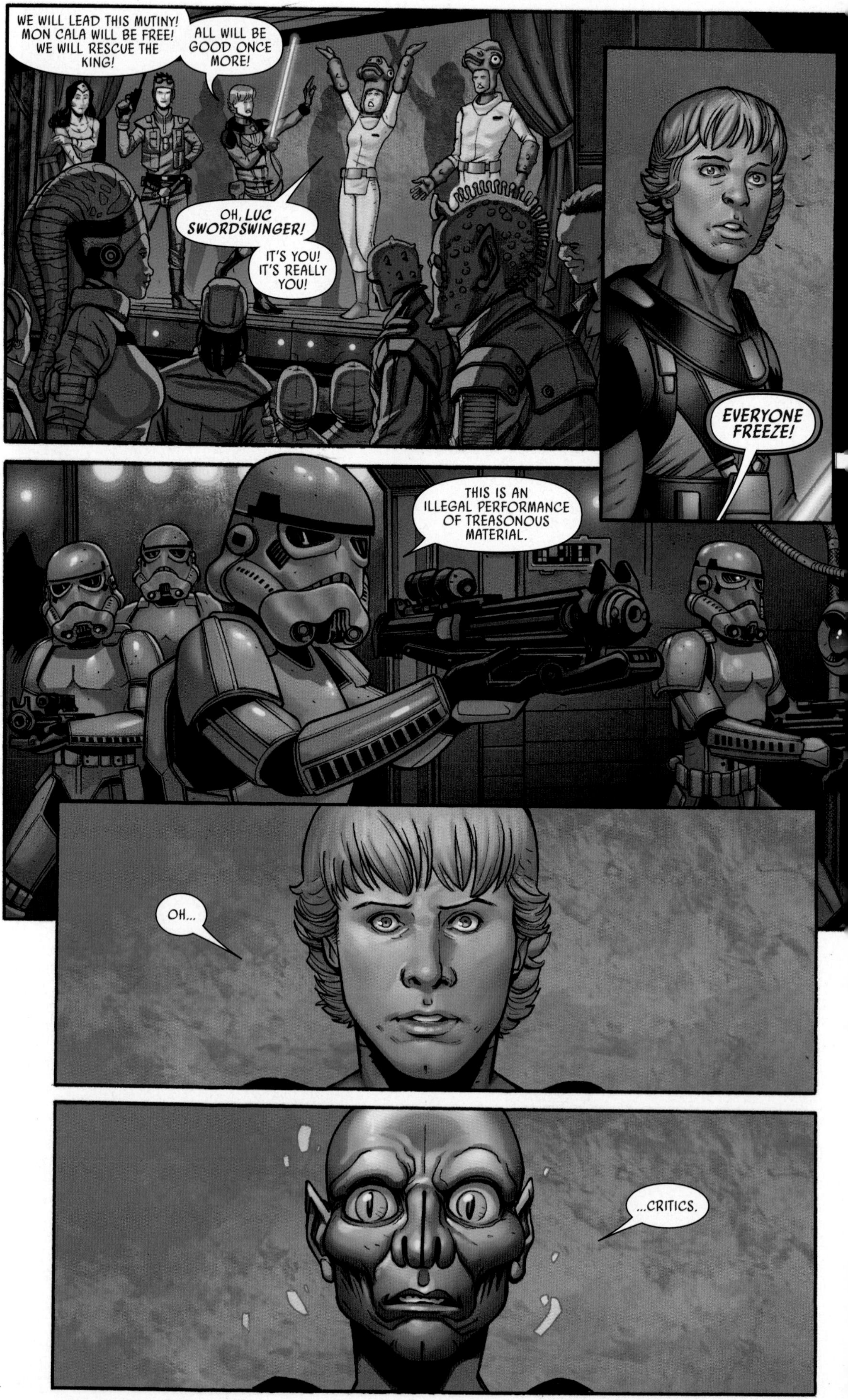
WE WILL LEAD THIS MUTINY! MON CALA WILL BE FREE! WE WILL RESCUE THE KING!
ALL WILL BE GOOD ONCE MORE!
OH, LUC SWORDSWINGER!
IT'S YOU! IT'S REALLY YOU!
EVERYONE FREEZE!
THIS IS AN ILLEGAL PERFORMANCE OF TREASONOUS MATERIAL.
OH...
...CRITICS.

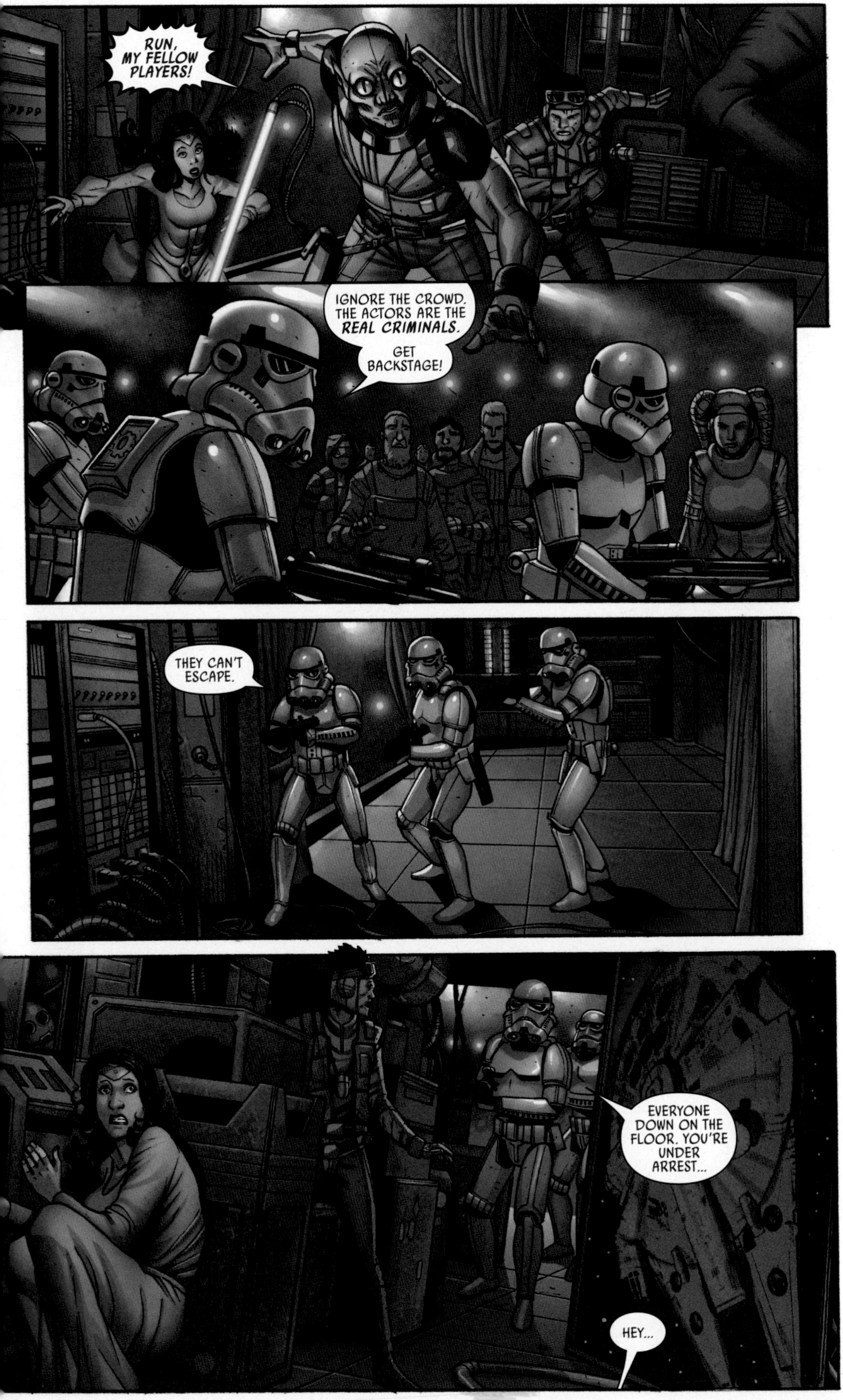
RUN, MY FELLOW PLAYERS!
IGNORE THE CROWD. THE ACTORS ARE THE REAL CRIMINALS.
GET BACKSTAGE!
THEY CAN'T ESCAPE.
EVERYONE DOWN ON THE FLOOR. YOU'RE UNDER ARREST...
HEY...

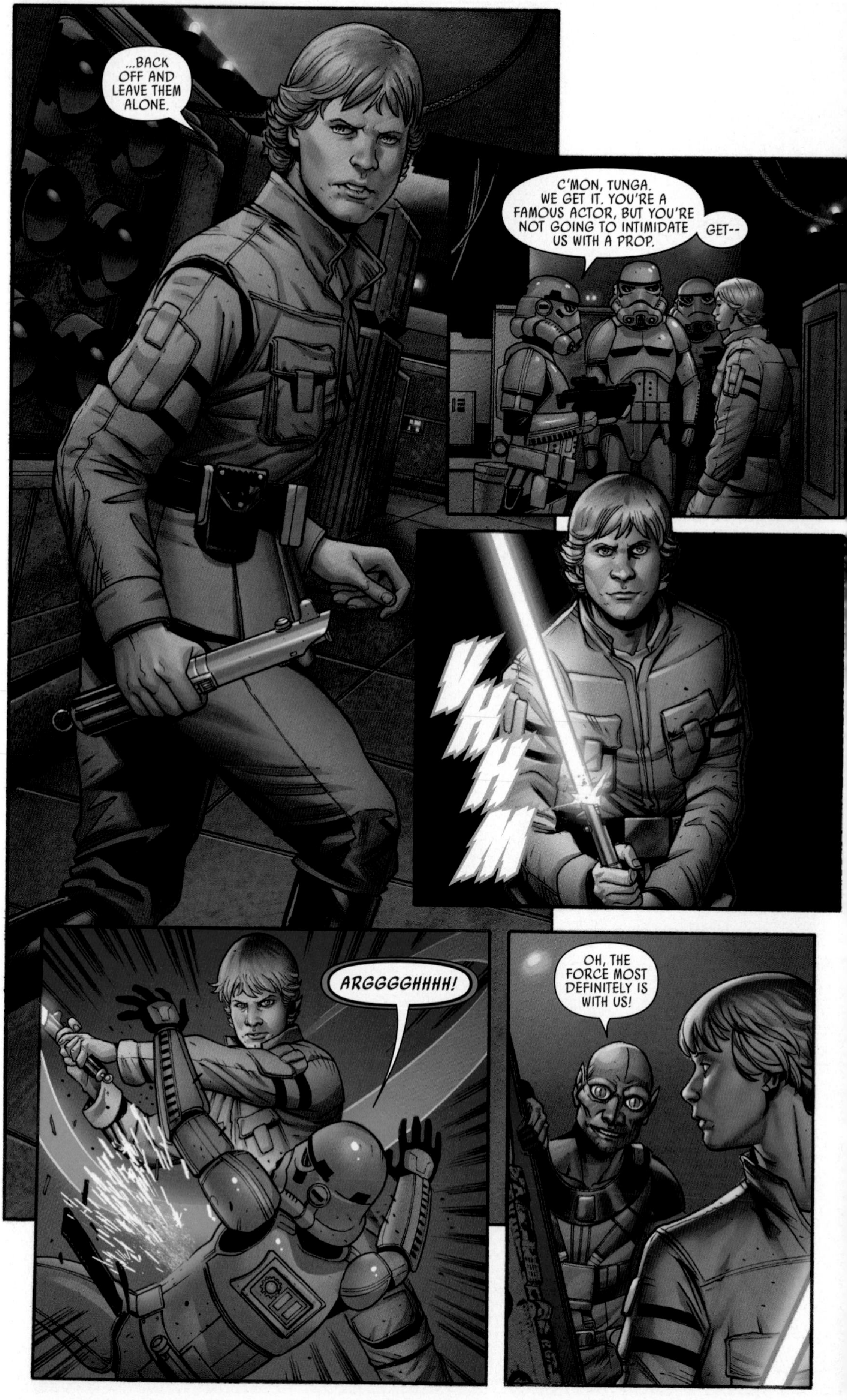
...BACK OFF AND LEAVE THEM ALONE.
C'MON, TUNGA. WE GET IT. YOU'RE A FAMOUS ACTOR, BUT YOU'RE NOT GOING TO INTIMIDATE US WITH A PROP.
GET--
VHHHM
ARGGGGHHHH!
OH, THE FORCE MOST DEFINITELY IS WITH US!

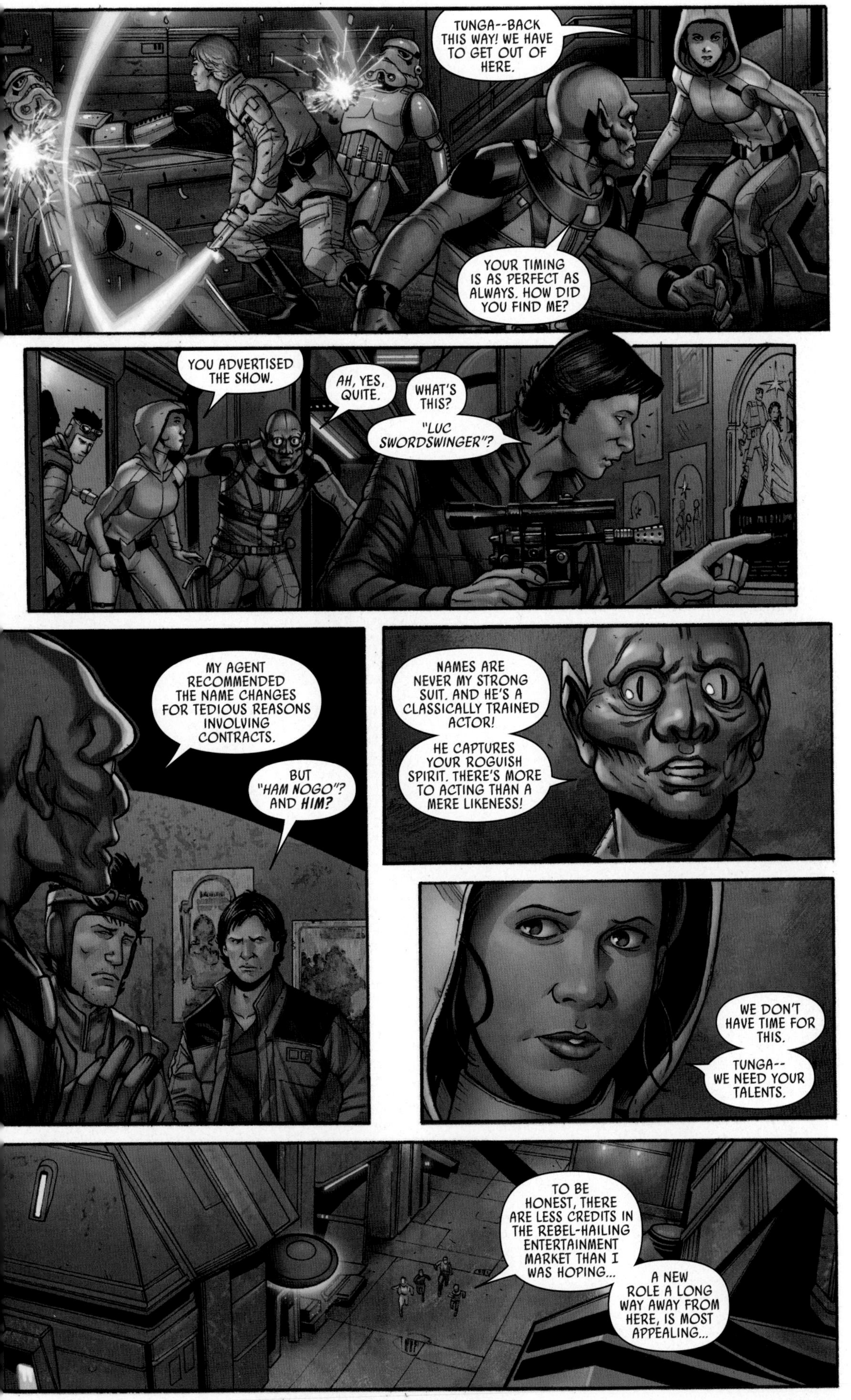
TUNGA--BACK THIS WAY! WE HAVE TO GET OUT OF HERE.
YOUR TIMING IS AS PERFECT AS ALWAYS. HOW DID YOU FIND ME?
YOU ADVERTISED THE SHOW.
AH, YES, QUITE.
WHAT'S THIS?
"LUC SWORDSWINGER"?
MY AGENT RECOMMENDED THE NAME CHANGES FOR TEDIOUS REASONS INVOLVING CONTRACTS.
BUT "HAM NOGO"? AND HIM?
NAMES ARE NEVER MY STRONG SUIT. AND HE'S A CLASSICALLY TRAINED ACTOR!
HE CAPTURES YOUR ROGUISH SPIRIT. THERE'S MORE TO ACTING THAN A MERE LIKENESS!
WE DON'T HAVE TIME FOR THIS.
TUNGA-- WE NEED YOUR TALENTS.
TO BE HONEST, THERE ARE LESS CREDITS IN THE REBEL-HAILING ENTERTAINMENT MARKET THAN I WAS HOPING...
A NEW ROLE A LONG WAY AWAY FROM HERE, IS MOST APPEALING...

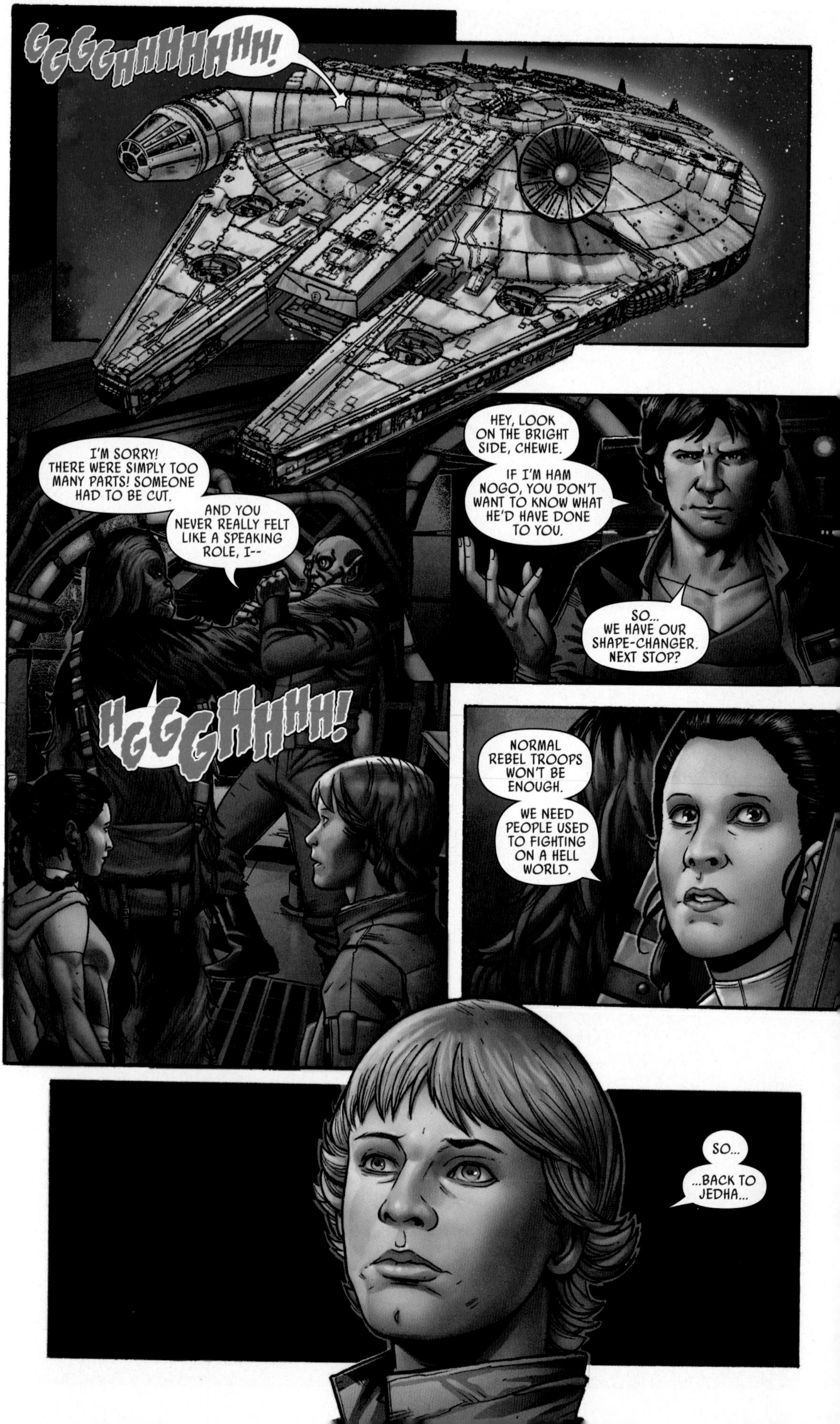
GGGGHHHHHHH!
I'M SORRY! THERE WERE SIMPLY TOO MANY PARTS! SOMEONE HAD TO BE CUT.
AND YOU NEVER REALLY FELT LIKE A SPEAKING ROLE, I--
HGGGHHHHH!
HEY, LOOK ON THE BRIGHT SIDE, CHEWIE.
IF I'M HAM NOGO, YOU DON'T WANT TO KNOW WHAT HE'D HAVE DONE TO YOU.
SO... WE HAVE OUR SHAPE-CHANGER. NEXT STOP?
NORMAL REBEL TROOPS WON'T BE ENOUGH.
WE NEED PEOPLE USED TO FIGHTING ON A HELL WORLD.
SO...
...BACK TO JEDHA...

Jedha.

THEY'RE OUT THERE!

WE'VE GOT TO GET CLEAR WITH THE SHIPMENT!

WAIT-- MOVEMENT! ON THE RIDGE TO THE SOUTH!

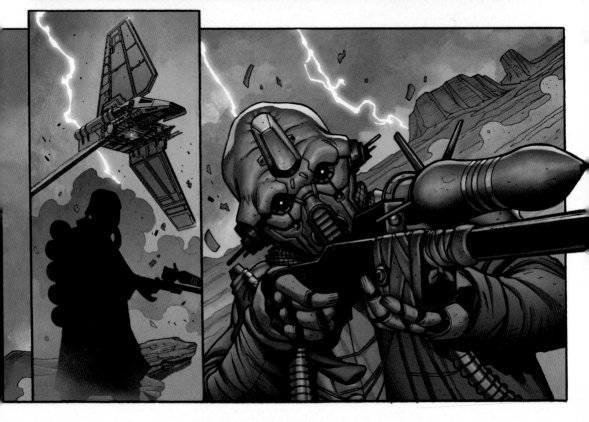

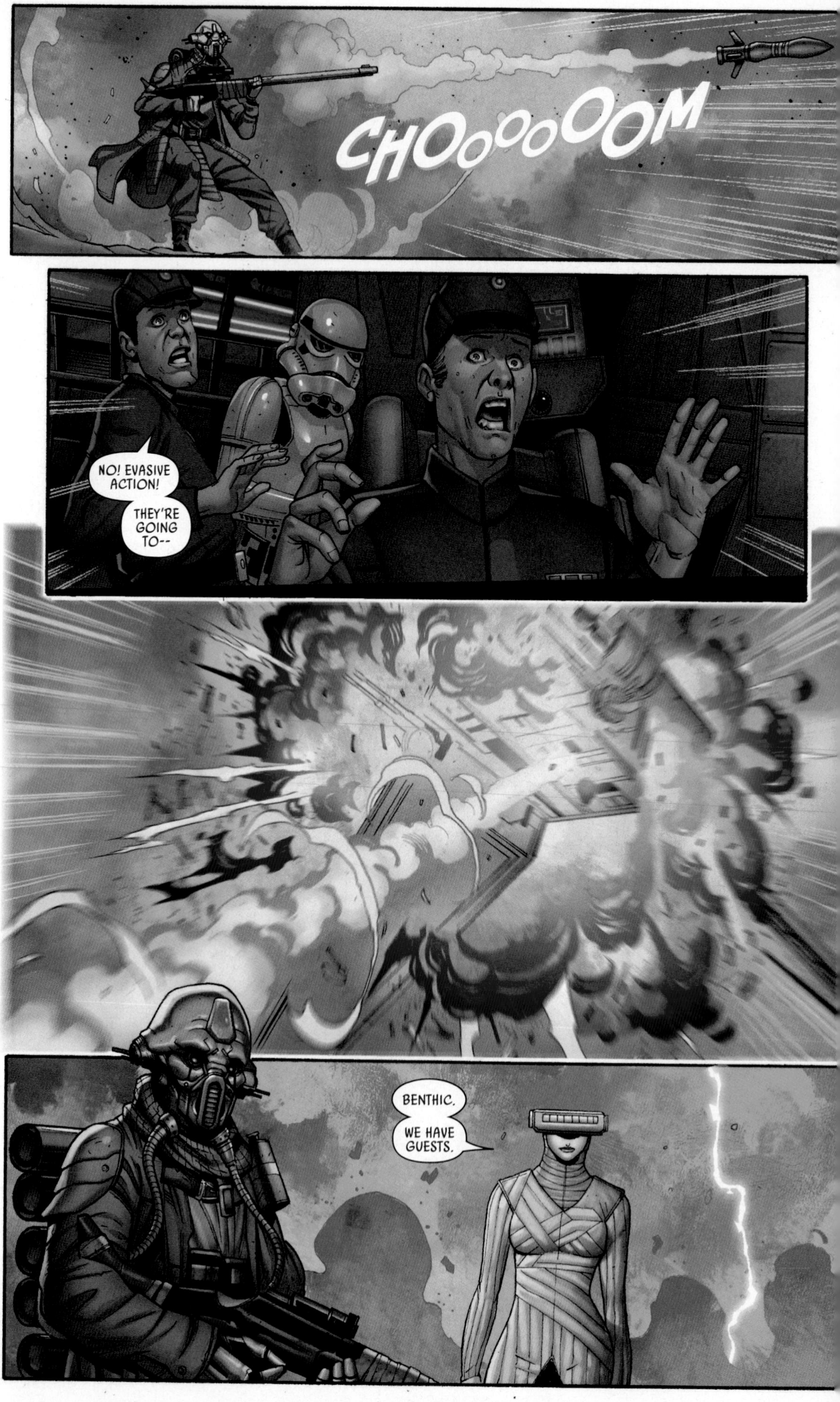
CHOOOOOOM
NO! EVASIVE ACTION!
THEY'RE GOING TO--
BENTHIC.
WE HAVE GUESTS.

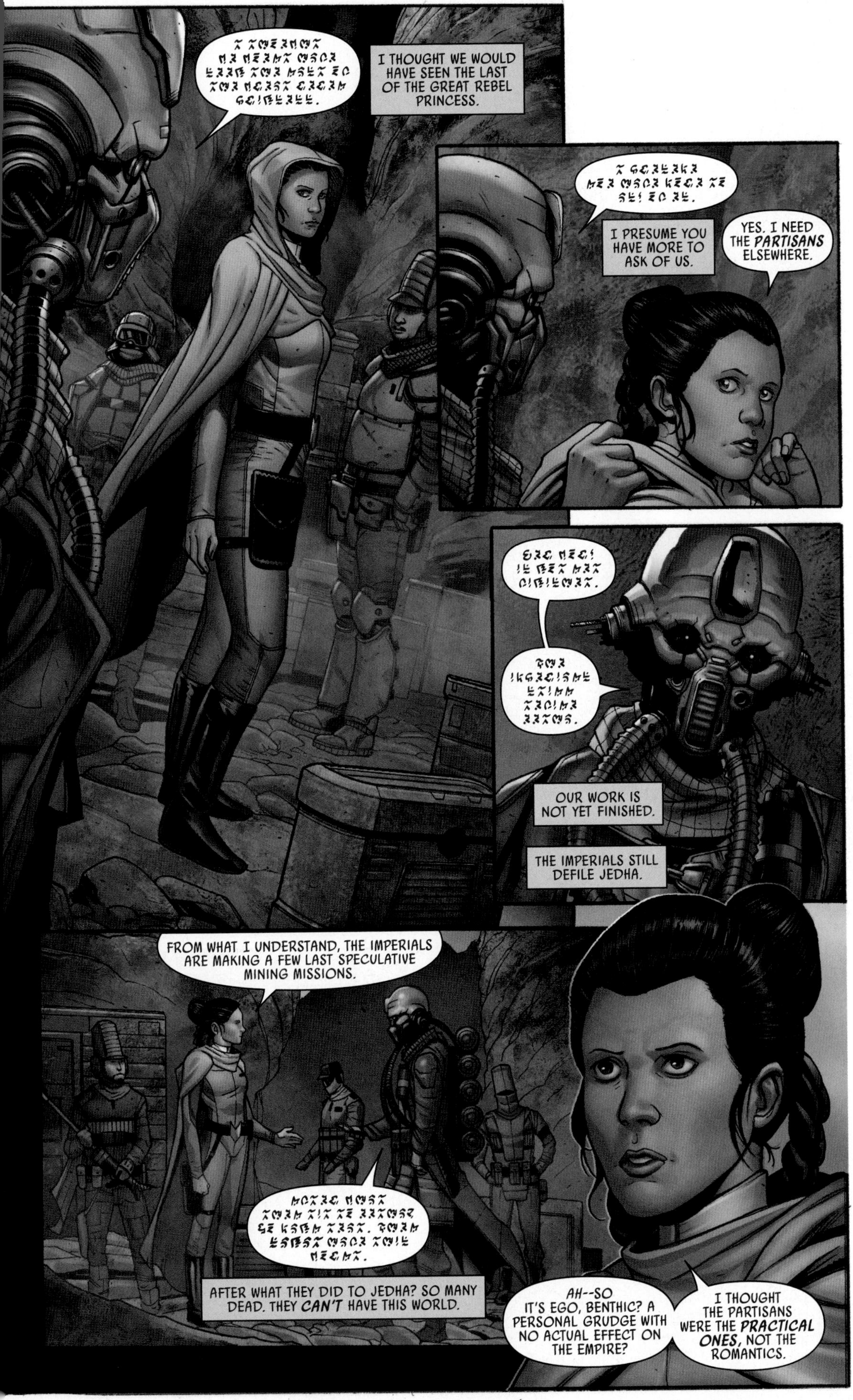
I THOUGHT WE WOULD HAVE SEEN THE LAST OF THE GREAT REBEL PRINCESS.
I PRESUME YOU HAVE MORE TO ASK OF US.
YES. I NEED THE PARTISANS ELSEWHERE.
OUR WORK IS NOT YET FINISHED.
THE IMPERIALS STILL DEFILE JEDHA.
FROM WHAT I UNDERSTAND, THE IMPERIALS ARE MAKING A FEW LAST SPECULATIVE MINING MISSIONS.
AFTER WHAT THEY DID TO JEDHA? SO MANY DEAD. THEY CAN'T HAVE THIS WORLD.
AH--SO IT'S EGO, BENTHIC? A PERSONAL GRUDGE WITH NO ACTUAL EFFECT ON THE EMPIRE?
I THOUGHT THE PARTISANS WERE THE PRACTICAL ONES, NOT THE ROMANTICS.

ᛁᛒᛖᛃᛗᚦᛁᛖᚻ ᚨᛖ. ᛋᚻᛖᛖ ᛒᛖᚦ ᚷᛟᛋᛖᚦᛁᛖᛋ.

INSULTING US. *ALSO* NOT PRACTICAL.

YOU STAY HERE, AND YOU DENY THE EMPEROR *TRINKETS.*

YOU COME WITH *ME,* YOU DENY THEM THE RICHES OF A *WHOLE WORLD.*

SHHH-K

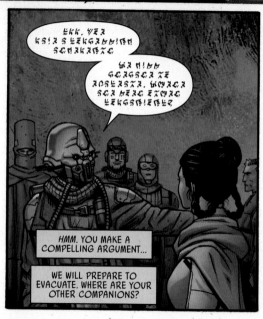

ᛖᚦᚦ, ᚢᛖᚹ ᚲᛋᛁᚨ ᛋ ᛖᛖᚲᛗᛃᛗᛁᛖᚻ ᛋᛟᛗᚨᚲᛁᛖᛏᛟ

ᚹᚨ ᚻᛁᛗᛗ ᚷᛟᚨᚷᛋᛟᚨ ᛏᛖ ᚨᛟᛋᛖᚨᛋᛏᚨ. ᚻᛟᚢᛟᚨ ᛋᛟᚨ ᛗᛖᚨᚷ ᛖᛏᚹᛟᚷ ᛖᛖᚲᛋᚨᛒᛁᛖᛒᛖᛏ

HMM. YOU MAKE A COMPELLING ARGUMENT...

WE WILL PREPARE TO EVACUATE. WHERE ARE YOUR OTHER COMPANIONS?

LUKE...HAD *OTHER BUSINESS* HERE.

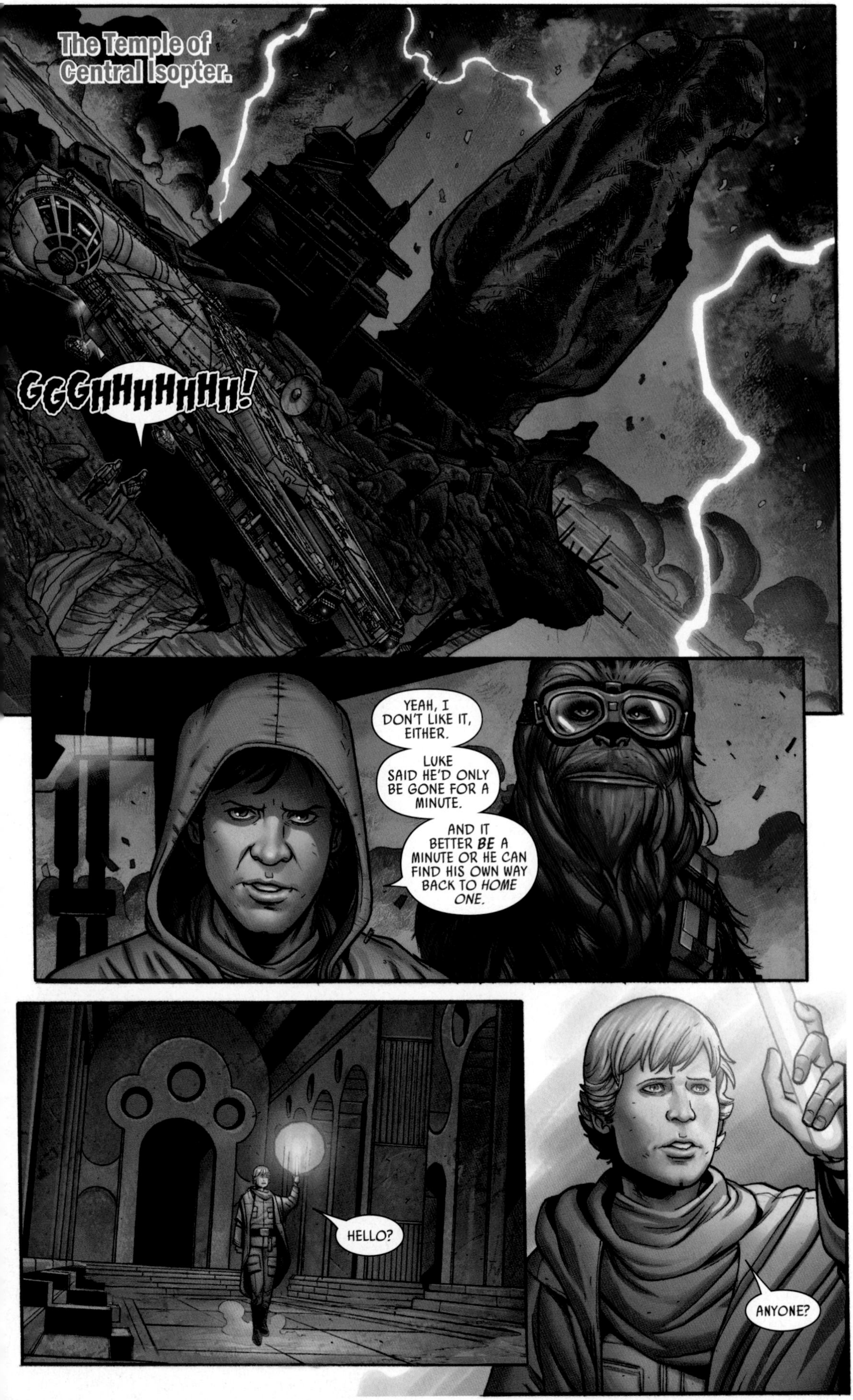
The Temple of Central Isopter.
GGGHHHHHHH!
YEAH, I DON'T LIKE IT, EITHER.
LUKE SAID HE'D ONLY BE GONE FOR A MINUTE.
AND IT BETTER BE A MINUTE OR HE CAN FIND HIS OWN WAY BACK TO HOME ONE.
HELLO?
ANYONE?

THE PLACE IS DESERTED.

THE CULT OF CENTRAL ISOPTER IS GONE.

WHO CAN BLAME THEM? THE ONLY PEOPLE LEFT ON THIS DYING DUSTBALL ARE THE IMPERIALS DUMB ENOUGH TO TRY MINING IT AND THE PARTISANS DUMB ENOUGH TO TRY AND STOP THEM.

OF COURSE THEY'RE GONE! AND WE SHOULD BE TOO!

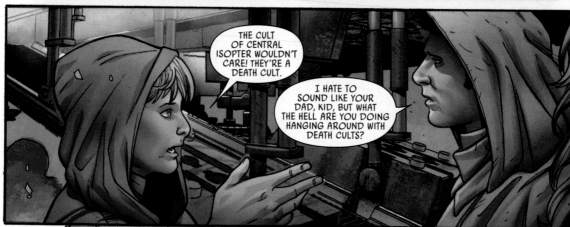

THE CULT OF CENTRAL ISOPTER WOULDN'T CARE! THEY'RE A DEATH CULT.

I HATE TO SOUND LIKE YOUR DAD, KID, BUT WHAT THE HELL ARE YOU DOING HANGING AROUND WITH DEATH CULTS?

THEY WERE...WARPED, BUT THEY DID TRY TO TEACH ME ABOUT THE DANGERS OF THE FORCE. IT ALMOST CONSUMED ME. IT DID CONSUME MY FRIEND.

I WAS THINKING OF HOW ANGRY I AM AT TRIOS AND WANTED THEIR ADVICE AND... WELL, THEY'RE GONE!

THEY HUNT DISASTERS TO WITNESS THEM. THEY THINK IT'S ALL PART OF THE FORCE.

THE WORLD IS STILL HERE AND DYING. THIS IS WHAT THEY LIVE FOR...

...I CAN'T SEE WHY THEY'D LEAVE NOW.

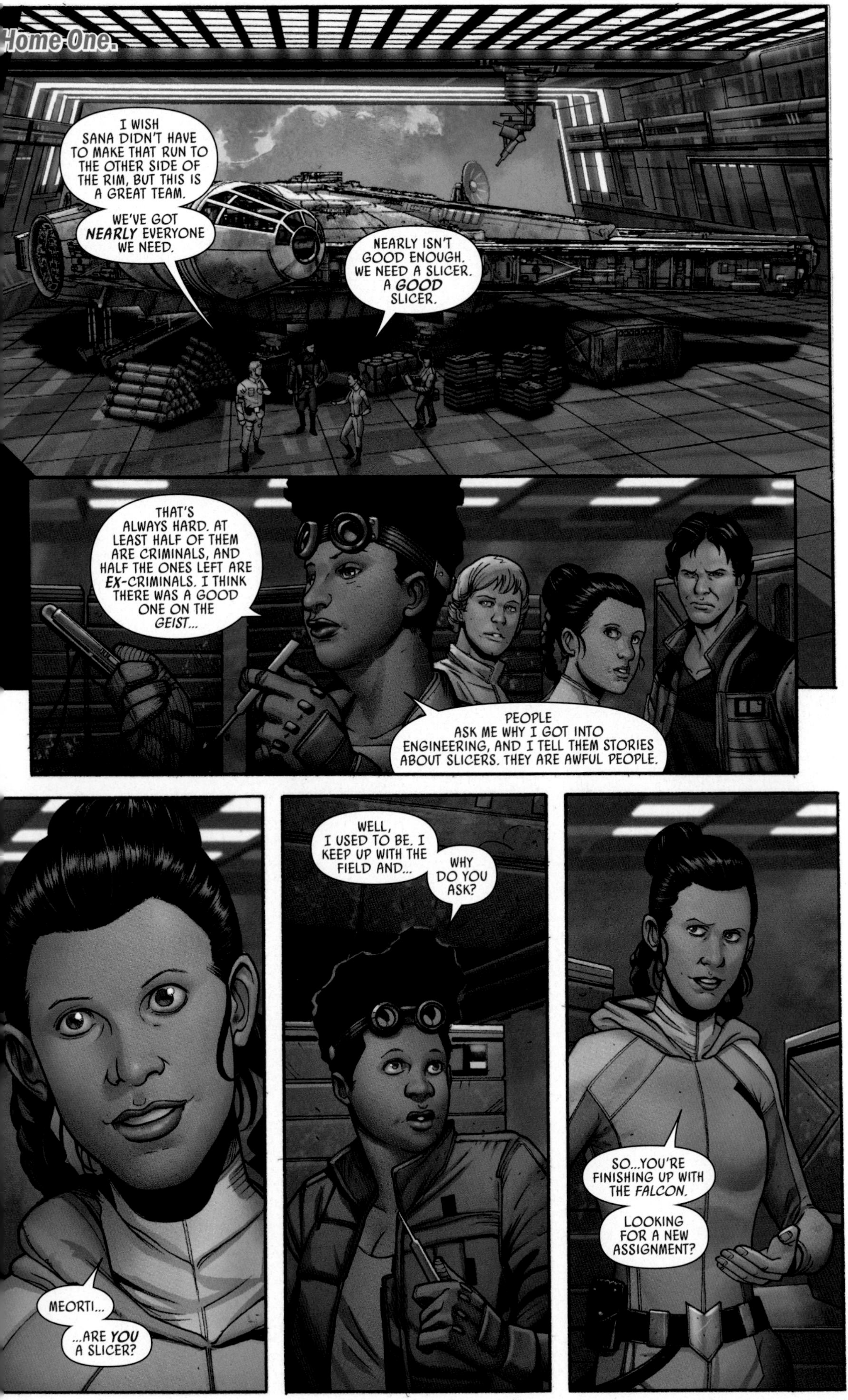
Home One.
I WISH SANA DIDN'T HAVE TO MAKE THAT RUN TO THE OTHER SIDE OF THE RIM, BUT THIS IS A GREAT TEAM.
WE'VE GOT NEARLY EVERYONE WE NEED.
NEARLY ISN'T GOOD ENOUGH. WE NEED A SLICER. A GOOD SLICER.
THAT'S ALWAYS HARD. AT LEAST HALF OF THEM ARE CRIMINALS, AND HALF THE ONES LEFT ARE EX-CRIMINALS. I THINK THERE WAS A GOOD ONE ON THE GEIST...
PEOPLE ASK ME WHY I GOT INTO ENGINEERING, AND I TELL THEM STORIES ABOUT SLICERS. THEY ARE AWFUL PEOPLE.
MEORTI...
...ARE YOU A SLICER?
WELL, I USED TO BE. I KEEP UP WITH THE FIELD AND...
WHY DO YOU ASK?
SO...YOU'RE FINISHING UP WITH THE FALCON.
LOOKING FOR A NEW ASSIGNMENT?

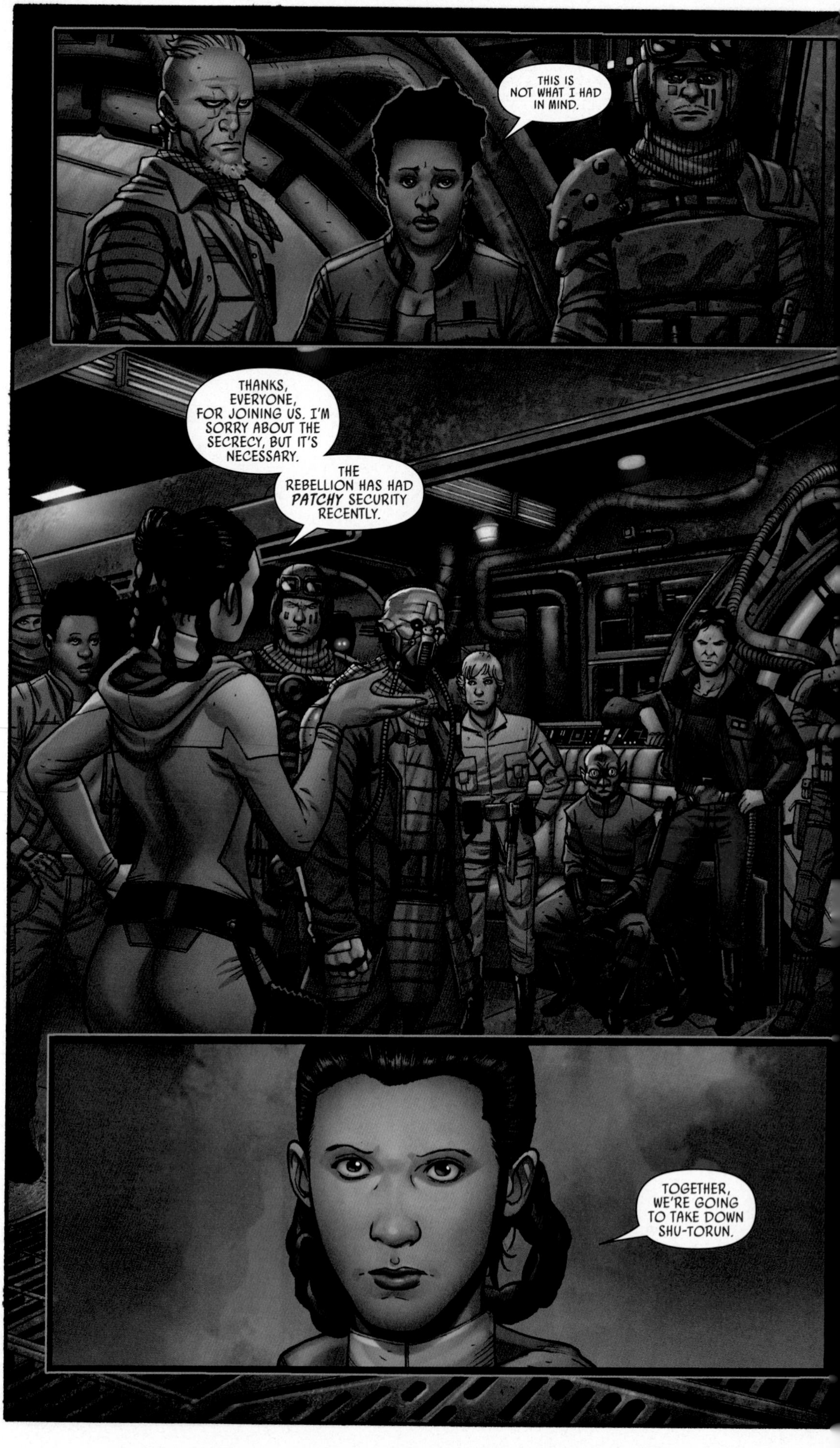
THIS IS NOT WHAT I HAD IN MIND.
THANKS, EVERYONE, FOR JOINING US. I'M SORRY ABOUT THE SECRECY, BUT IT'S NECESSARY.
THE REBELLION HAS HAD *PATCHY* SECURITY RECENTLY.
TOGETHER, WE'RE GOING TO TAKE DOWN SHU-TORUN.

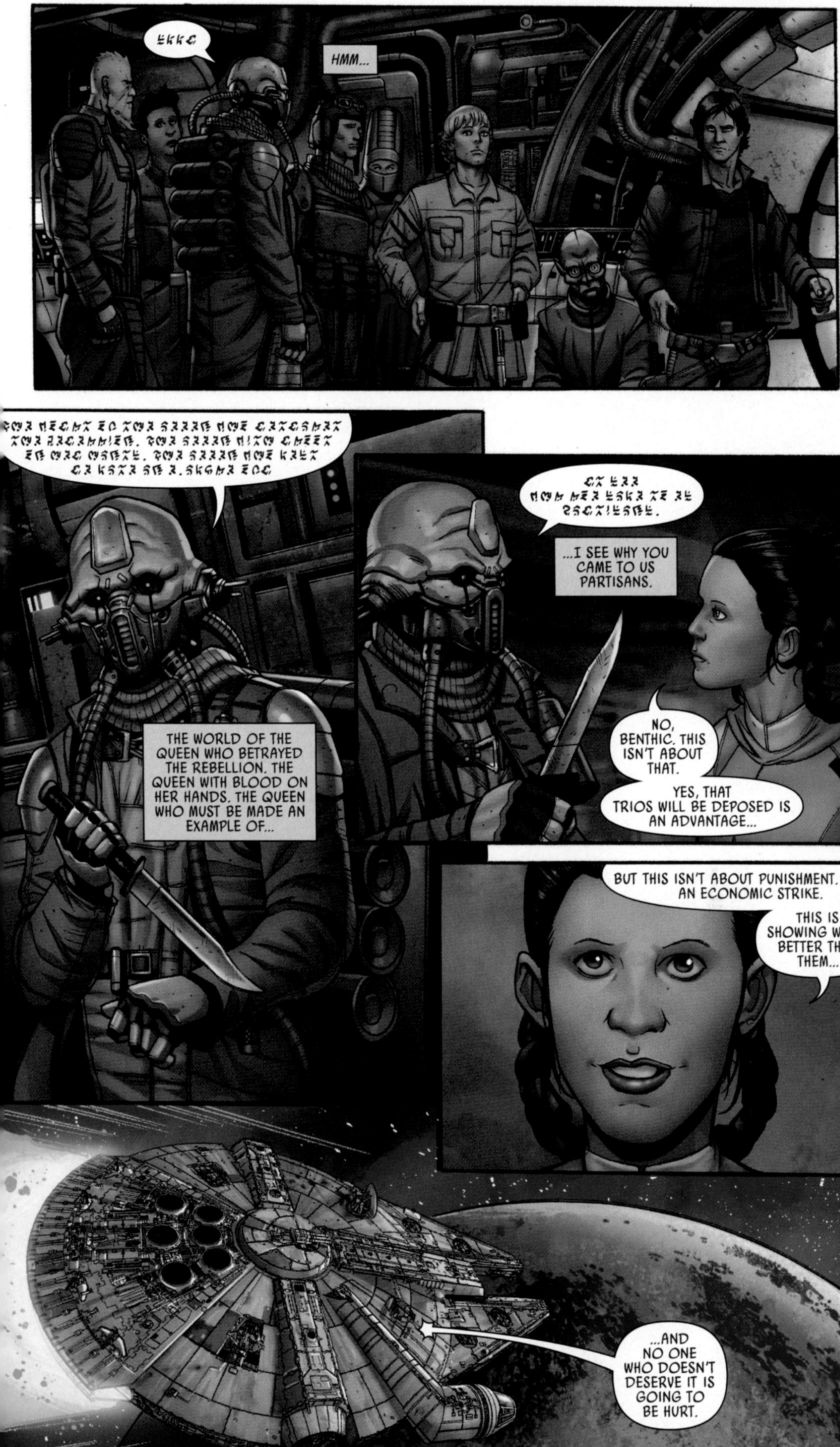
HMM...
THE WORLD OF THE QUEEN WHO BETRAYED THE REBELLION. THE QUEEN WITH BLOOD ON HER HANDS. THE QUEEN WHO MUST BE MADE AN EXAMPLE OF...
...I SEE WHY YOU CAME TO US PARTISANS.
NO, BENTHIC. THIS ISN'T ABOUT THAT.
YES, THAT TRIOS WILL BE DEPOSED IS AN ADVANTAGE...
BUT THIS ISN'T ABOUT PUNISHMENT. THIS IS AN ECONOMIC STRIKE.
THIS IS SHOWING WE'RE BETTER THAN THEM...
...AND NO ONE WHO DOESN'T DESERVE IT IS GOING TO BE HURT.

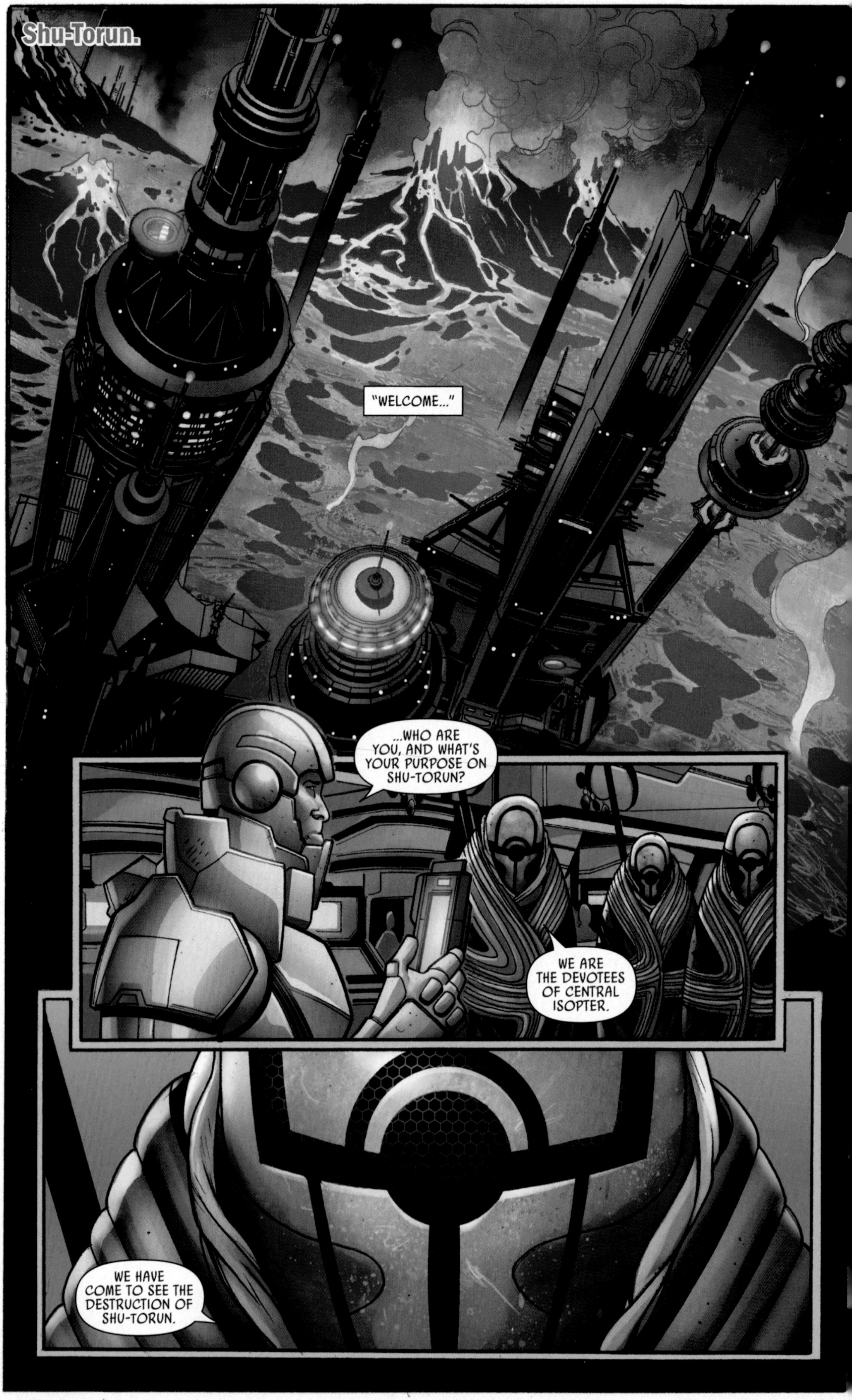
Shu-Torun.
"WELCOME..."
...WHO ARE YOU, AND WHAT'S YOUR PURPOSE ON SHU-TORUN?
WE ARE THE DEVOTEES OF CENTRAL ISOPTER.
WE HAVE COME TO SEE THE DESTRUCTION OF SHU-TORUN.

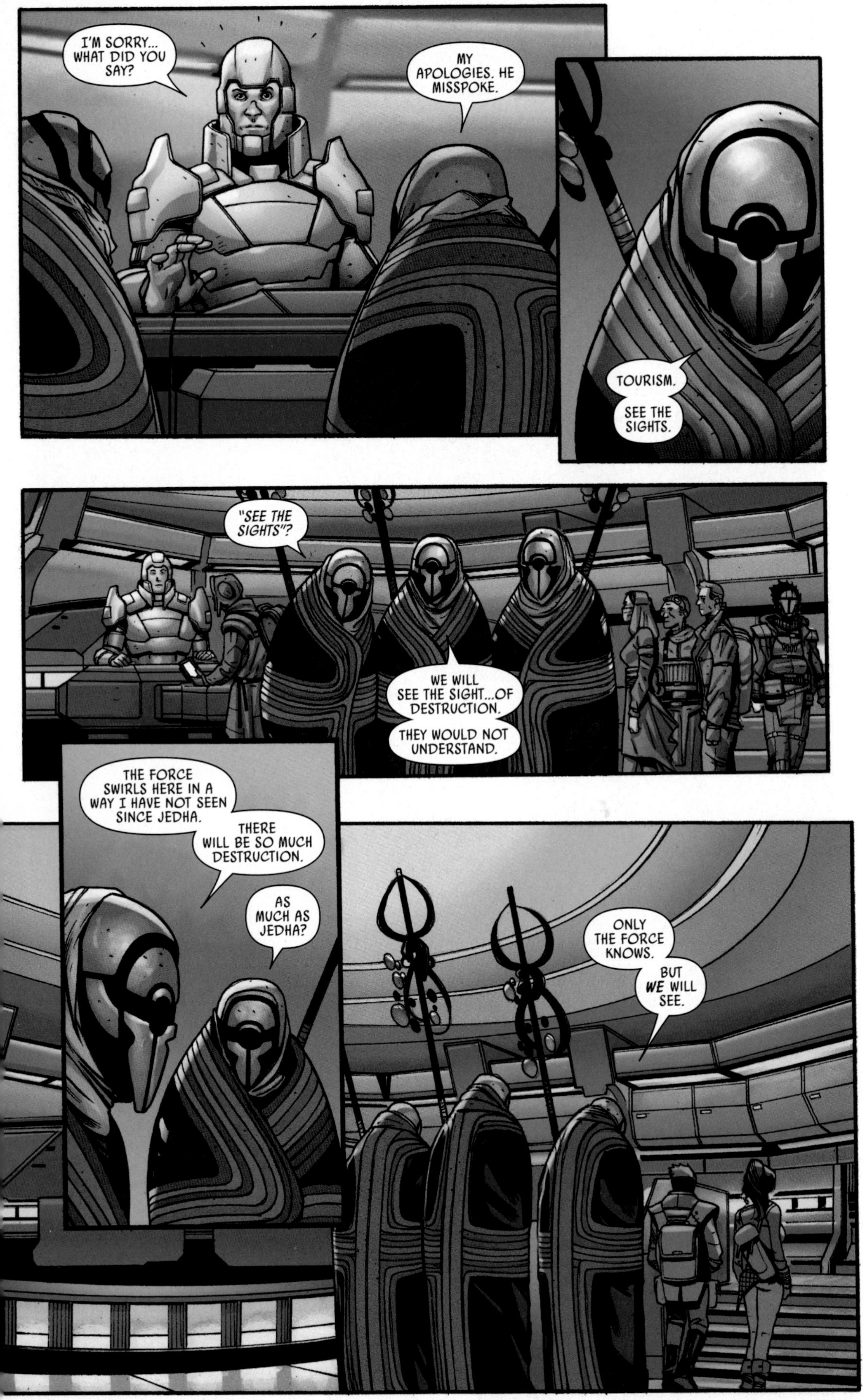

I'M SORRY... WHAT DID YOU SAY?
MY APOLOGIES. HE MISSPOKE.
TOURISM.
SEE THE SIGHTS.
"SEE THE SIGHTS"?
WE WILL SEE THE SIGHT...OF DESTRUCTION.
THEY WOULD NOT UNDERSTAND.
THE FORCE SWIRLS HERE IN A WAY I HAVE NOT SEEN SINCE JEDHA.
THERE WILL BE SO MUCH DESTRUCTION.
AS MUCH AS JEDHA?
ONLY THE FORCE KNOWS.
BUT WE WILL SEE.

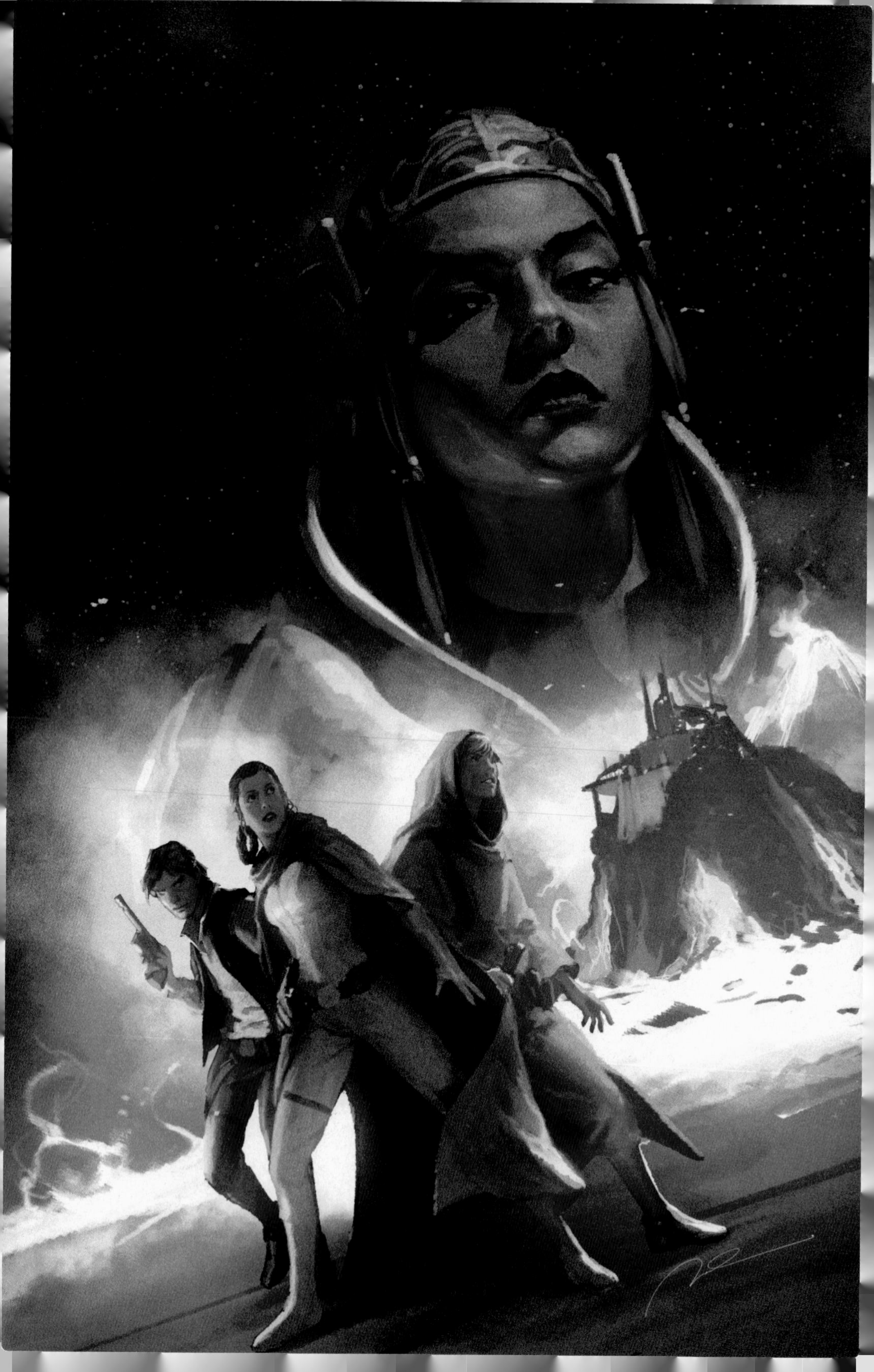

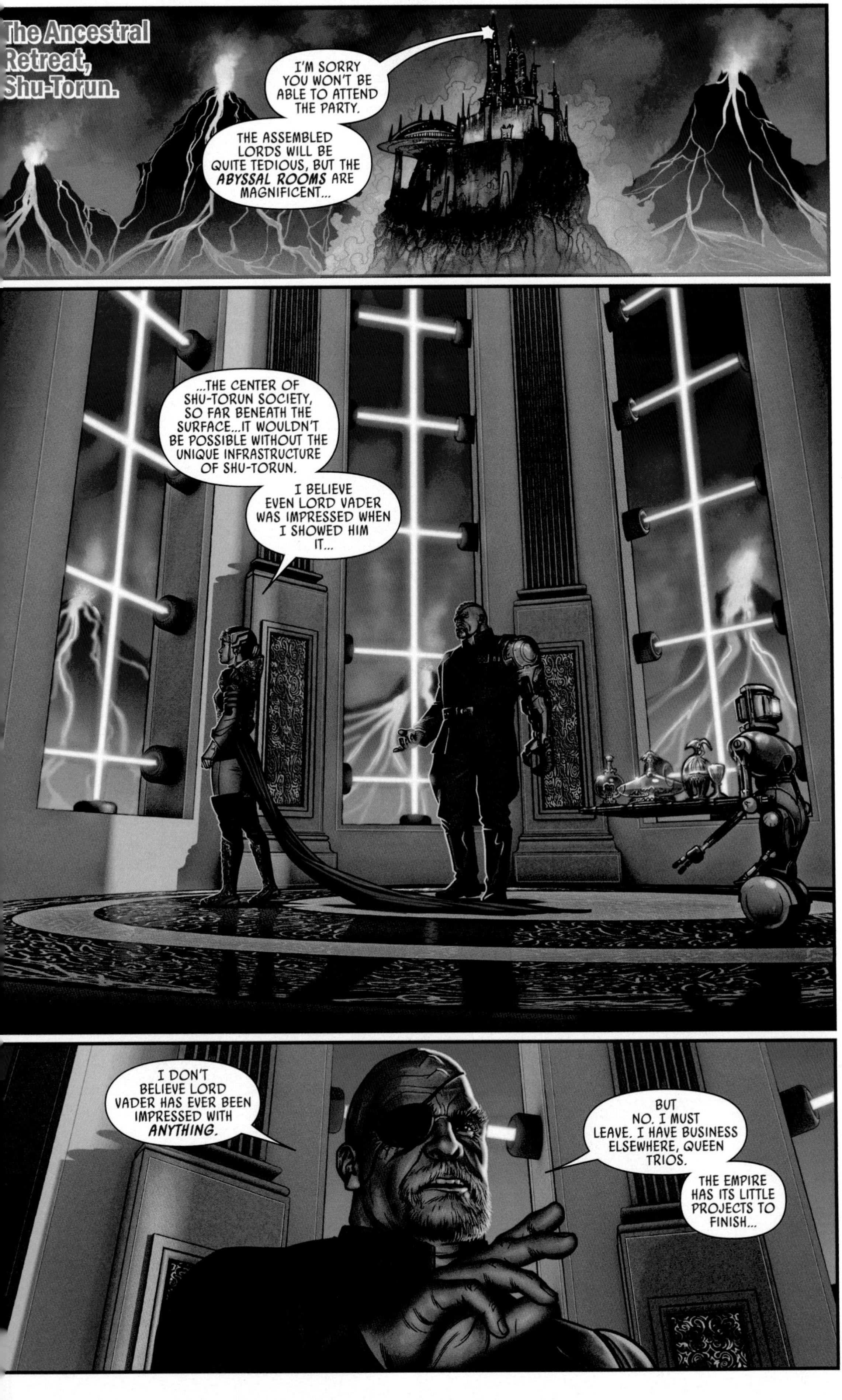
The Ancestral Retreat, Shu-Torun.
I'M SORRY YOU WON'T BE ABLE TO ATTEND THE PARTY.
THE ASSEMBLED LORDS WILL BE QUITE TEDIOUS, BUT THE ABYSSAL ROOMS ARE MAGNIFICENT...
...THE CENTER OF SHU-TORUN SOCIETY, SO FAR BENEATH THE SURFACE...IT WOULDN'T BE POSSIBLE WITHOUT THE UNIQUE INFRASTRUCTURE OF SHU-TORUN.
I BELIEVE EVEN LORD VADER WAS IMPRESSED WHEN I SHOWED HIM IT...
I DON'T BELIEVE LORD VADER HAS EVER BEEN IMPRESSED WITH ANYTHING.
BUT NO. I MUST LEAVE. I HAVE BUSINESS ELSEWHERE, QUEEN TRIOS.
THE EMPIRE HAS ITS LITTLE PROJECTS TO FINISH...

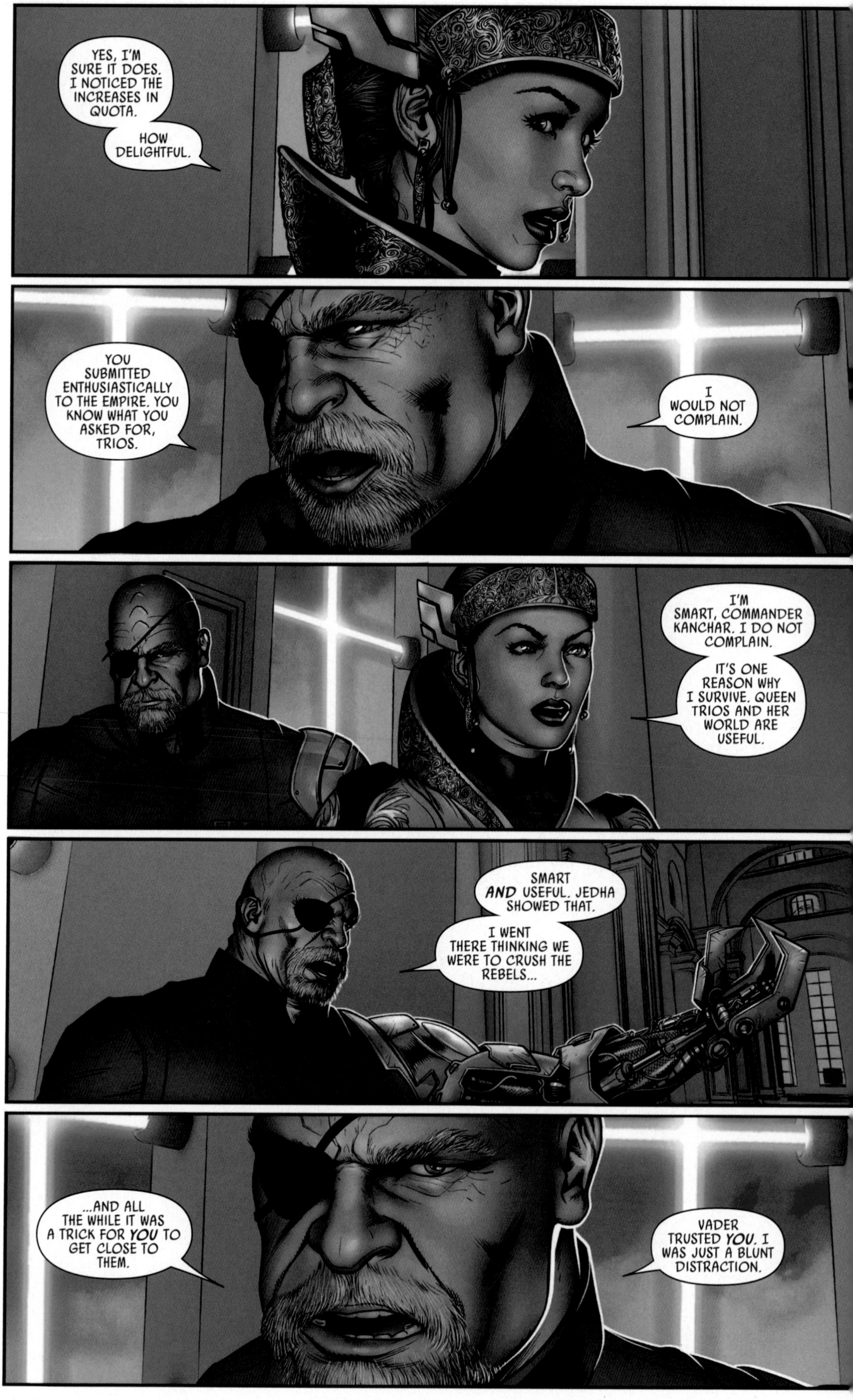

YES, I'M SURE IT DOES. I NOTICED THE INCREASES IN QUOTA.
HOW DELIGHTFUL.
YOU SUBMITTED ENTHUSIASTICALLY TO THE EMPIRE. YOU KNOW WHAT YOU ASKED FOR, TRIOS.
I WOULD NOT COMPLAIN.
I'M SMART, COMMANDER KANCHAR. I DO NOT COMPLAIN.
IT'S ONE REASON WHY I SURVIVE. QUEEN TRIOS AND HER WORLD ARE USEFUL.
SMART *AND* USEFUL. JEDHA SHOWED THAT.
I WENT THERE THINKING WE WERE TO CRUSH THE REBELS...
...AND ALL THE WHILE IT WAS A TRICK FOR *YOU* TO GET CLOSE TO THEM.
VADER TRUSTED *YOU*. I WAS JUST A BLUNT DISTRACTION.

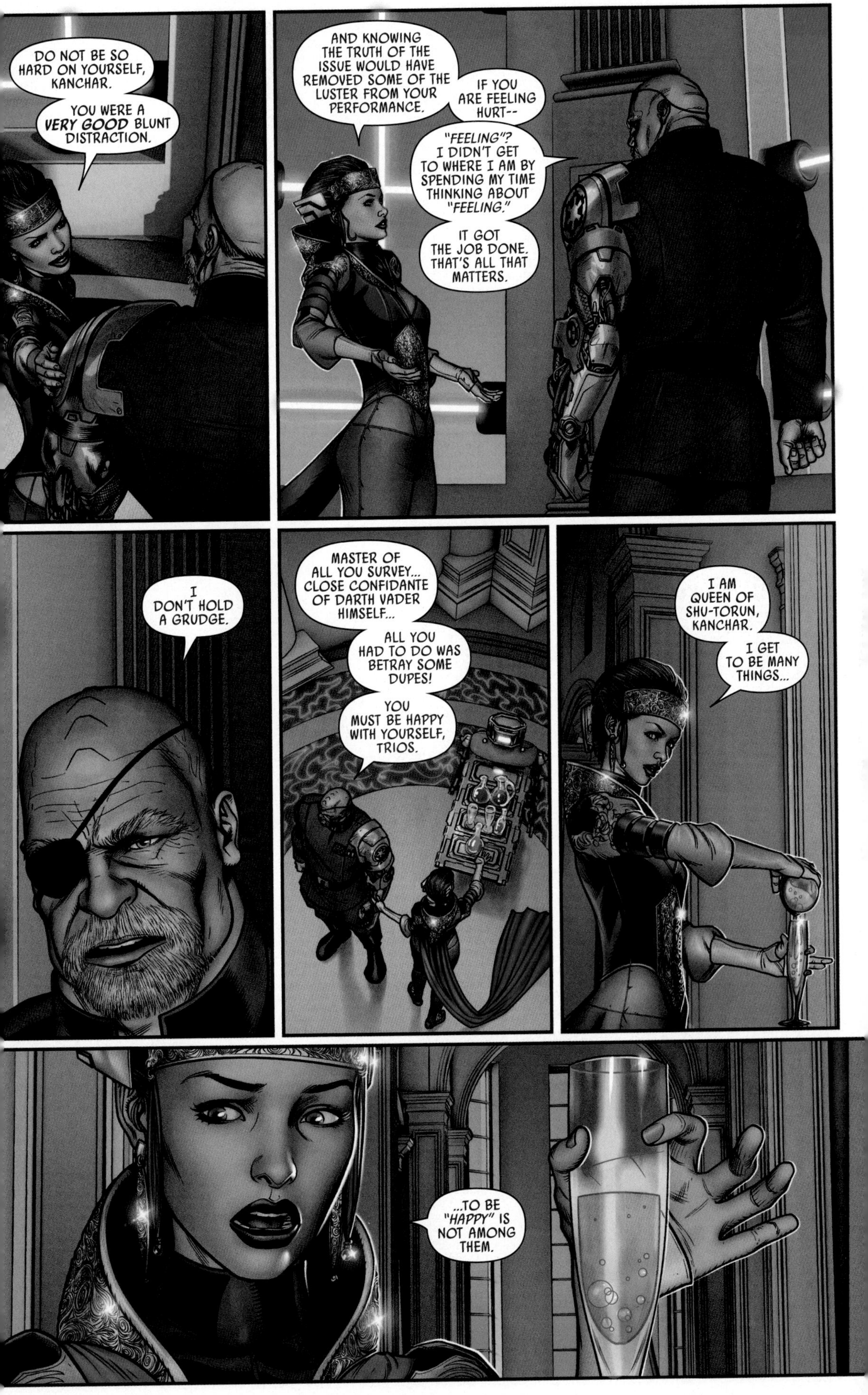
DO NOT BE SO HARD ON YOURSELF, KANCHAR.
YOU WERE A VERY GOOD BLUNT DISTRACTION.
AND KNOWING THE TRUTH OF THE ISSUE WOULD HAVE REMOVED SOME OF THE LUSTER FROM YOUR PERFORMANCE.
IF YOU ARE FEELING HURT--
"FEELING"? I DIDN'T GET TO WHERE I AM BY SPENDING MY TIME THINKING ABOUT "FEELING."
IT GOT THE JOB DONE. THAT'S ALL THAT MATTERS.
I DON'T HOLD A GRUDGE.
MASTER OF ALL YOU SURVEY... CLOSE CONFIDANTE OF DARTH VADER HIMSELF...
ALL YOU HAD TO DO WAS BETRAY SOME DUPES!
YOU MUST BE HAPPY WITH YOURSELF, TRIOS.
I AM QUEEN OF SHU-TORUN, KANCHAR.
I GET TO BE MANY THINGS...
...TO BE "HAPPY" IS NOT AMONG THEM.

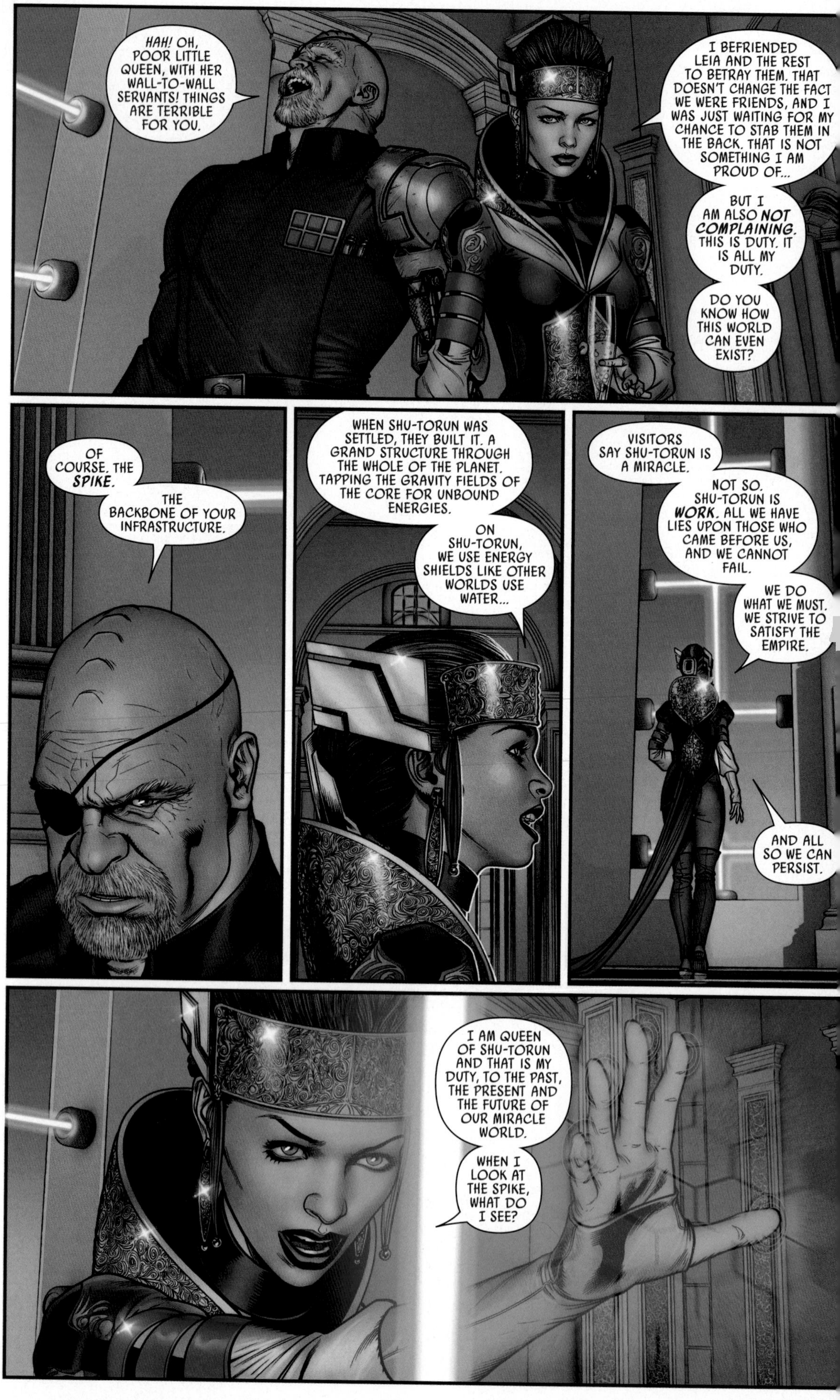

HAH! OH, POOR LITTLE QUEEN, WITH HER WALL-TO-WALL SERVANTS! THINGS ARE TERRIBLE FOR YOU.
I BEFRIENDED LEIA AND THE REST TO BETRAY THEM. THAT DOESN'T CHANGE THE FACT WE WERE FRIENDS, AND I WAS JUST WAITING FOR MY CHANCE TO STAB THEM IN THE BACK. THAT IS NOT SOMETHING I AM PROUD OF...
BUT I AM ALSO **NOT COMPLAINING.** THIS IS DUTY. IT IS ALL MY DUTY.
DO YOU KNOW HOW THIS WORLD CAN EVEN EXIST?
OF COURSE. THE ***SPIKE***.
THE BACKBONE OF YOUR INFRASTRUCTURE.
WHEN SHU-TORUN WAS SETTLED, THEY BUILT IT. A GRAND STRUCTURE THROUGH THE WHOLE OF THE PLANET. TAPPING THE GRAVITY FIELDS OF THE CORE FOR UNBOUND ENERGIES.
ON SHU-TORUN, WE USE ENERGY SHIELDS LIKE OTHER WORLDS USE WATER...
VISITORS SAY SHU-TORUN IS A MIRACLE.
NOT SO. SHU-TORUN IS ***WORK***. ALL WE HAVE LIES UPON THOSE WHO CAME BEFORE US, AND WE CANNOT FAIL.
WE DO WHAT WE MUST. WE STRIVE TO SATISFY THE EMPIRE.
AND ALL SO WE CAN PERSIST.
I AM QUEEN OF SHU-TORUN AND THAT IS MY DUTY, TO THE PAST, THE PRESENT AND THE FUTURE OF OUR MIRACLE WORLD.
WHEN I LOOK AT THE SPIKE, WHAT DO I SEE?

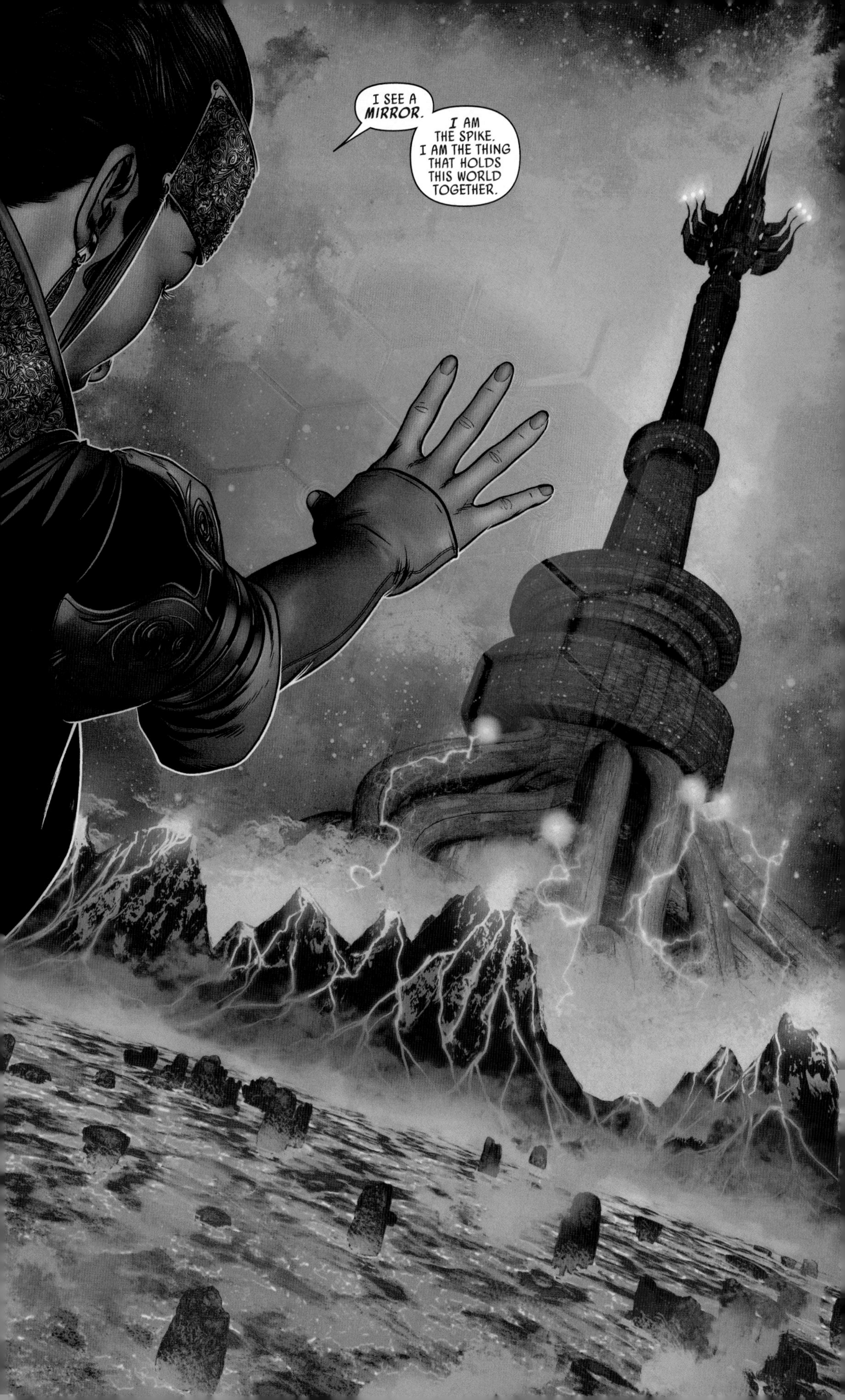
I SEE A MIRROR.
I AM THE SPIKE. I AM THE THING THAT HOLDS THIS WORLD TOGETHER.

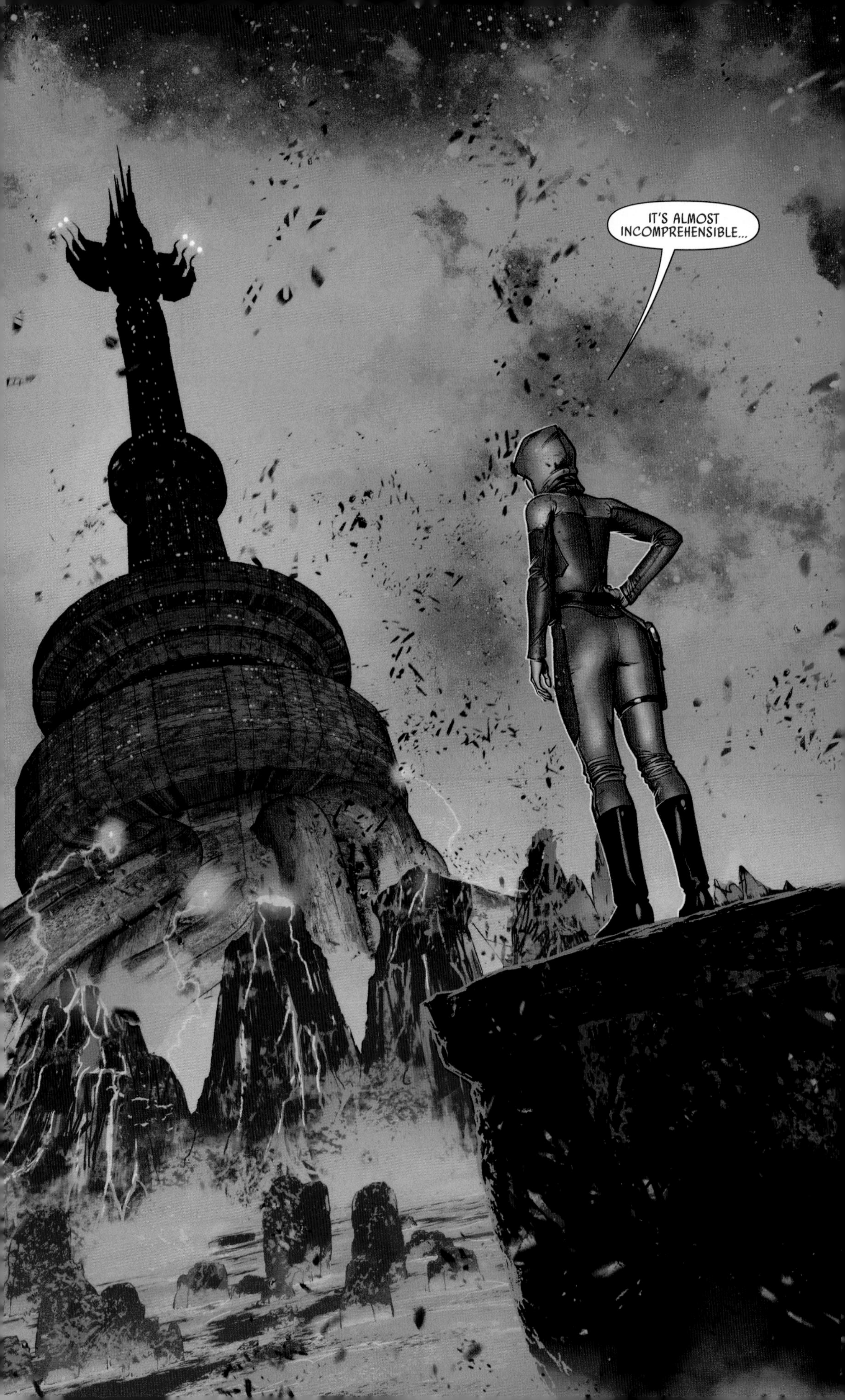
IT'S ALMOST INCOMPREHENSIBLE...

WE'RE GOING TO TAKE DOWN *THAT* AND SHU-TORUN WITH IT...

DON'T SAY YOU'RE GETTING COLD FEET, PRINCESS.

IT'S NOT TOO LATE TO BACK OUT AND DO SOMETHING LESS SUICIDAL INSTEAD.

SUICIDAL?!

IT'S NOT. HAN JUST LIKES TO BE DRAMATIC.

IT'S A GOOD PLAN.

ᚻᛠᚷ ᛉᛁᛊᛏᚢ ᛁᛉ ᛊ ᛉᚷᚻᚳᛗ ᛉᚲᚢᛁᛊᚻ.

AND DEATH IS A SMALL THING.

OH MY! ALL THIS *POSTURING*...

...I THOUGHT I WAS THE GREAT ACTOR, BUT YOU, MY TUBE-FACED FRIEND, ARE INCREDIBLE.

CAN WE SKIP ALL THE "WE ARE SUCH WONDERFUL HEROES" AND GET TO HOW WE'RE GOING TO CAUSE A GRAND SPLASH ON THE GALACTIC STAGE, HMM?

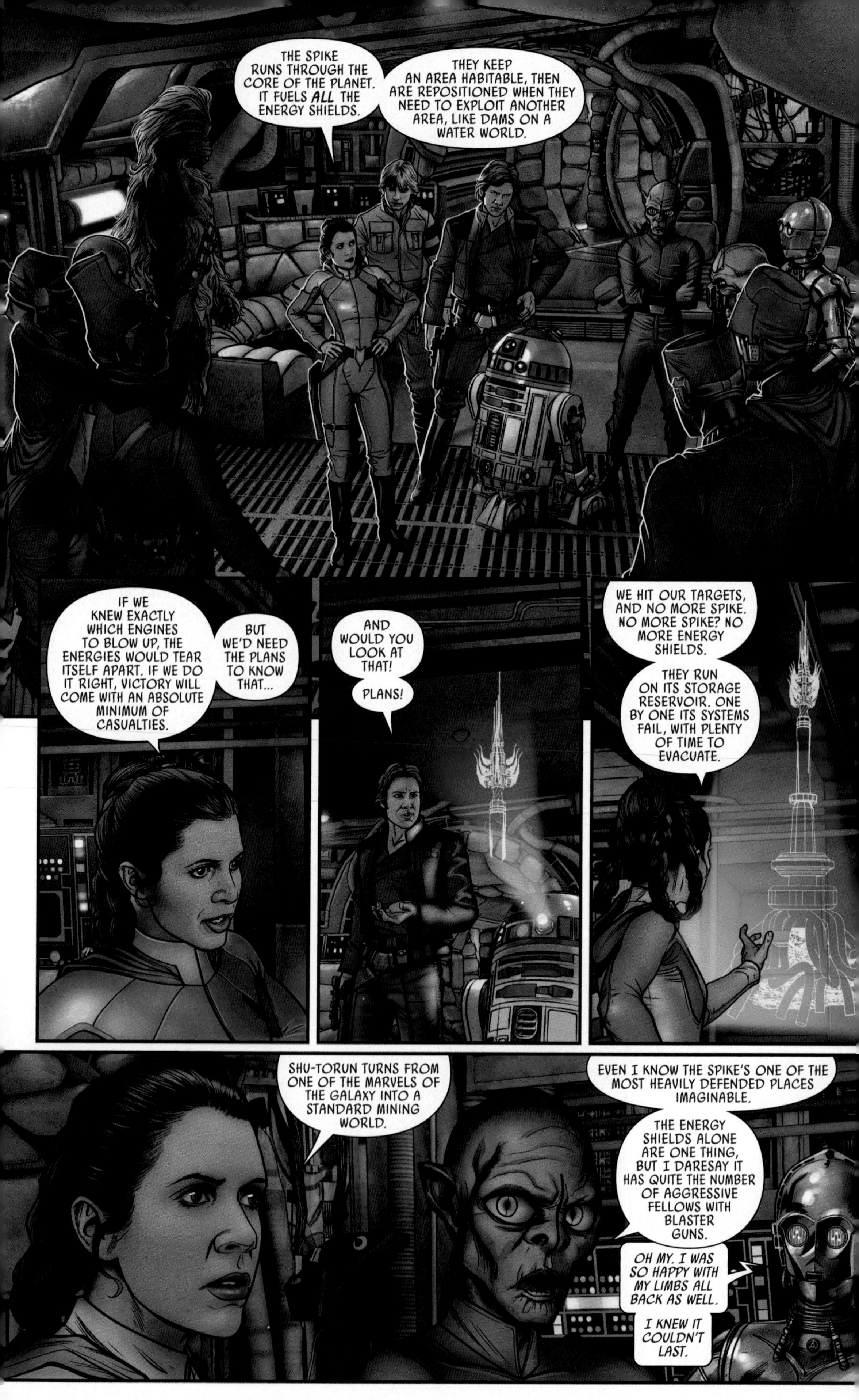

THE SPIKE RUNS THROUGH THE CORE OF THE PLANET. IT FUELS ALL THE ENERGY SHIELDS.
THEY KEEP AN AREA HABITABLE, THEN ARE REPOSITIONED WHEN THEY NEED TO EXPLOIT ANOTHER AREA, LIKE DAMS ON A WATER WORLD.
IF WE KNEW EXACTLY WHICH ENGINES TO BLOW UP, THE ENERGIES WOULD TEAR ITSELF APART. IF WE DO IT RIGHT, VICTORY WILL COME WITH AN ABSOLUTE MINIMUM OF CASUALTIES.
BUT WE'D NEED THE PLANS TO KNOW THAT...
AND WOULD YOU LOOK AT THAT!
PLANS!
WE HIT OUR TARGETS, AND NO MORE SPIKE. NO MORE SPIKE? NO MORE ENERGY SHIELDS.
THEY RUN ON ITS STORAGE RESERVOIR. ONE BY ONE ITS SYSTEMS FAIL, WITH PLENTY OF TIME TO EVACUATE.
SHU-TORUN TURNS FROM ONE OF THE MARVELS OF THE GALAXY INTO A STANDARD MINING WORLD.
EVEN I KNOW THE SPIKE'S ONE OF THE MOST HEAVILY DEFENDED PLACES IMAGINABLE.
THE ENERGY SHIELDS ALONE ARE ONE THING, BUT I DARESAY IT HAS QUITE THE NUMBER OF AGGRESSIVE FELLOWS WITH BLASTER GUNS.
OH MY. I WAS SO HAPPY WITH MY LIMBS ALL BACK AS WELL.
I KNEW IT COULDN'T LAST.

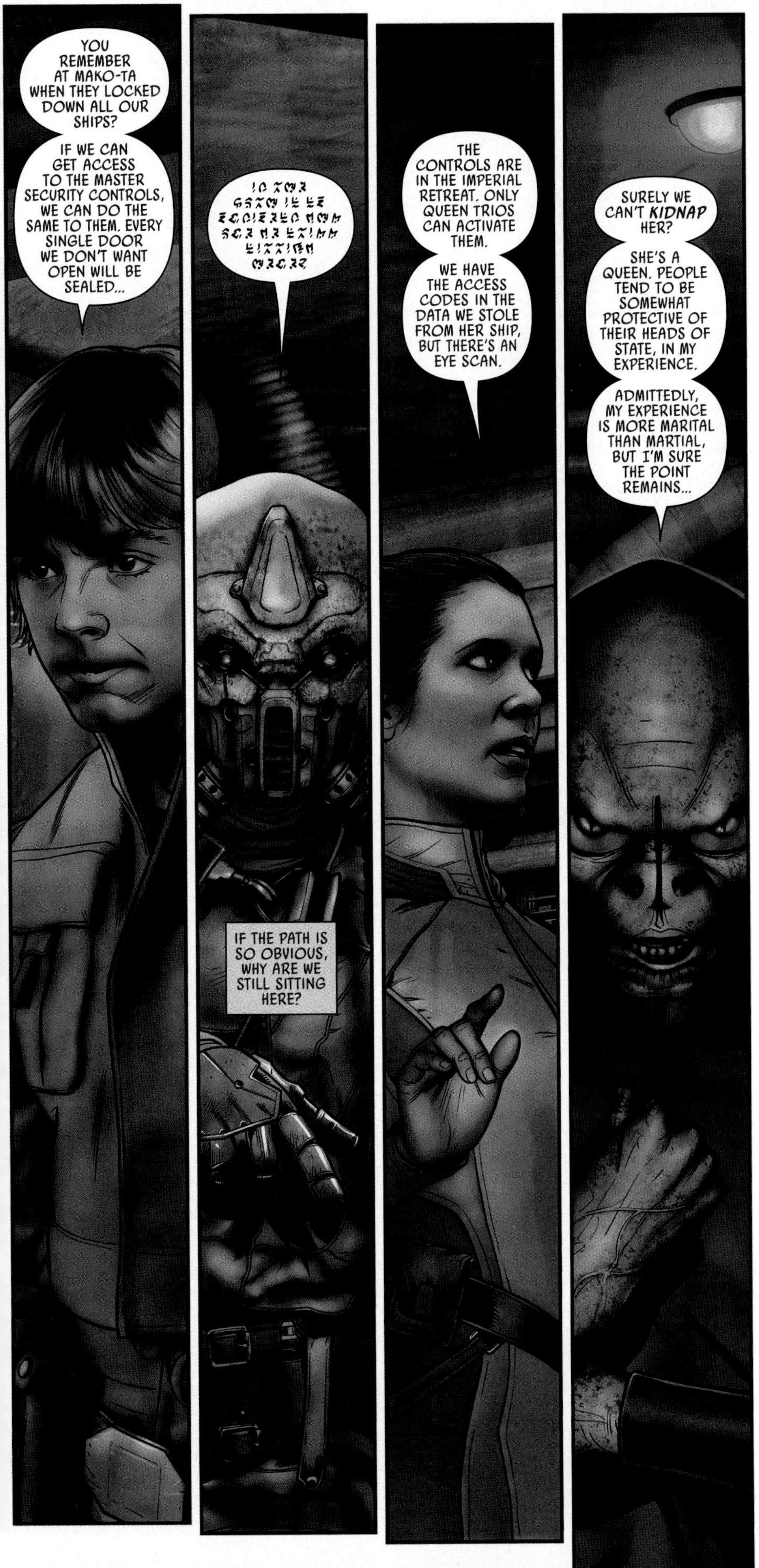
YOU REMEMBER AT MAKO-TA WHEN THEY LOCKED DOWN ALL OUR SHIPS?
IF WE CAN GET ACCESS TO THE MASTER SECURITY CONTROLS, WE CAN DO THE SAME TO THEM. EVERY SINGLE DOOR WE DON'T WANT OPEN WILL BE SEALED...
IF THE PATH IS SO OBVIOUS, WHY ARE WE STILL SITTING HERE?
THE CONTROLS ARE IN THE IMPERIAL RETREAT. ONLY QUEEN TRIOS CAN ACTIVATE THEM.
WE HAVE THE ACCESS CODES IN THE DATA WE STOLE FROM HER SHIP, BUT THERE'S AN EYE SCAN.
SURELY WE CAN'T *KIDNAP* HER?
SHE'S A QUEEN. PEOPLE TEND TO BE SOMEWHAT PROTECTIVE OF THEIR HEADS OF STATE, IN MY EXPERIENCE.
ADMITTEDLY, MY EXPERIENCE IS MORE MARITAL THAN MARTIAL, BUT I'M SURE THE POINT REMAINS...

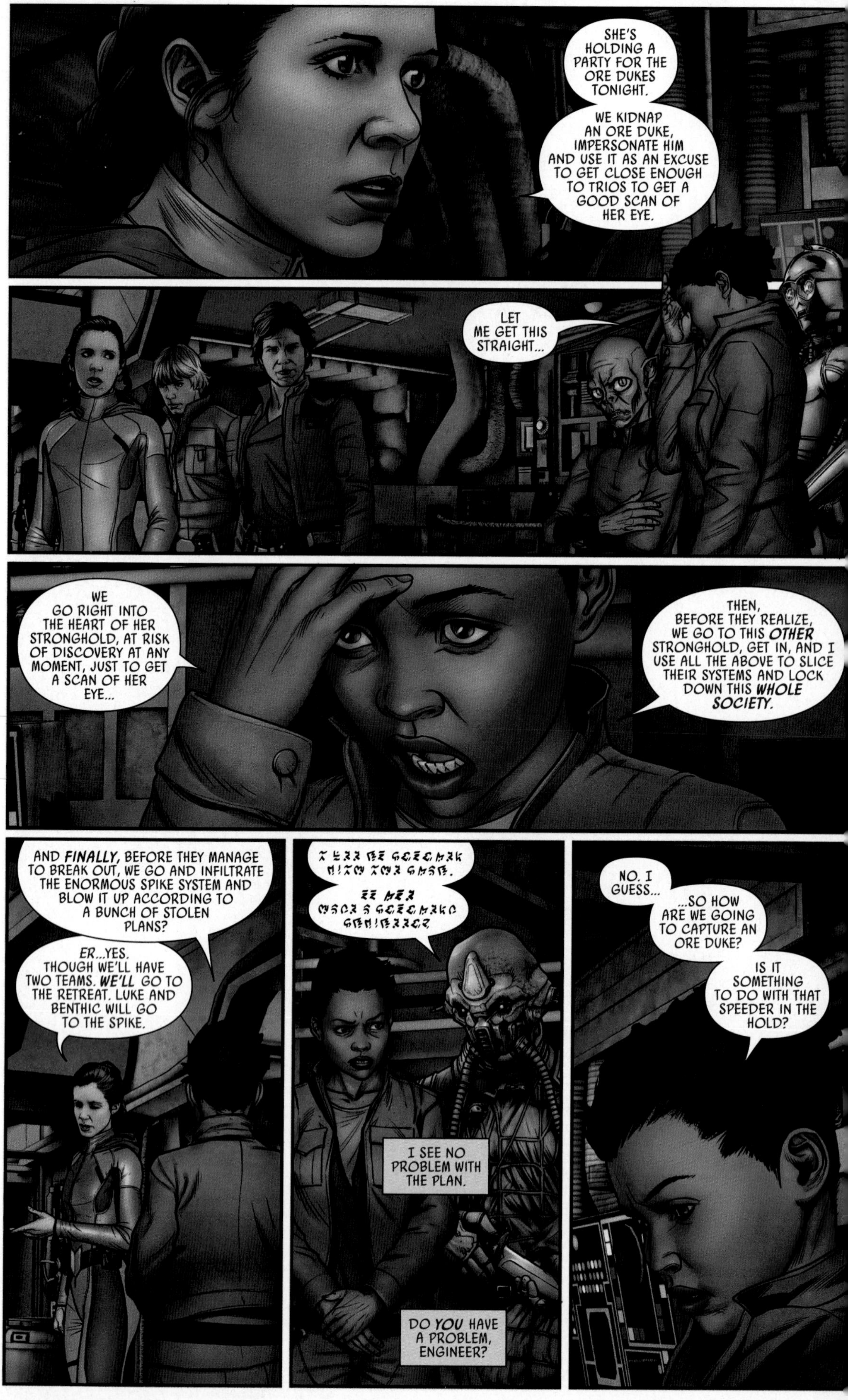
SHE'S HOLDING A PARTY FOR THE ORE DUKES TONIGHT.
WE KIDNAP AN ORE DUKE, IMPERSONATE HIM AND USE IT AS AN EXCUSE TO GET CLOSE ENOUGH TO TRIOS TO GET A GOOD SCAN OF HER EYE.
LET ME GET THIS STRAIGHT...
WE GO RIGHT INTO THE HEART OF HER STRONGHOLD, AT RISK OF DISCOVERY AT ANY MOMENT, JUST TO GET A SCAN OF HER EYE...
THEN, BEFORE THEY REALIZE, WE GO TO THIS OTHER STRONGHOLD, GET IN, AND I USE ALL THE ABOVE TO SLICE THEIR SYSTEMS AND LOCK DOWN THIS WHOLE SOCIETY.
AND FINALLY, BEFORE THEY MANAGE TO BREAK OUT, WE GO AND INFILTRATE THE ENORMOUS SPIKE SYSTEM AND BLOW IT UP ACCORDING TO A BUNCH OF STOLEN PLANS?
ER...YES. THOUGH WE'LL HAVE TWO TEAMS. WE'LL GO TO THE RETREAT. LUKE AND BENTHIC WILL GO TO THE SPIKE.
I SEE NO PROBLEM WITH THE PLAN.
DO YOU HAVE A PROBLEM, ENGINEER?
NO. I GUESS...
...SO HOW ARE WE GOING TO CAPTURE AN ORE DUKE?
IS IT SOMETHING TO DO WITH THAT SPEEDER IN THE HOLD?

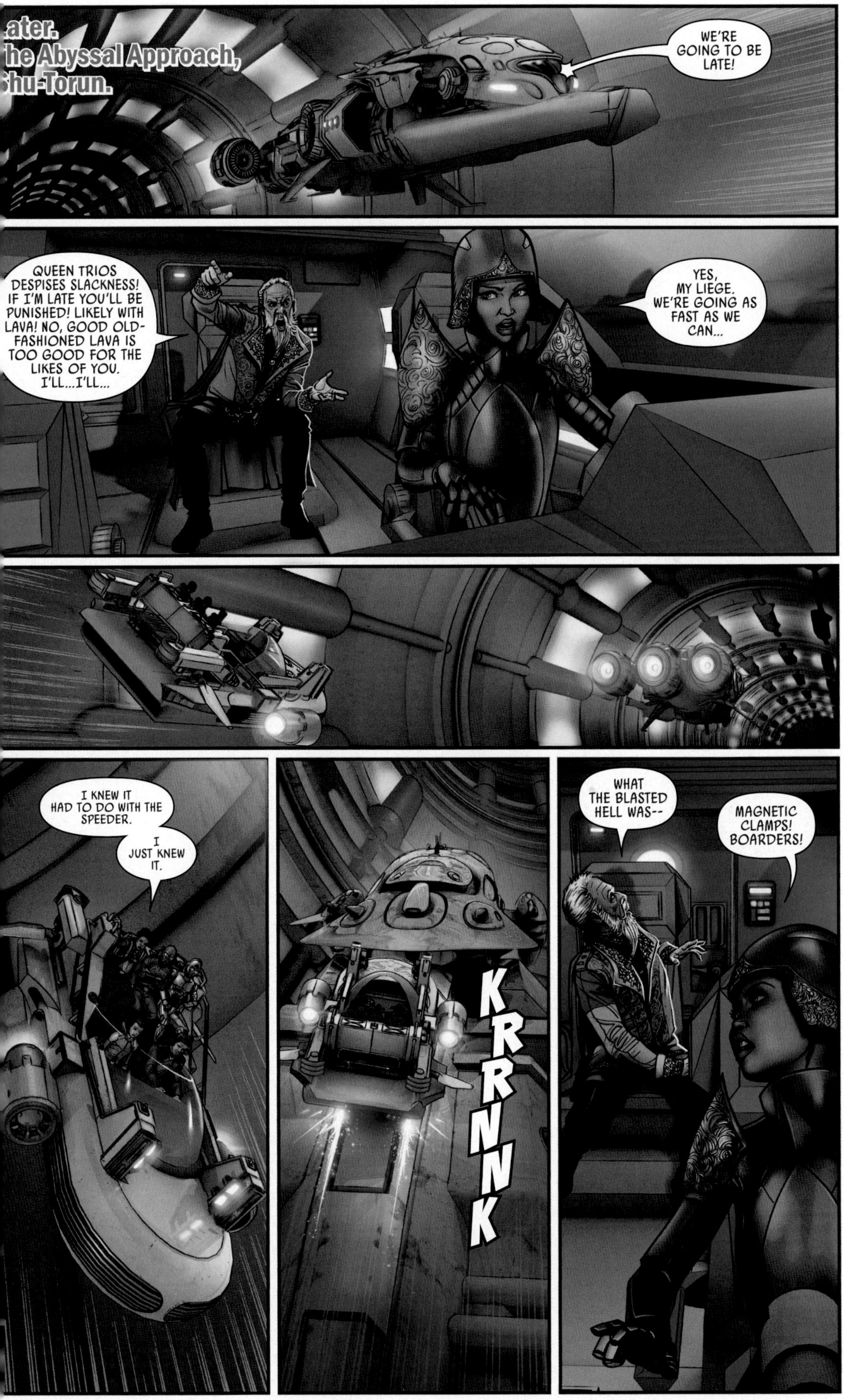
ater.
he Abyssal Approach,
hu-Torun.
WE'RE GOING TO BE LATE!
QUEEN TRIOS DESPISES SLACKNESS! IF I'M LATE YOU'LL BE PUNISHED! LIKELY WITH LAVA! NO, GOOD OLD-FASHIONED LAVA IS TOO GOOD FOR THE LIKES OF YOU. I'LL...I'LL...
YES, MY LIEGE. WE'RE GOING AS FAST AS WE CAN...
I KNEW IT HAD TO DO WITH THE SPEEDER.
I JUST KNEW IT.
KRRNNK
WHAT THE BLASTED HELL WAS--
MAGNETIC CLAMPS! BOARDERS!

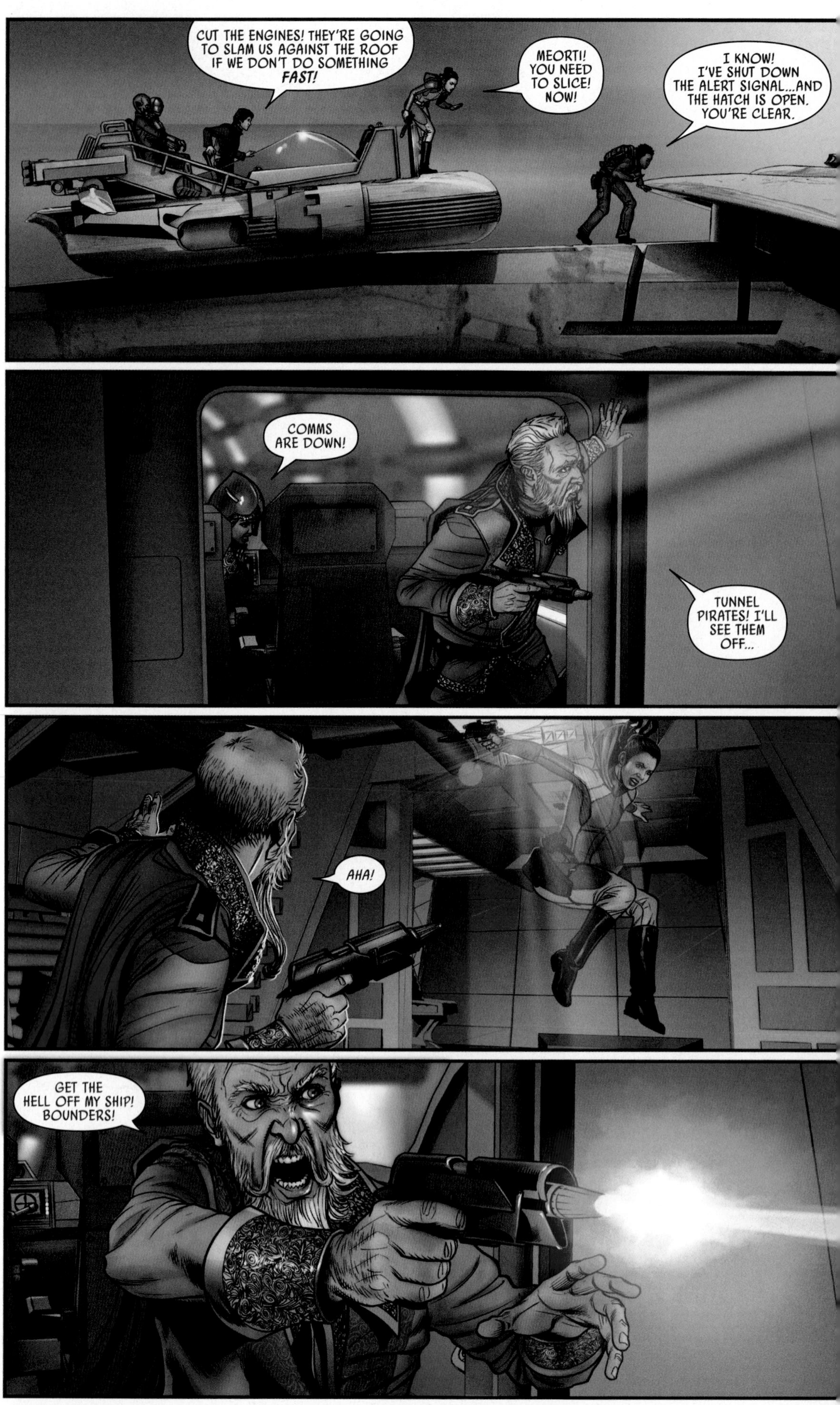
CUT THE ENGINES! THEY'RE GOING TO SLAM US AGAINST THE ROOF IF WE DON'T DO SOMETHING FAST!
MEORTI! YOU NEED TO SLICE! NOW!
I KNOW! I'VE SHUT DOWN THE ALERT SIGNAL...AND THE HATCH IS OPEN. YOU'RE CLEAR.
COMMS ARE DOWN!
TUNNEL PIRATES! I'LL SEE THEM OFF...
AHA!
GET THE HELL OFF MY SHIP! BOUNDERS!

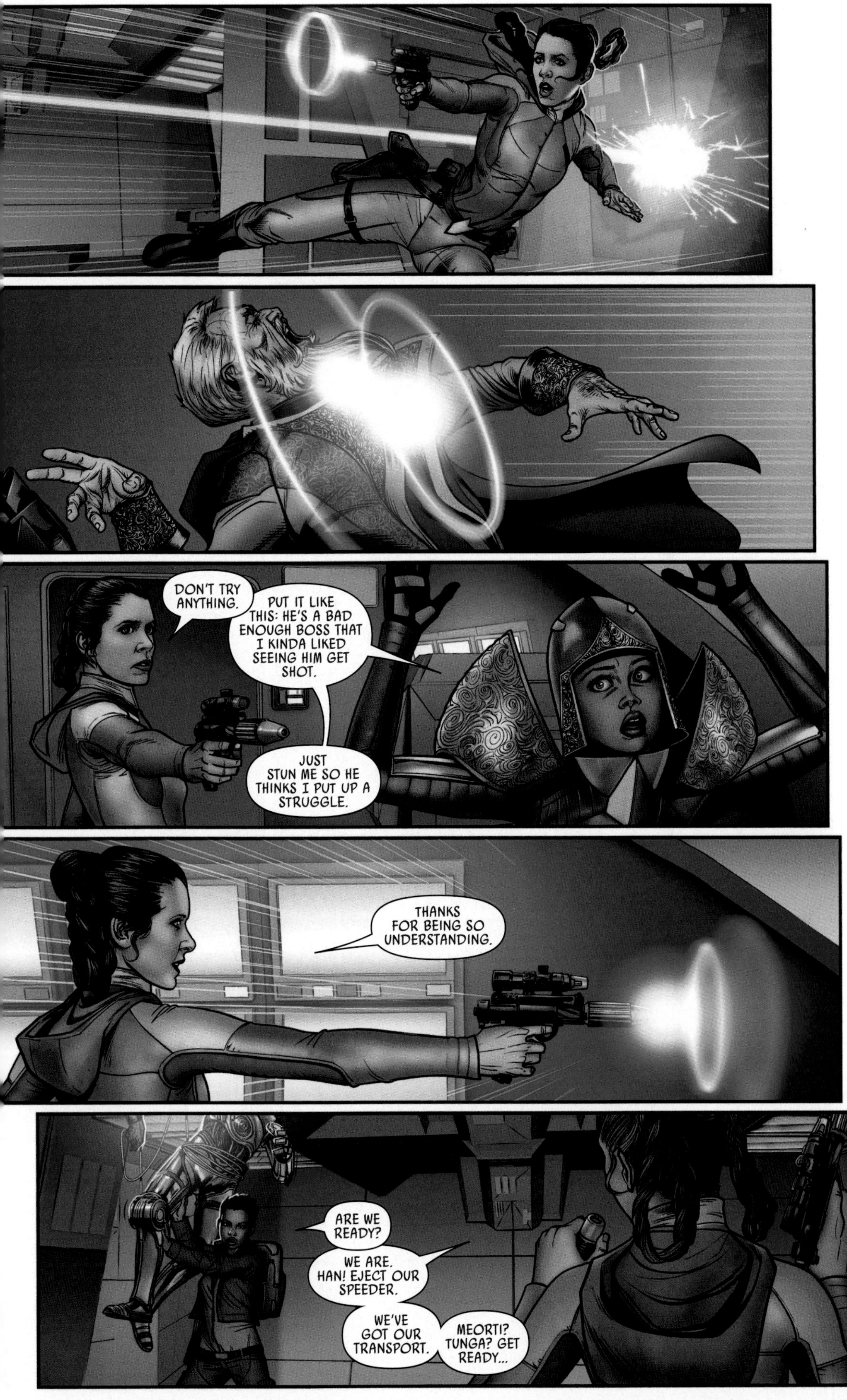
DON'T TRY ANYTHING.
PUT IT LIKE THIS: HE'S A BAD ENOUGH BOSS THAT I KINDA LIKED SEEING HIM GET SHOT.
JUST STUN ME SO HE THINKS I PUT UP A STRUGGLE.
THANKS FOR BEING SO UNDERSTANDING.
ARE WE READY?
WE ARE. HAN! EJECT OUR SPEEDER.
WE'VE GOT OUR TRANSPORT.
MEORTI? TUNGA? GET READY...

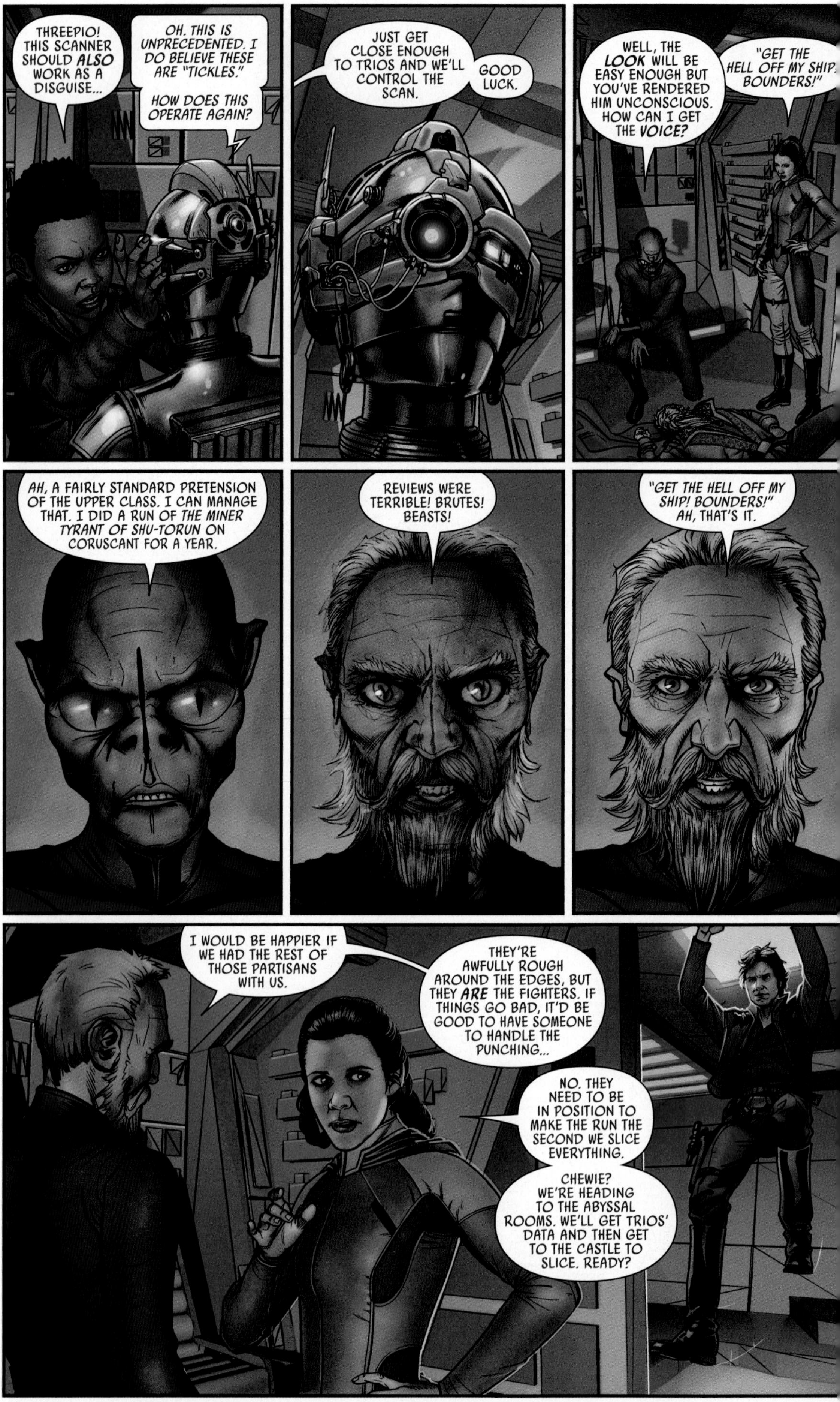
THREEPIO! THIS SCANNER SHOULD ALSO WORK AS A DISGUISE...
OH. THIS IS UNPRECEDENTED. I DO BELIEVE THESE ARE "TICKLES."
HOW DOES THIS OPERATE AGAIN?
JUST GET CLOSE ENOUGH TO TRIOS AND WE'LL CONTROL THE SCAN.
GOOD LUCK.
WELL, THE LOOK WILL BE EASY ENOUGH BUT YOU'VE RENDERED HIM UNCONSCIOUS. HOW CAN I GET THE VOICE?
"GET THE HELL OFF MY SHIP, BOUNDERS!"
AH, A FAIRLY STANDARD PRETENSION OF THE UPPER CLASS. I CAN MANAGE THAT. I DID A RUN OF THE MINER TYRANT OF SHU-TORUN ON CORUSCANT FOR A YEAR.
REVIEWS WERE TERRIBLE! BRUTES! BEASTS!
"GET THE HELL OFF MY SHIP! BOUNDERS!" AH, THAT'S IT.
I WOULD BE HAPPIER IF WE HAD THE REST OF THOSE PARTISANS WITH US.
THEY'RE AWFULLY ROUGH AROUND THE EDGES, BUT THEY ARE THE FIGHTERS. IF THINGS GO BAD, IT'D BE GOOD TO HAVE SOMEONE TO HANDLE THE PUNCHING...
NO. THEY NEED TO BE IN POSITION TO MAKE THE RUN THE SECOND WE SLICE EVERYTHING.
CHEWIE? WE'RE HEADING TO THE ABYSSAL ROOMS. WE'LL GET TRIOS' DATA AND THEN GET TO THE CASTLE TO SLICE. READY?

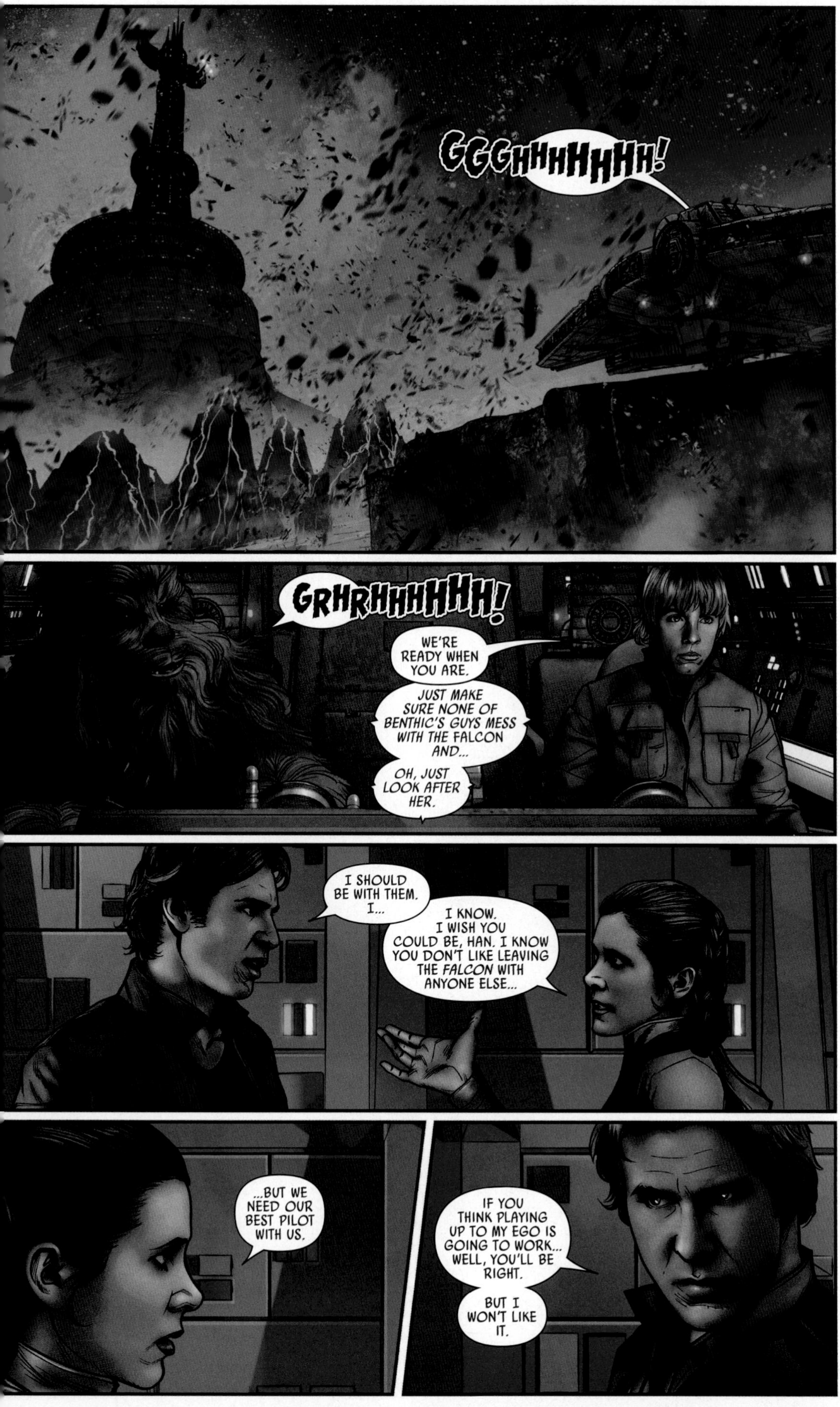
GGGHHHHHHH!
GRHRHHHHHH!
WE'RE READY WHEN YOU ARE.
JUST MAKE SURE NONE OF BENTHIC'S GUYS MESS WITH THE FALCON AND...
OH, JUST LOOK AFTER HER.
I SHOULD BE WITH THEM. I...
I KNOW. I WISH YOU COULD BE, HAN. I KNOW YOU DON'T LIKE LEAVING THE *FALCON* WITH ANYONE ELSE...
...BUT WE NEED OUR BEST PILOT WITH US.
IF YOU THINK PLAYING UP TO MY EGO IS GOING TO WORK... WELL, YOU'LL BE RIGHT.
BUT I WON'T LIKE IT.

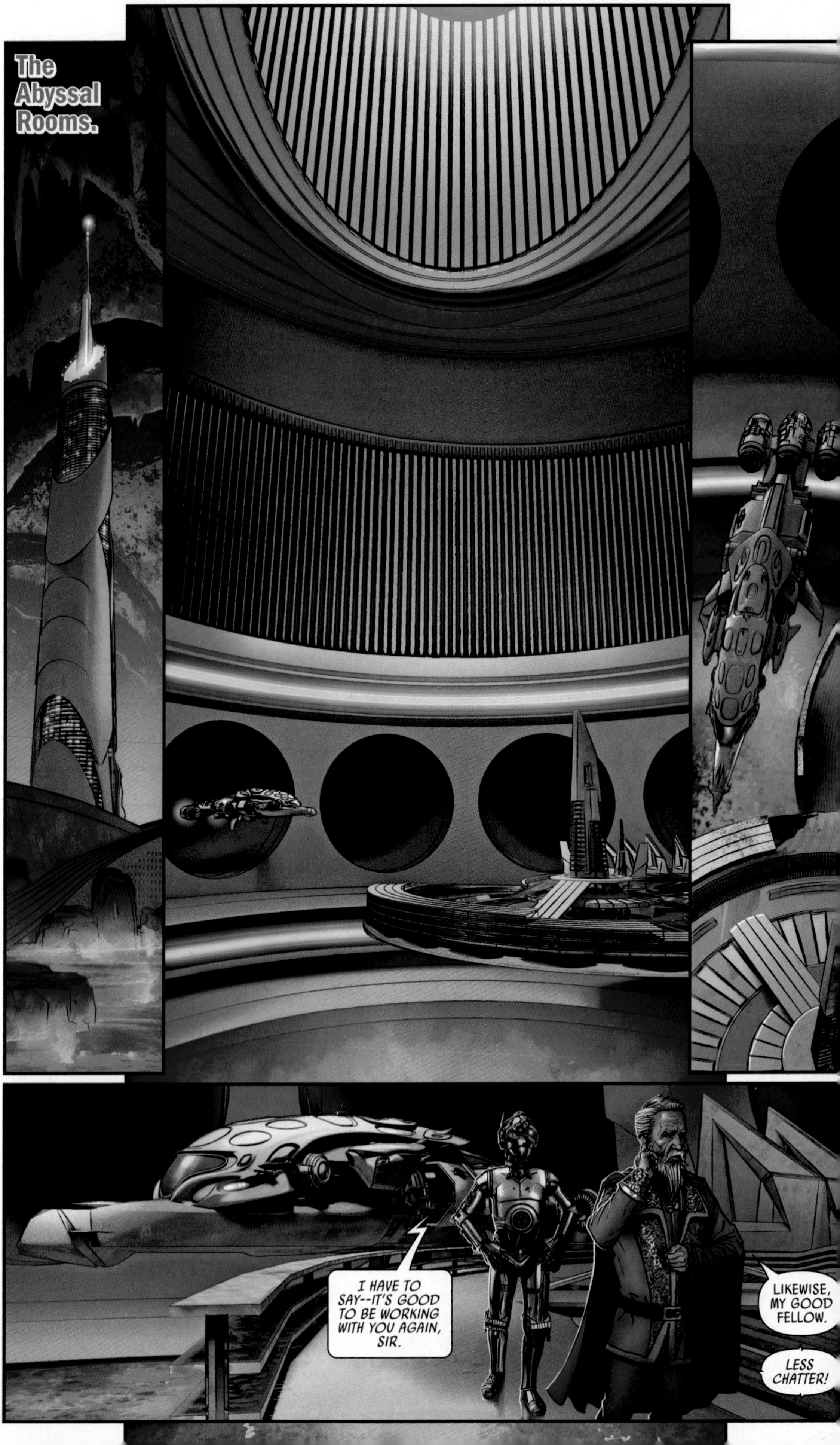

The Abyssal Rooms.
I HAVE TO SAY--IT'S GOOD TO BE WORKING WITH YOU AGAIN, SIR.
LIKEWISE, MY GOOD FELLOW.
LESS CHATTER!

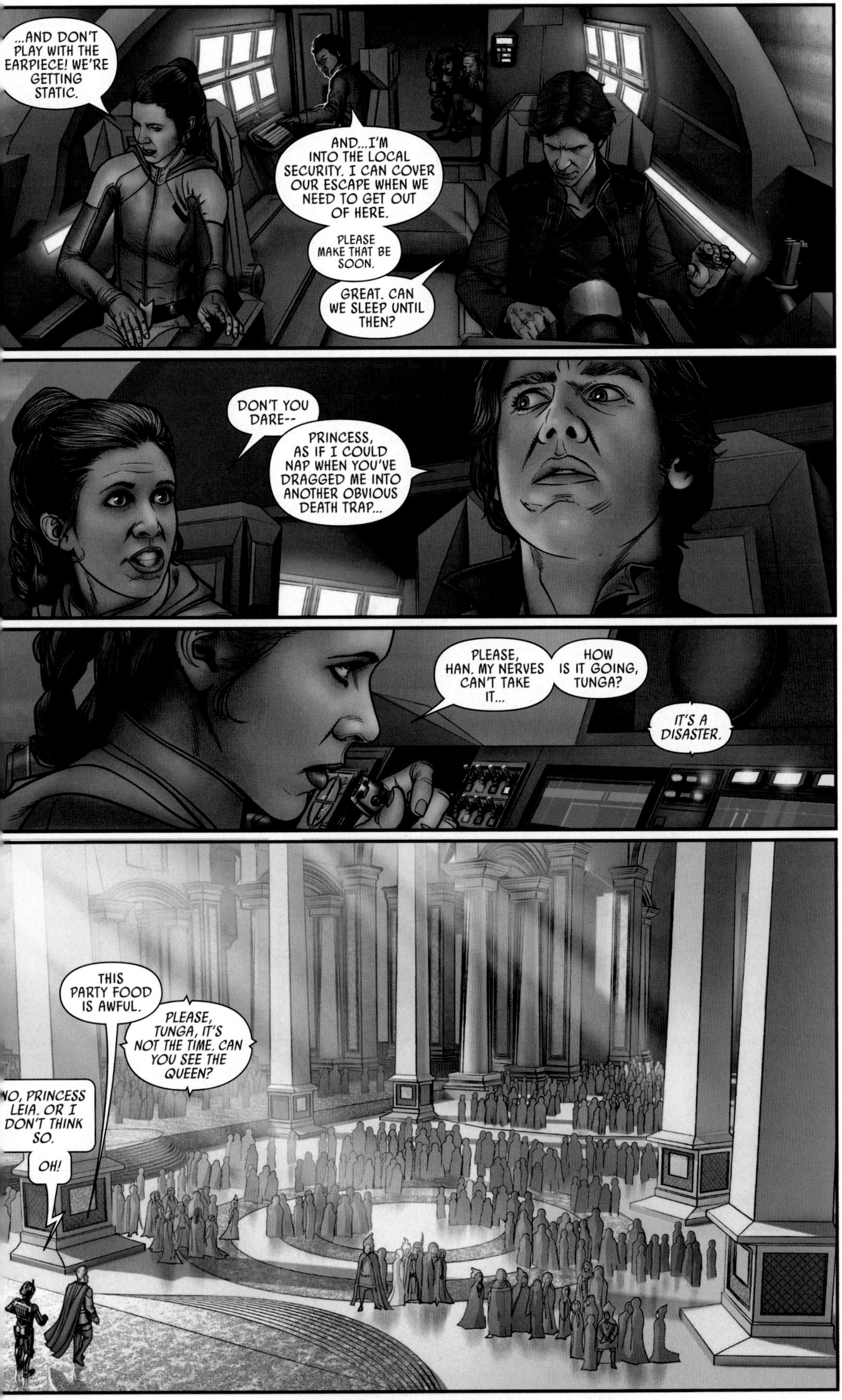

...AND DON'T PLAY WITH THE EARPIECE! WE'RE GETTING STATIC.
AND...I'M INTO THE LOCAL SECURITY. I CAN COVER OUR ESCAPE WHEN WE NEED TO GET OUT OF HERE.
PLEASE MAKE THAT BE SOON.
GREAT. CAN WE SLEEP UNTIL THEN?
DON'T YOU DARE--
PRINCESS, AS IF I COULD NAP WHEN YOU'VE DRAGGED ME INTO ANOTHER OBVIOUS DEATH TRAP...
PLEASE, HAN. MY NERVES CAN'T TAKE IT...
HOW IS IT GOING, TUNGA?
IT'S A DISASTER.
THIS PARTY FOOD IS AWFUL.
PLEASE, TUNGA, IT'S NOT THE TIME. CAN YOU SEE THE QUEEN?
NO, PRINCESS LEIA. OR I DON'T THINK SO.
OH!

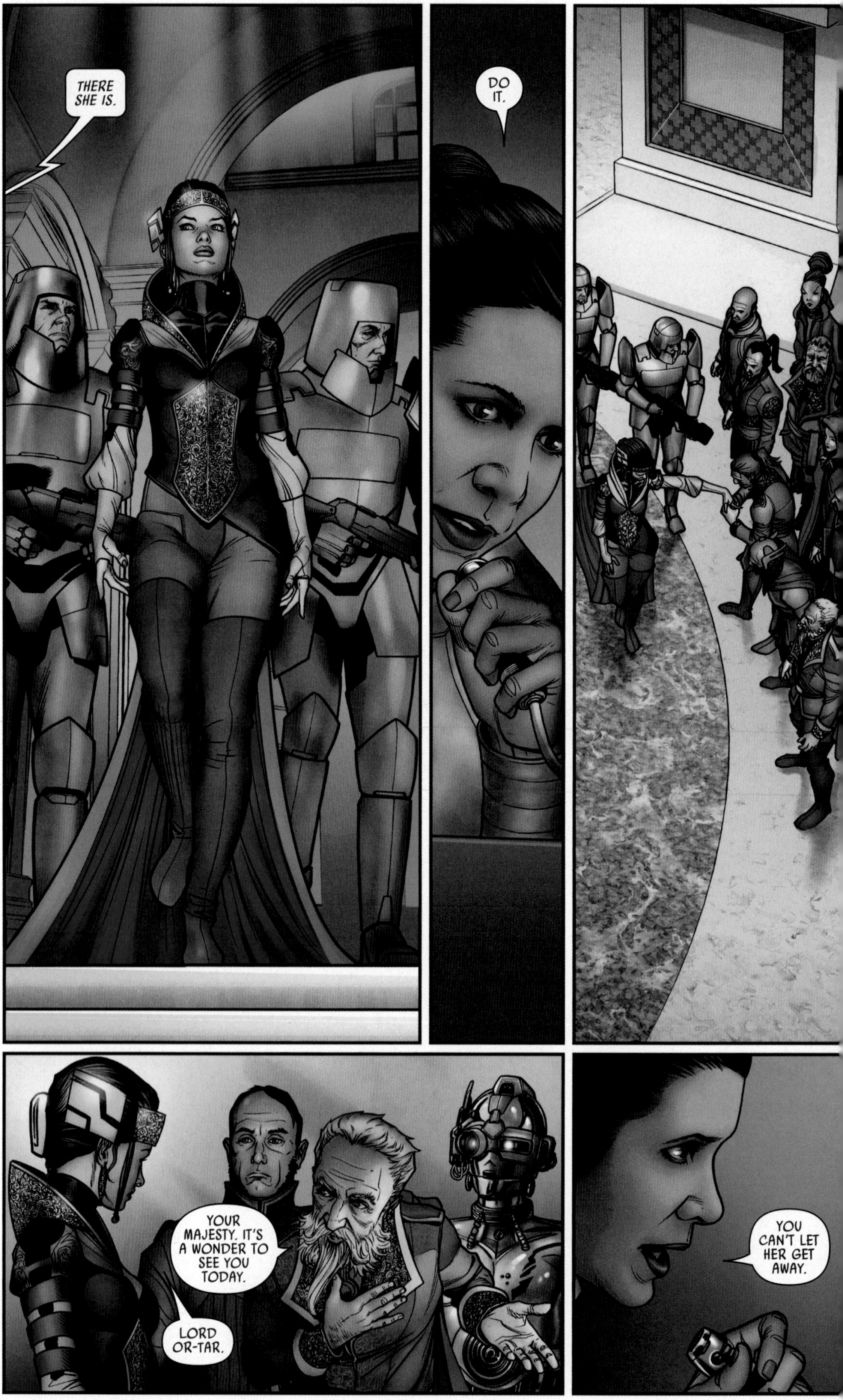
THERE SHE IS.
DO IT.
YOUR MAJESTY. IT'S A WONDER TO SEE YOU TODAY.
LORD OR-TAR.
YOU CAN'T LET HER GET AWAY.

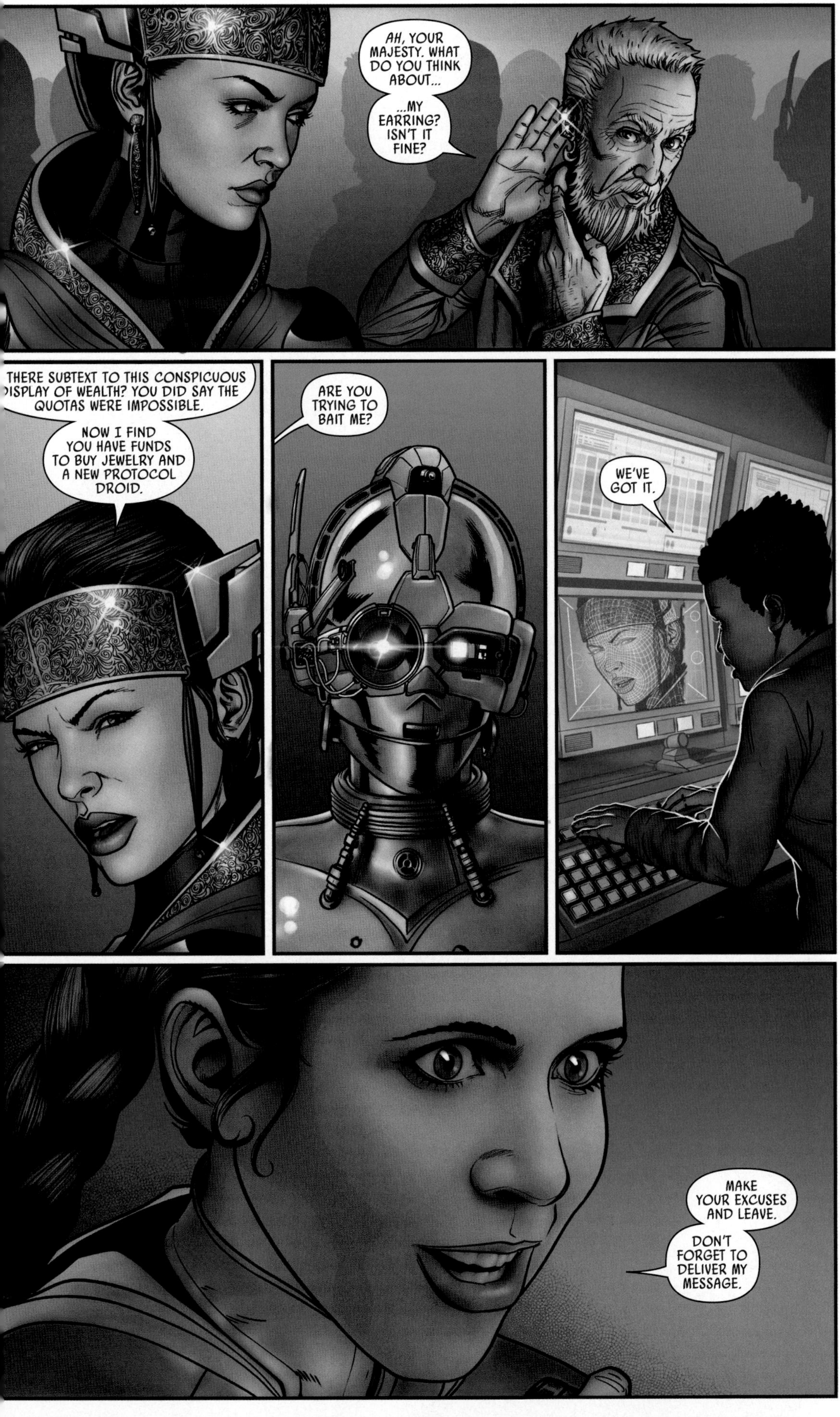
AH, YOUR MAJESTY. WHAT DO YOU THINK ABOUT...
...MY EARRING? ISN'T IT FINE?
THERE SUBTEXT TO THIS CONSPICUOUS DISPLAY OF WEALTH? YOU DID SAY THE QUOTAS WERE IMPOSSIBLE.
NOW I FIND YOU HAVE FUNDS TO BUY JEWELRY AND A NEW PROTOCOL DROID.
ARE YOU TRYING TO BAIT ME?
WE'VE GOT IT.
MAKE YOUR EXCUSES AND LEAVE.
DON'T FORGET TO DELIVER MY MESSAGE.

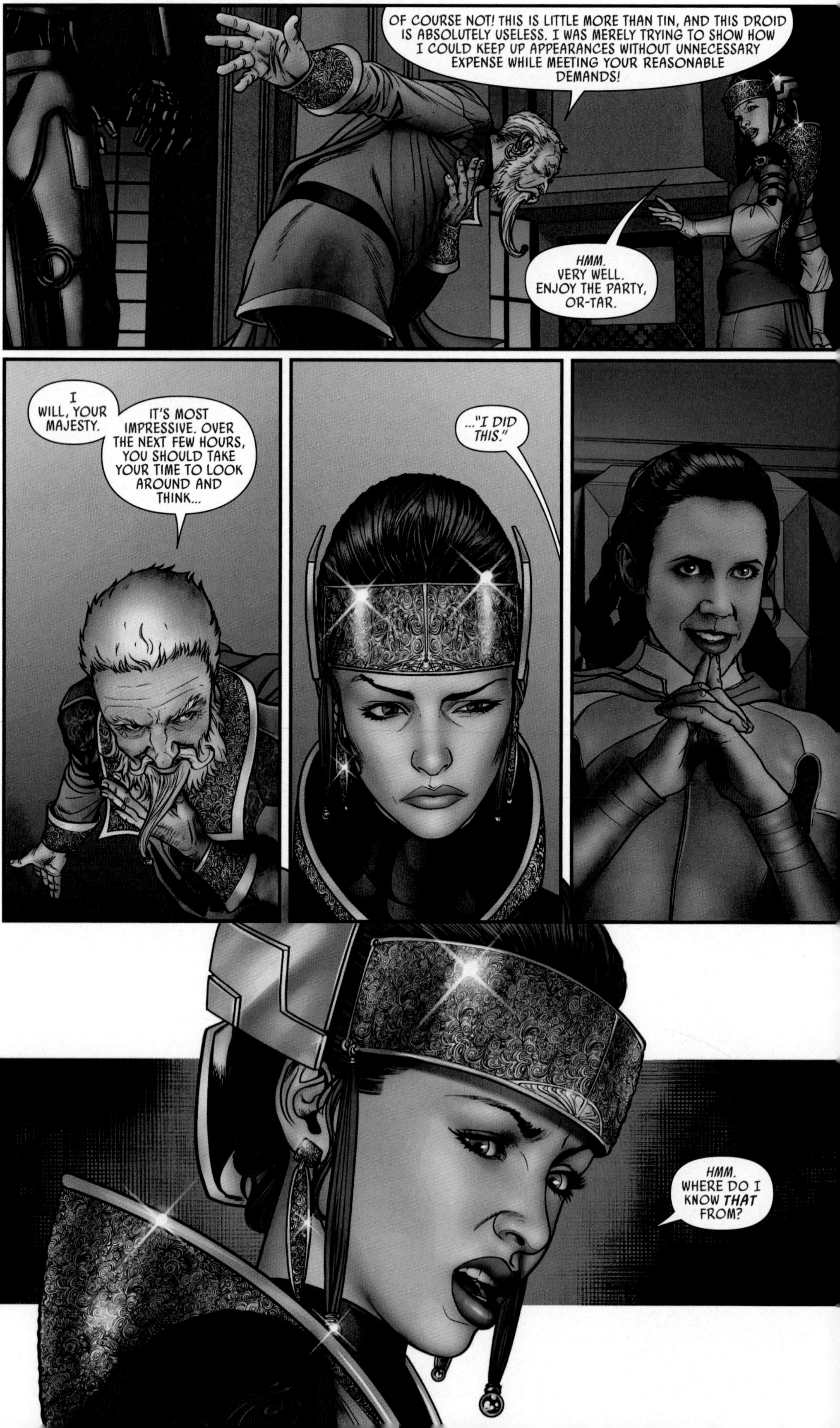
OF COURSE NOT! THIS IS LITTLE MORE THAN TIN, AND THIS DROID IS ABSOLUTELY USELESS. I WAS MERELY TRYING TO SHOW HOW I COULD KEEP UP APPEARANCES WITHOUT UNNECESSARY EXPENSE WHILE MEETING YOUR REASONABLE DEMANDS!
HMM. VERY WELL. ENJOY THE PARTY, OR-TAR.
I WILL, YOUR MAJESTY.
IT'S MOST IMPRESSIVE. OVER THE NEXT FEW HOURS, YOU SHOULD TAKE YOUR TIME TO LOOK AROUND AND THINK...
..."I DID THIS."
HMM. WHERE DO I KNOW THAT FROM?

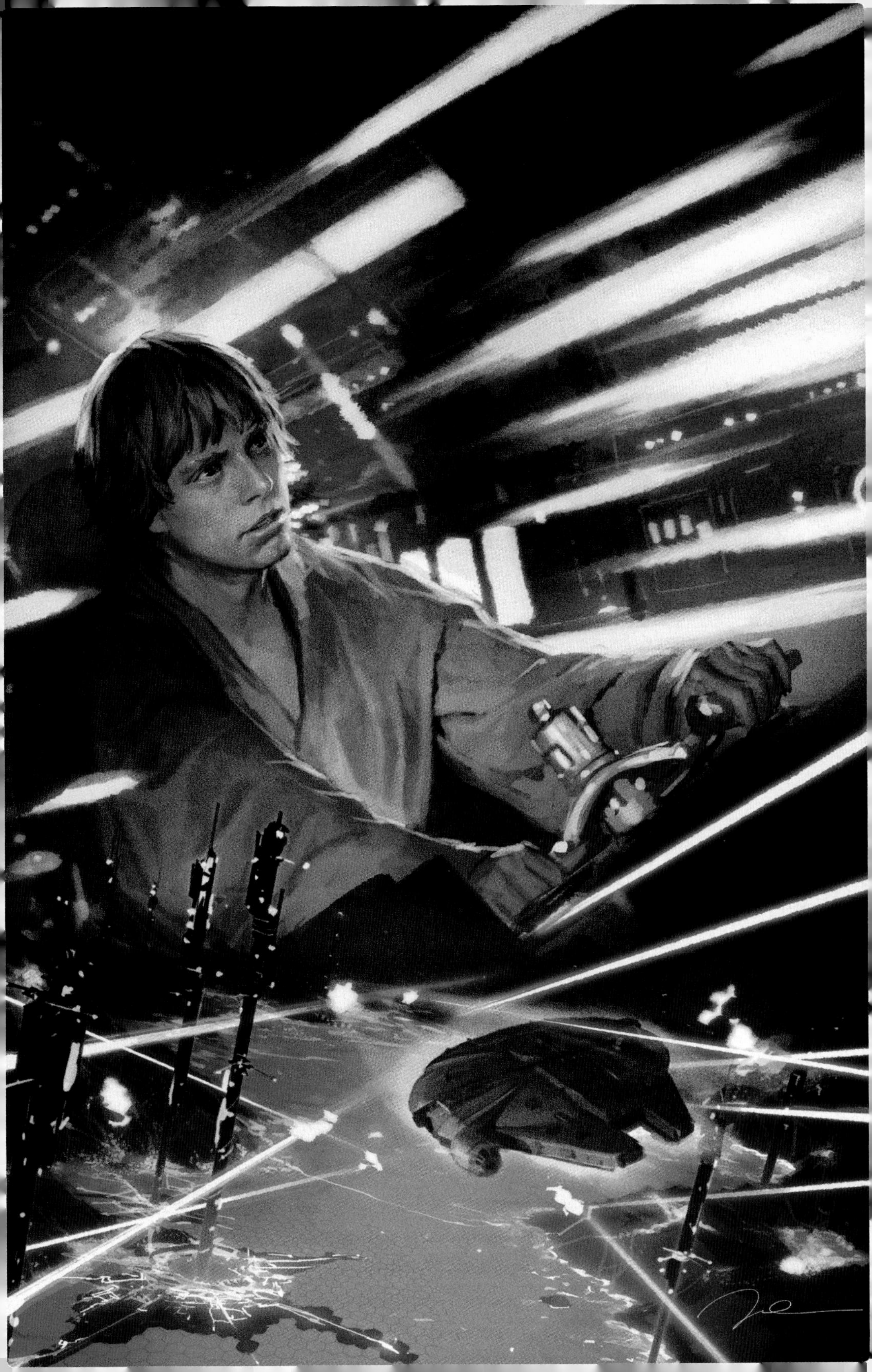

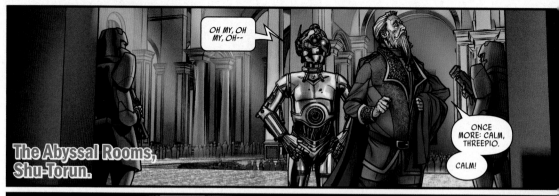

OH MY, OH MY, OH--

The Abyssal Rooms, Shu-Torun.

ONCE MORE: CALM, THREEPIO.

CALM!

HASTE WILL ATTRACT ATTENTION. WALK LIKE YOU OWN THE PLACE. YOU NEED TO SORT OF *EXUDE* PRIVILEGE AND POWER.

EXUDE, MY DEAR DROID. *EXUDE!*

I THINK I'M EXUDING LUBRICANT FROM ALL MY JOINTS, SIR.

WE COULD BE DISCOVERED AT ANY MOMENT!

YET WE WEREN'T. WAS THE SCAN OF THE QUEEN'S EYE SUITABLE? IF SO, CAN WE PLEASE BE GETTING OUT OF HERE, HMM?

THE READ IS GOOD. I'VE SLICED THE DOCKING SECURITY. THEY'LL THINK WE'RE STILL HERE UNLESS THEY MANUALLY COME TO CHECK.

SHOULD BUY US MORE TIME TO...I DON'T KNOW...*NOT BE HERE!*

DON'T WORRY, MEORTI, WE'RE LEAVING.

TUNGA, CHANGE BACK TO YOUR NORMAL FORM. YOU NEED TO GET READY FOR THE RETREAT.

AND THIS PLACE IS WEIRD ENOUGH WITHOUT TWO CLONES OF CRUSTY OLD BARONS AROUND THE PLACE...

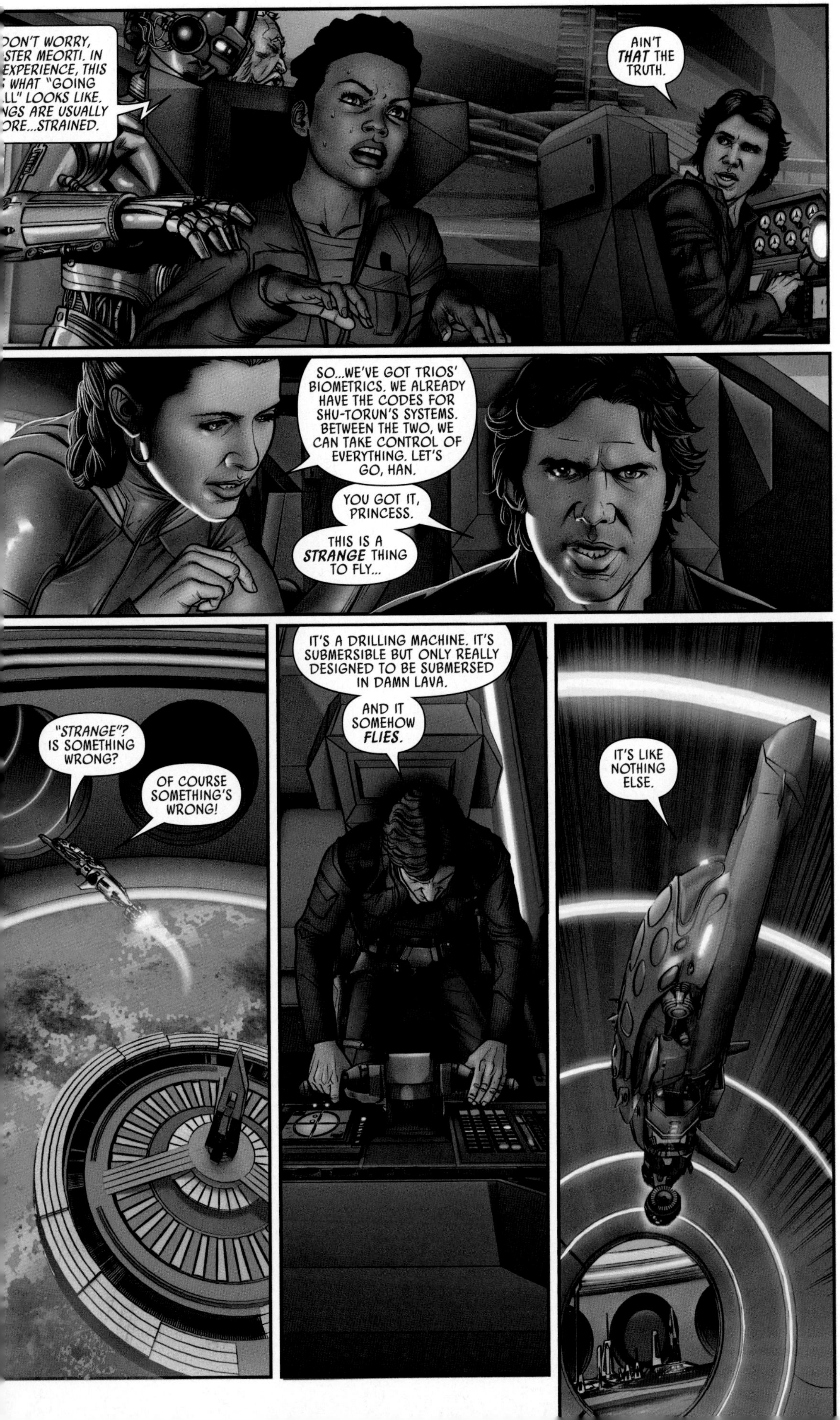
DON'T WORRY, STER MEORTI. IN EXPERIENCE, THIS S WHAT "GOING LL" LOOKS LIKE. NGS ARE USUALLY ORE...STRAINED.
AIN'T THAT THE TRUTH.
SO...WE'VE GOT TRIOS' BIOMETRICS. WE ALREADY HAVE THE CODES FOR SHU-TORUN'S SYSTEMS. BETWEEN THE TWO, WE CAN TAKE CONTROL OF EVERYTHING. LET'S GO, HAN.
YOU GOT IT, PRINCESS.
THIS IS A STRANGE THING TO FLY...
"STRANGE"? IS SOMETHING WRONG?
OF COURSE SOMETHING'S WRONG!
IT'S A DRILLING MACHINE. IT'S SUBMERSIBLE BUT ONLY REALLY DESIGNED TO BE SUBMERSED IN DAMN LAVA.
AND IT SOMEHOW FLIES.
IT'S LIKE NOTHING ELSE.

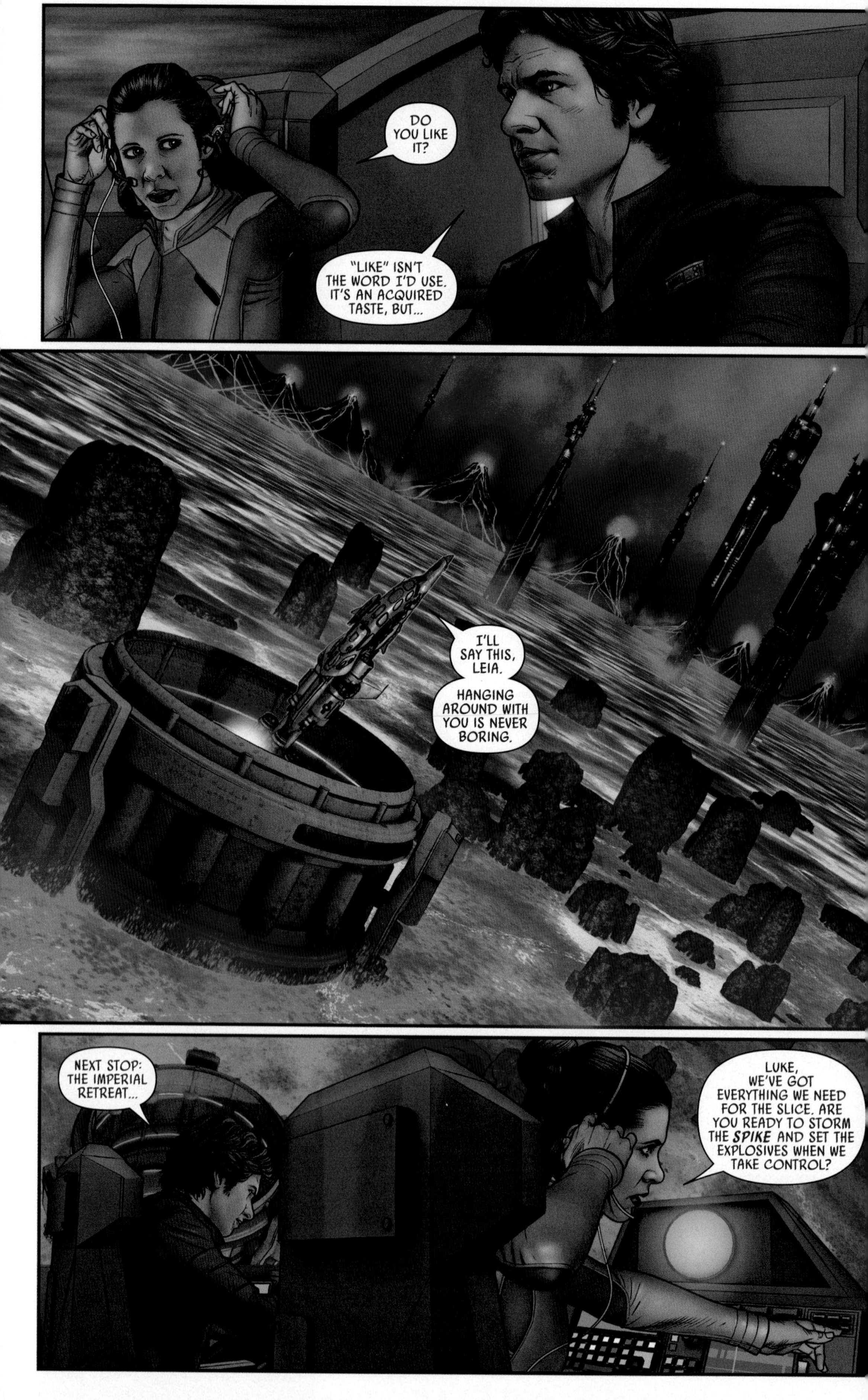
DO YOU LIKE IT?
"LIKE" ISN'T THE WORD I'D USE. IT'S AN ACQUIRED TASTE, BUT...
I'LL SAY THIS, LEIA.
HANGING AROUND WITH YOU IS NEVER BORING.
NEXT STOP: THE IMPERIAL RETREAT...
LUKE, WE'VE GOT EVERYTHING WE NEED FOR THE SLICE. ARE YOU READY TO STORM THE SPIKE AND SET THE EXPLOSIVES WHEN WE TAKE CONTROL?

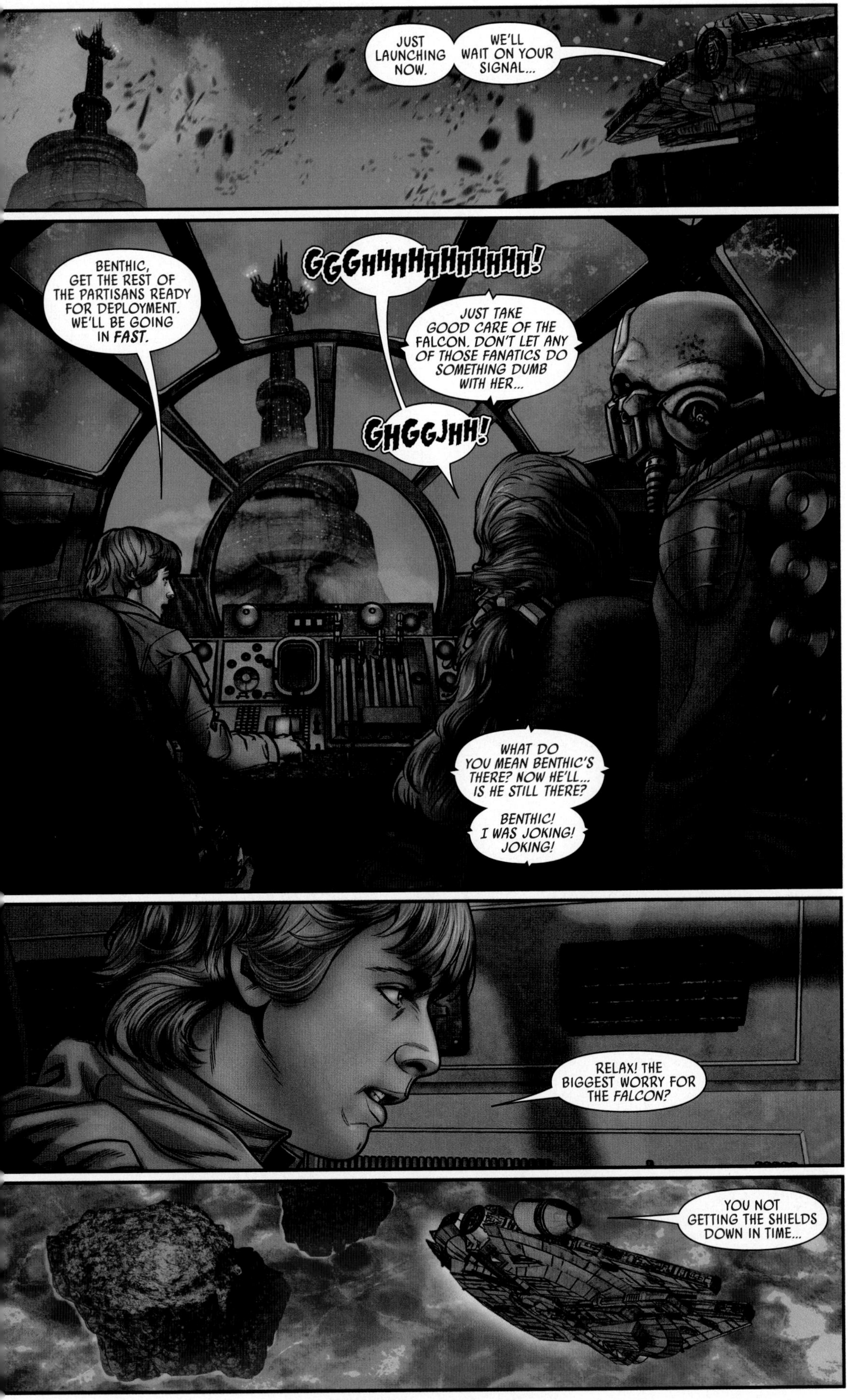
JUST LAUNCHING NOW.
WE'LL WAIT ON YOUR SIGNAL...
BENTHIC, GET THE REST OF THE PARTISANS READY FOR DEPLOYMENT. WE'LL BE GOING IN FAST.
GGGHHHHHHHHHH!
JUST TAKE GOOD CARE OF THE FALCON. DON'T LET ANY OF THOSE FANATICS DO SOMETHING DUMB WITH HER...
GHGGJHH!
WHAT DO YOU MEAN BENTHIC'S THERE? NOW HE'LL... IS HE STILL THERE?
BENTHIC! I WAS JOKING! JOKING!
RELAX! THE BIGGEST WORRY FOR THE FALCON?
YOU NOT GETTING THE SHIELDS DOWN IN TIME...

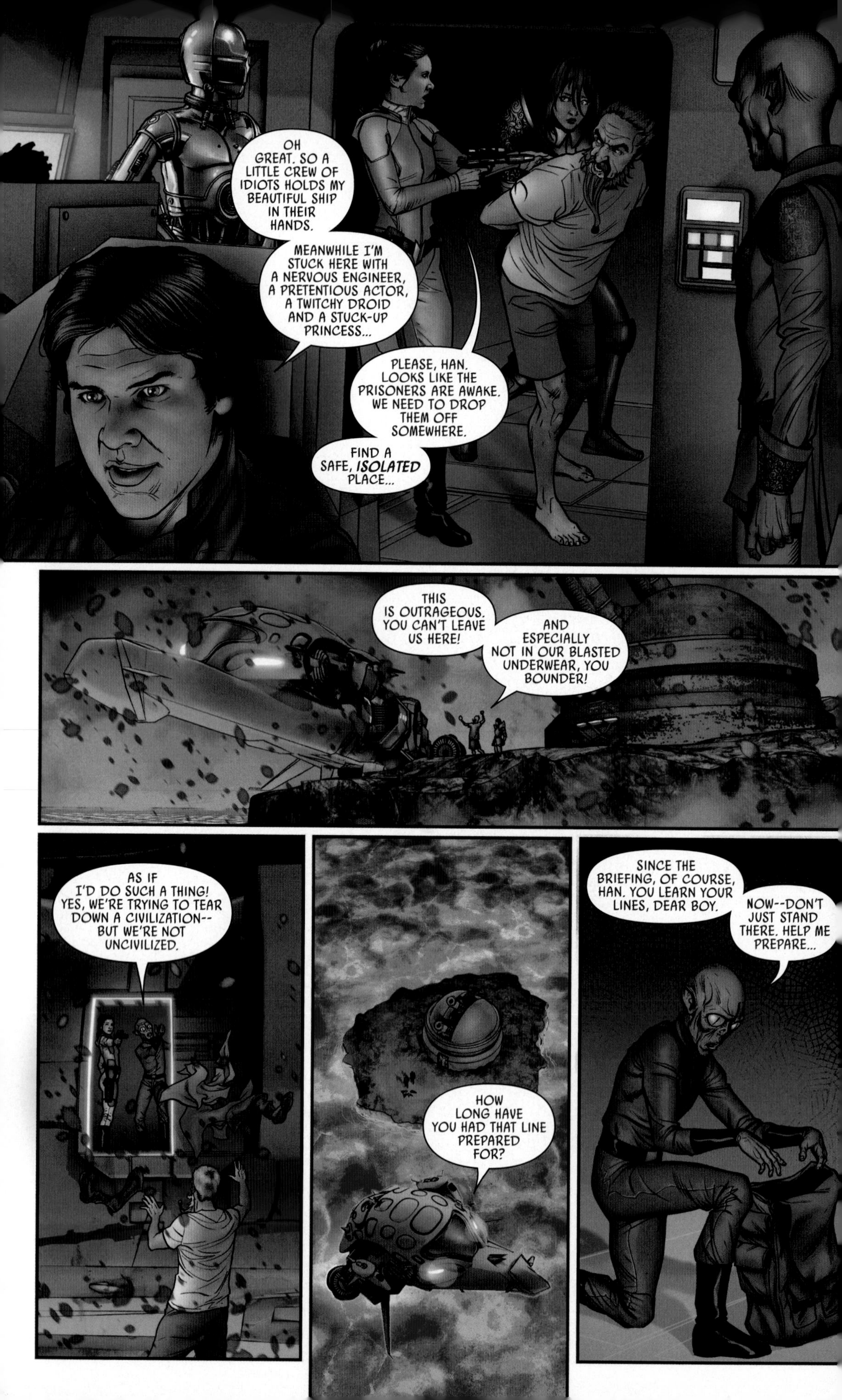
OH GREAT. SO A LITTLE CREW OF IDIOTS HOLDS MY BEAUTIFUL SHIP IN THEIR HANDS.
MEANWHILE I'M STUCK HERE WITH A NERVOUS ENGINEER, A PRETENTIOUS ACTOR, A TWITCHY DROID AND A STUCK-UP PRINCESS...
PLEASE, HAN. LOOKS LIKE THE PRISONERS ARE AWAKE. WE NEED TO DROP THEM OFF SOMEWHERE.
FIND A SAFE, *ISOLATED* PLACE...
THIS IS OUTRAGEOUS. YOU CAN'T LEAVE US HERE!
AND ESPECIALLY NOT IN OUR BLASTED UNDERWEAR, YOU BOUNDER!
AS IF I'D DO SUCH A THING! YES, WE'RE TRYING TO TEAR DOWN A CIVILIZATION--BUT WE'RE NOT UNCIVILIZED.
HOW LONG HAVE YOU HAD THAT LINE PREPARED FOR?
SINCE THE BRIEFING, OF COURSE, HAN. YOU LEARN YOUR LINES, DEAR BOY.
NOW--DON'T JUST STAND THERE. HELP ME PREPARE...

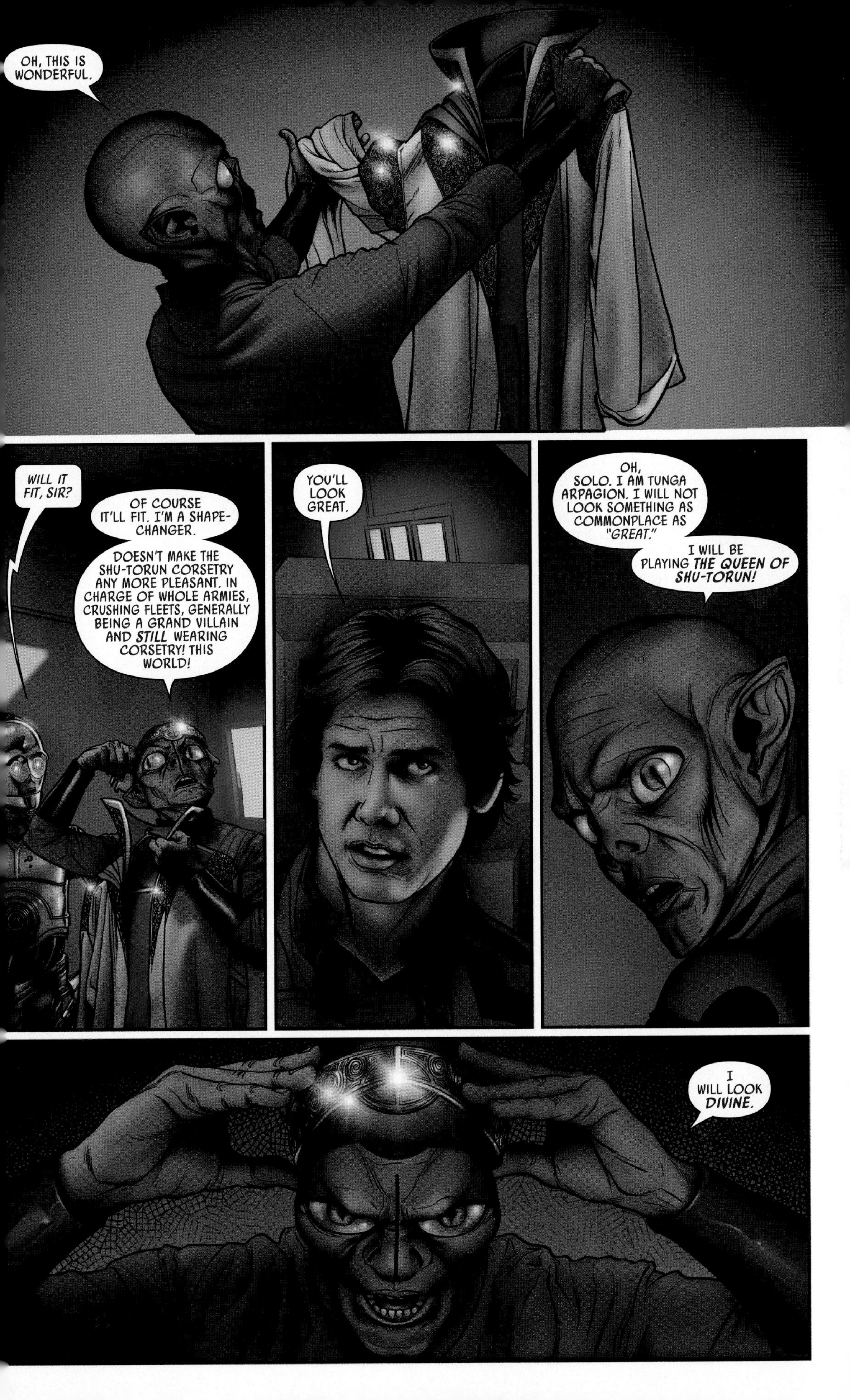
OH, THIS IS WONDERFUL.
WILL IT FIT, SIR?
OF COURSE IT'LL FIT. I'M A SHAPE-CHANGER.
DOESN'T MAKE THE SHU-TORUN CORSETRY ANY MORE PLEASANT. IN CHARGE OF WHOLE ARMIES, CRUSHING FLEETS, GENERALLY BEING A GRAND VILLAIN AND STILL WEARING CORSETRY! THIS WORLD!
YOU'LL LOOK GREAT.
OH, SOLO. I AM TUNGA ARPAGION. I WILL NOT LOOK SOMETHING AS COMMONPLACE AS "GREAT."
I WILL BE PLAYING THE QUEEN OF SHU-TORUN!
I WILL LOOK DIVINE.

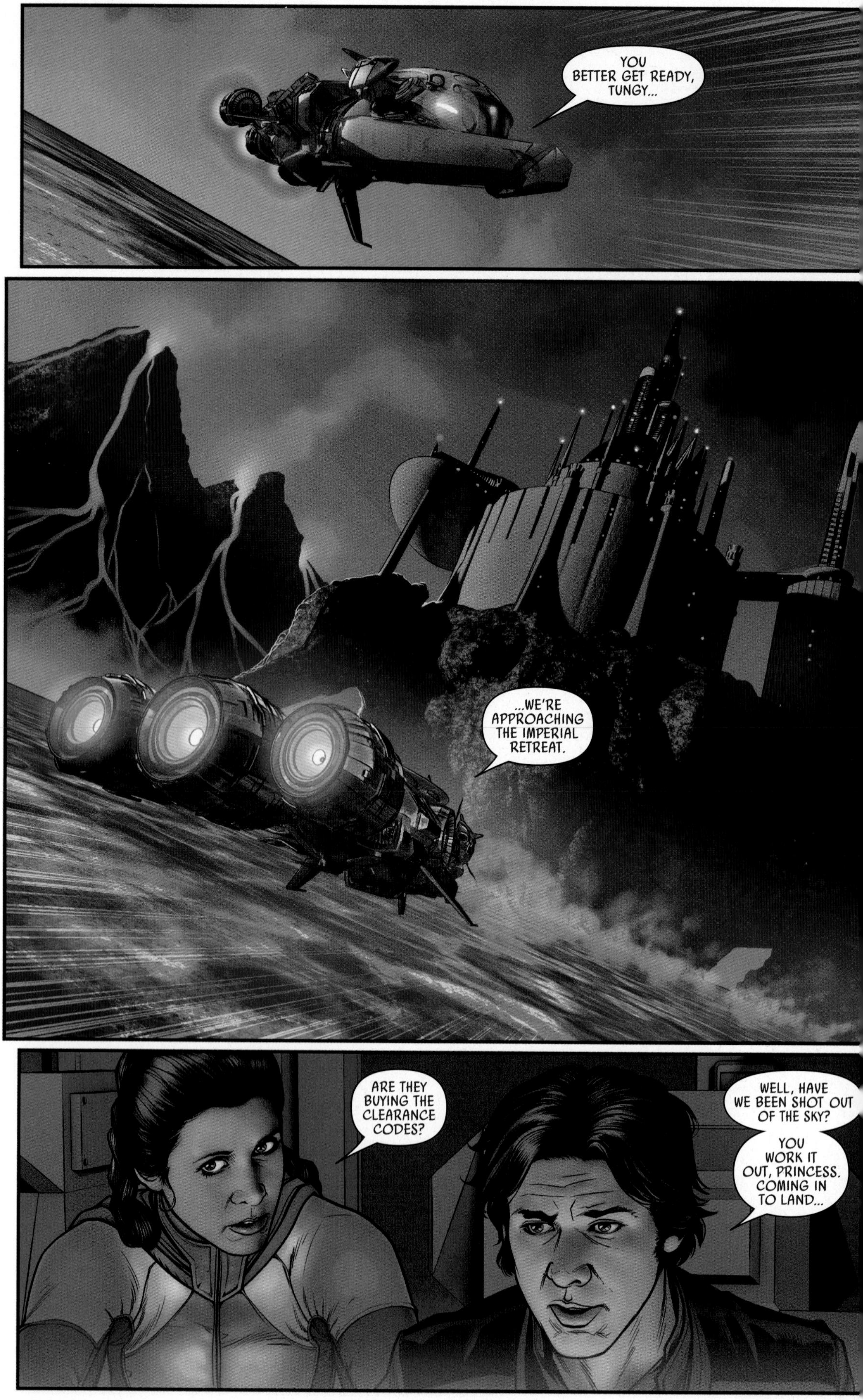

YOU BETTER GET READY, TUNGY...
...WE'RE APPROACHING THE IMPERIAL RETREAT.
ARE THEY BUYING THE CLEARANCE CODES?
WELL, HAVE WE BEEN SHOT OUT OF THE SKY?
YOU WORK IT OUT, PRINCESS. COMING IN TO LAND...

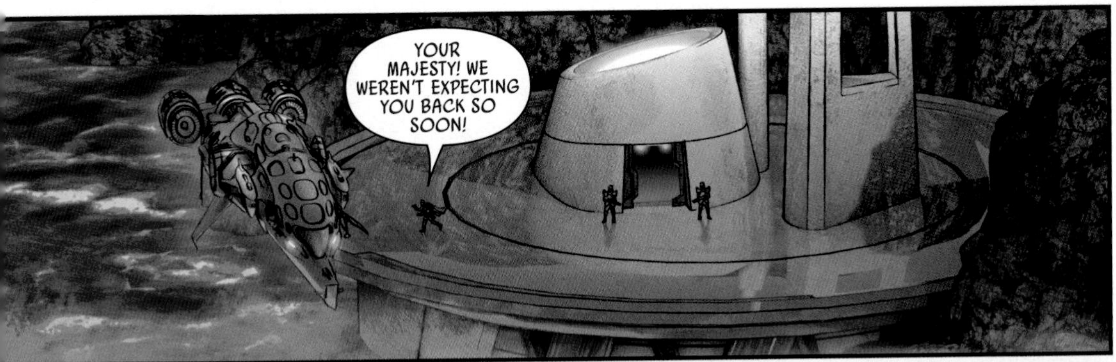
YOUR MAJESTY! WE WEREN'T EXPECTING YOU BACK SO SOON!

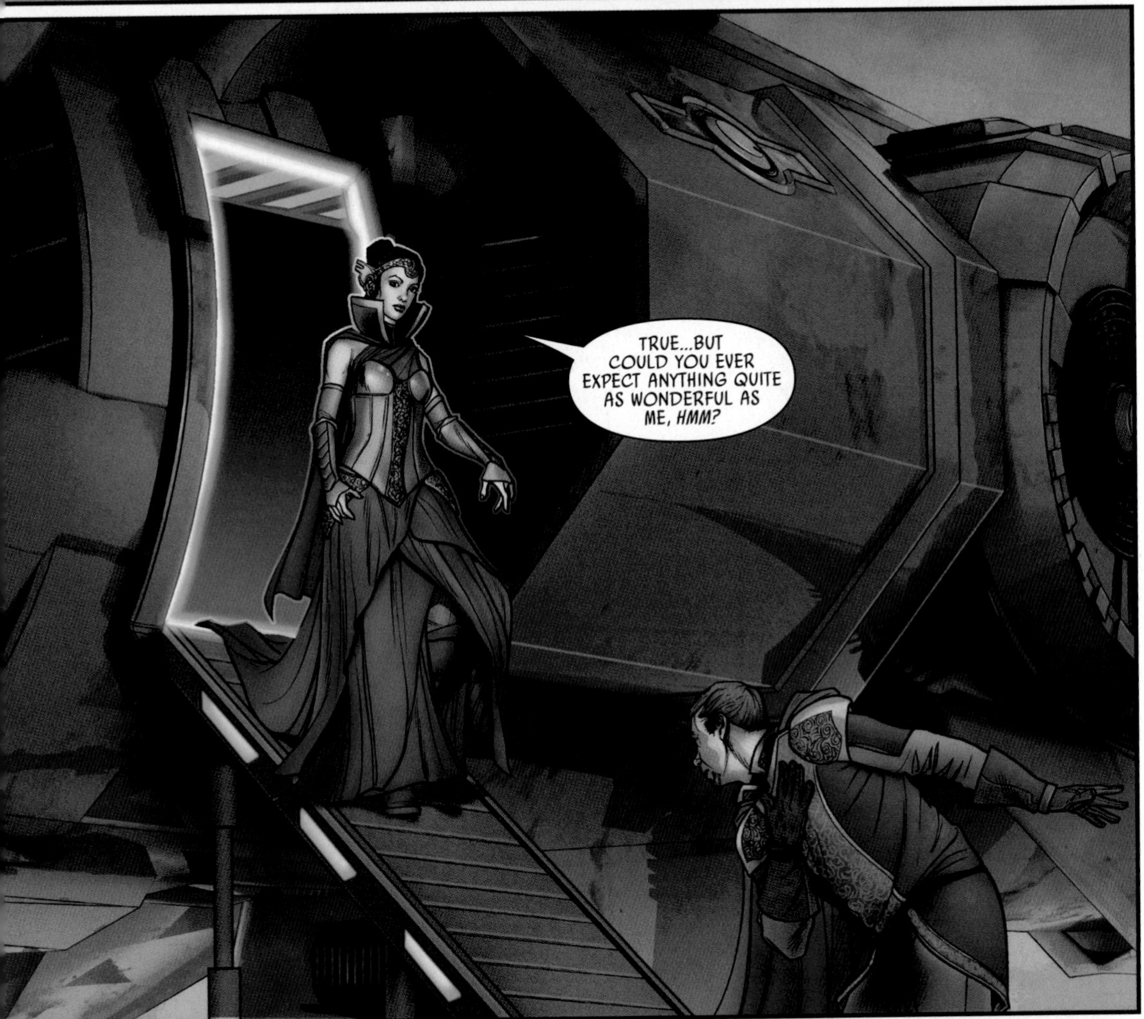
TRUE...BUT COULD YOU EVER EXPECT ANYTHING QUITE AS WONDERFUL AS ME, *HMM?*

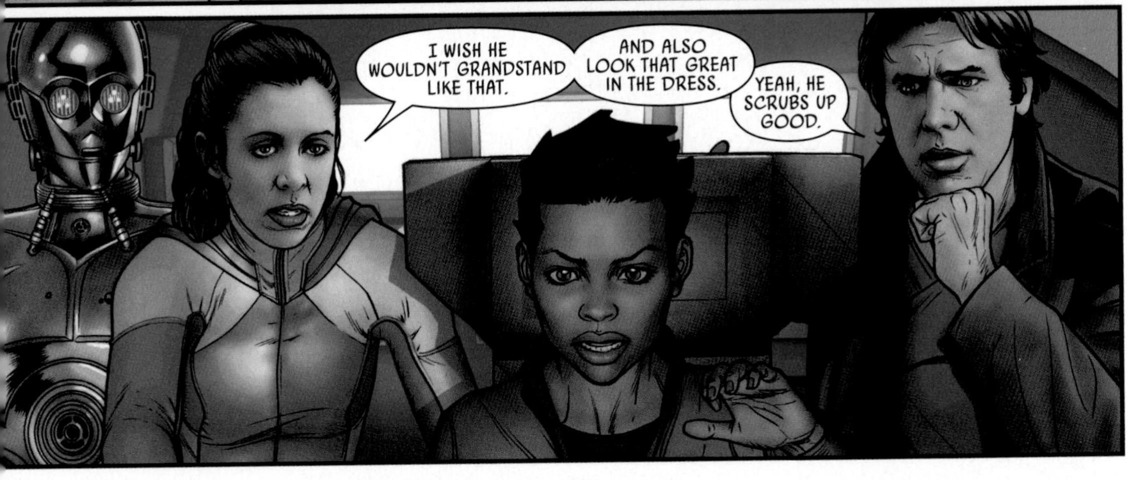
I WISH HE WOULDN'T GRANDSTAND LIKE THAT.
AND ALSO LOOK THAT GREAT IN THE DRESS.
YEAH, HE SCRUBS UP GOOD.

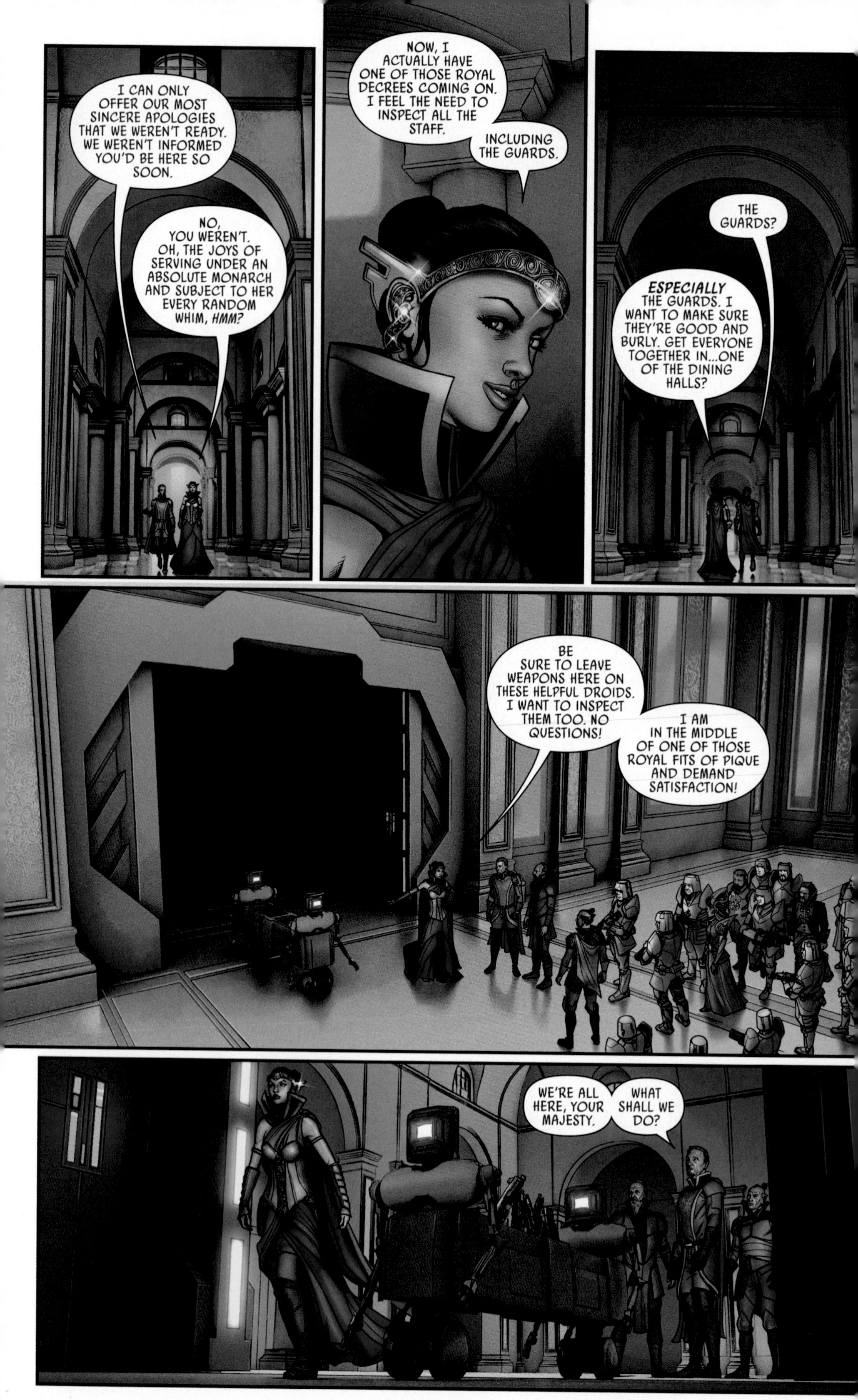
I CAN ONLY OFFER OUR MOST SINCERE APOLOGIES THAT WE WEREN'T READY. WE WEREN'T INFORMED YOU'D BE HERE SO SOON.
NO, YOU WEREN'T. OH, THE JOYS OF SERVING UNDER AN ABSOLUTE MONARCH AND SUBJECT TO HER EVERY RANDOM WHIM, *HMM?*
NOW, I ACTUALLY HAVE ONE OF THOSE ROYAL DECREES COMING ON. I FEEL THE NEED TO INSPECT ALL THE STAFF.
INCLUDING THE GUARDS.
THE GUARDS?
ESPECIALLY THE GUARDS. I WANT TO MAKE SURE THEY'RE GOOD AND BURLY. GET EVERYONE TOGETHER IN...ONE OF THE DINING HALLS?
BE SURE TO LEAVE WEAPONS HERE ON THESE HELPFUL DROIDS. I WANT TO INSPECT THEM TOO. NO QUESTIONS!
I AM IN THE MIDDLE OF ONE OF THOSE ROYAL FITS OF PIQUE AND DEMAND SATISFACTION!
WE'RE ALL HERE, YOUR MAJESTY.
WHAT SHALL WE DO?

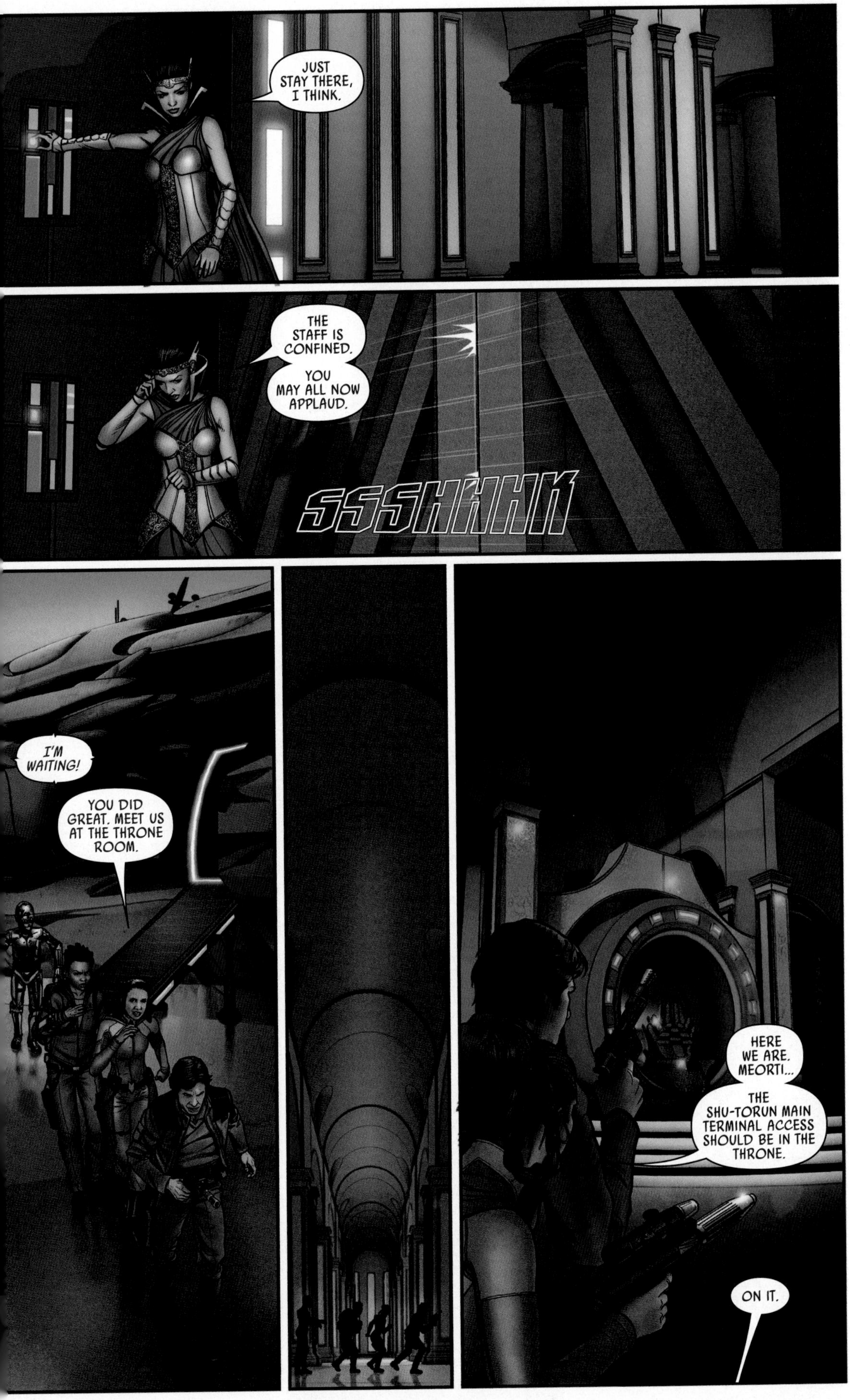
JUST STAY THERE, I THINK.
THE STAFF IS CONFINED.
YOU MAY ALL NOW APPLAUD.
SSSHHHK
I'M WAITING!
YOU DID GREAT. MEET US AT THE THRONE ROOM.
HERE WE ARE. MEORTI...
THE SHU-TORUN MAIN TERMINAL ACCESS SHOULD BE IN THE THRONE.
ON IT.

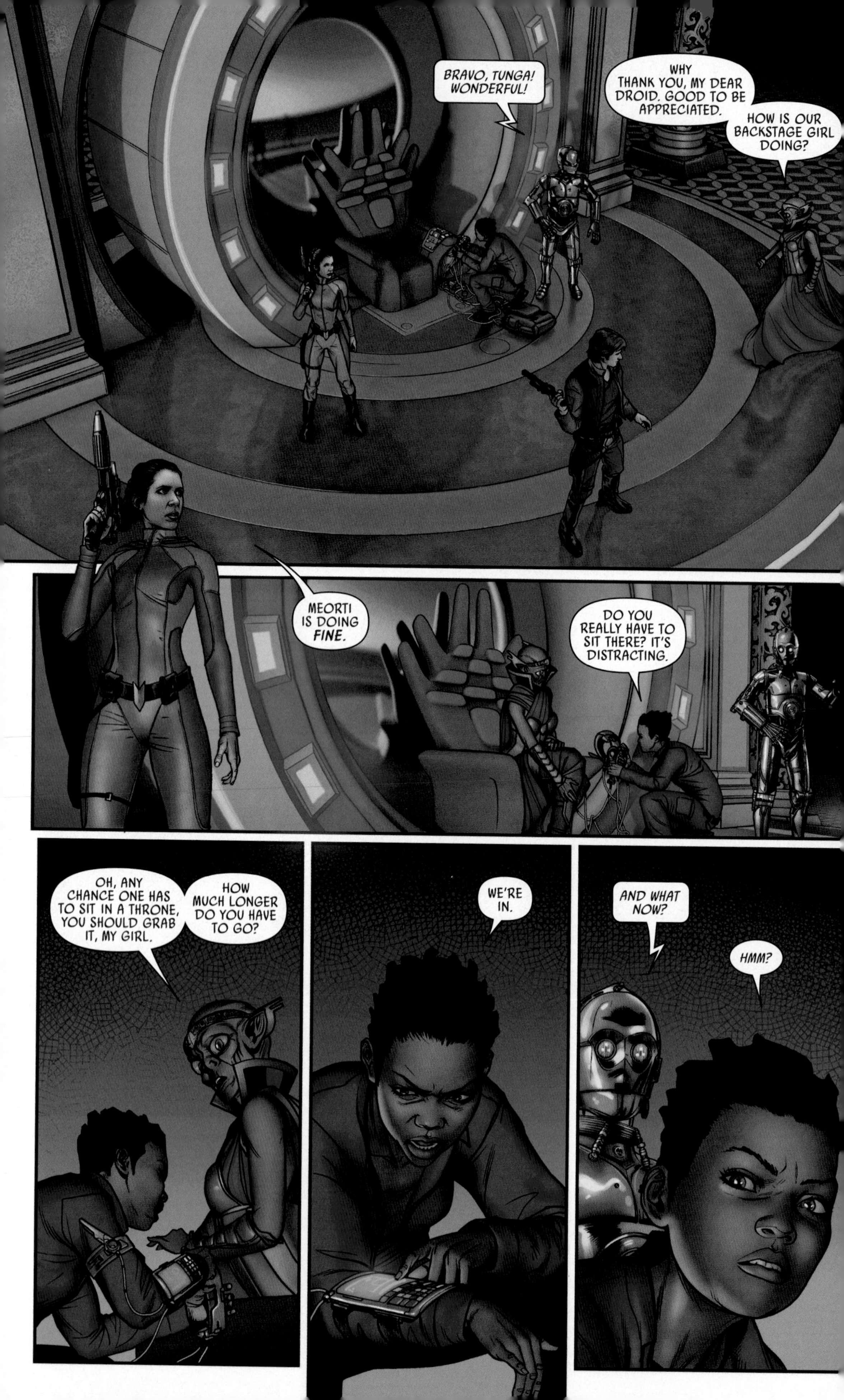
BRAVO, TUNGA! WONDERFUL!
WHY THANK YOU, MY DEAR DROID. GOOD TO BE APPRECIATED.
HOW IS OUR BACKSTAGE GIRL DOING?
MEORTI IS DOING FINE.
DO YOU REALLY HAVE TO SIT THERE? IT'S DISTRACTING.
OH, ANY CHANCE ONE HAS TO SIT IN A THRONE, YOU SHOULD GRAB IT, MY GIRL.
HOW MUCH LONGER DO YOU HAVE TO GO?
WE'RE IN.
AND WHAT NOW?
HMM?

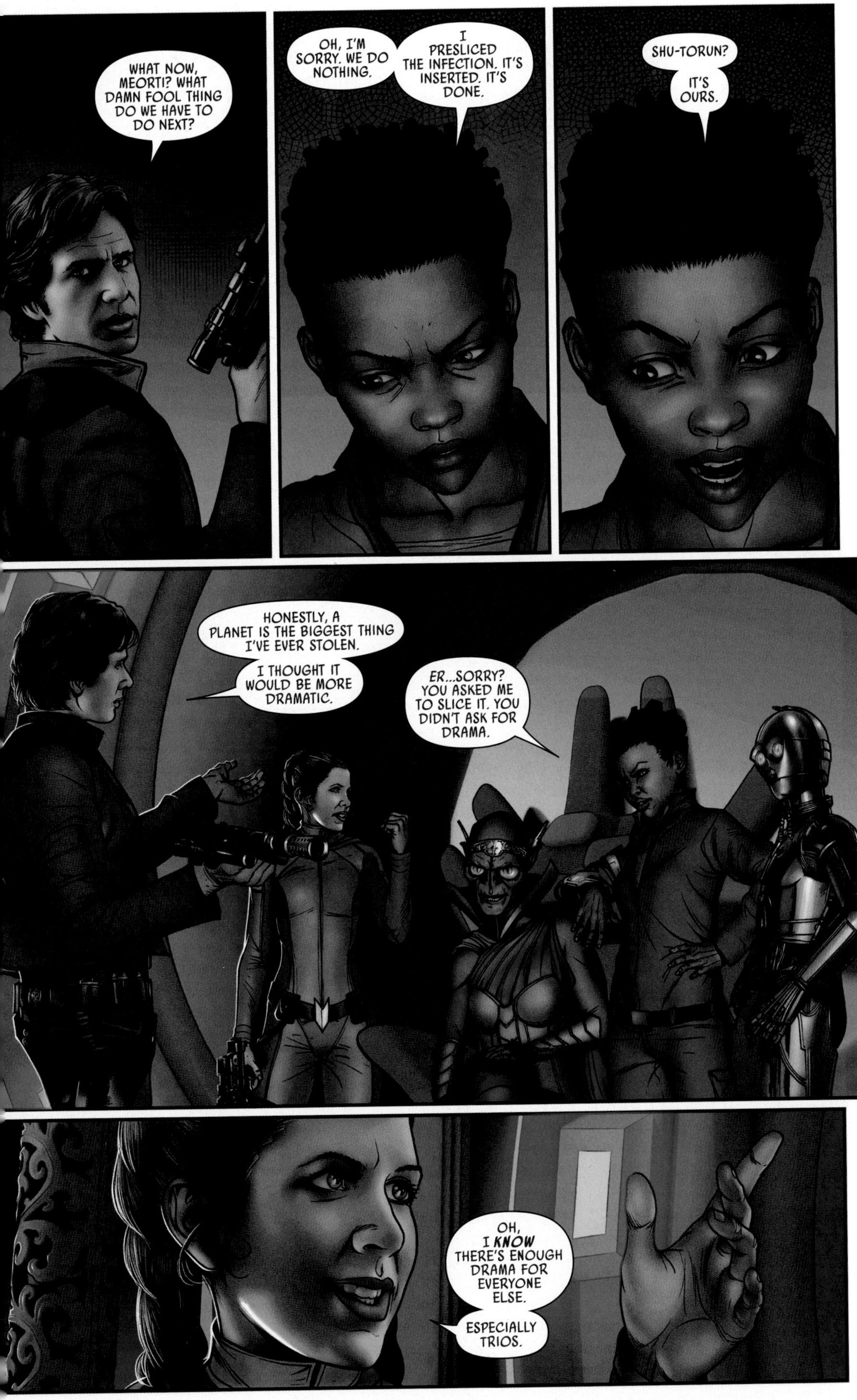
WHAT NOW, MEORTI? WHAT DAMN FOOL THING DO WE HAVE TO DO NEXT?
OH, I'M SORRY. WE DO NOTHING.
I PRESLICED THE INFECTION. IT'S INSERTED. IT'S DONE.
SHU-TORUN?
IT'S OURS.
HONESTLY, A PLANET IS THE BIGGEST THING I'VE EVER STOLEN.
I THOUGHT IT WOULD BE MORE DRAMATIC.
ER...SORRY? YOU ASKED ME TO SLICE IT. YOU DIDN'T ASK FOR DRAMA.
OH, I *KNOW* THERE'S ENOUGH DRAMA FOR EVERYONE ELSE.
ESPECIALLY TRIOS.

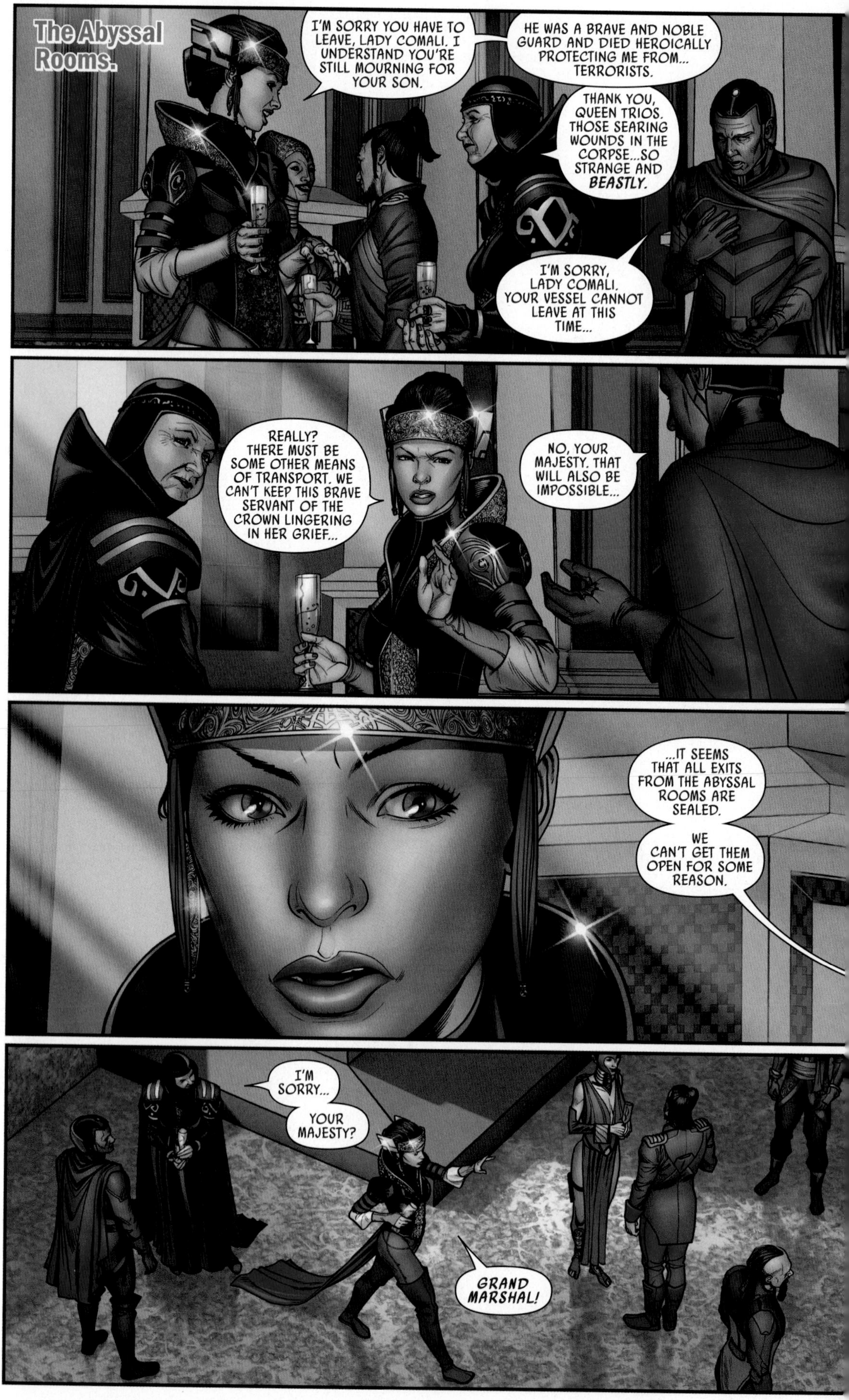

The Abyssal Rooms.
I'M SORRY YOU HAVE TO LEAVE, LADY COMALI. I UNDERSTAND YOU'RE STILL MOURNING FOR YOUR SON.
HE WAS A BRAVE AND NOBLE GUARD AND DIED HEROICALLY PROTECTING ME FROM... TERRORISTS.
THANK YOU, QUEEN TRIOS. THOSE SEARING WOUNDS IN THE CORPSE...SO STRANGE AND BEASTLY.
I'M SORRY, LADY COMALI. YOUR VESSEL CANNOT LEAVE AT THIS TIME...
REALLY? THERE MUST BE SOME OTHER MEANS OF TRANSPORT. WE CAN'T KEEP THIS BRAVE SERVANT OF THE CROWN LINGERING IN HER GRIEF...
NO, YOUR MAJESTY. THAT WILL ALSO BE IMPOSSIBLE...
...IT SEEMS THAT ALL EXITS FROM THE ABYSSAL ROOMS ARE SEALED.
WE CAN'T GET THEM OPEN FOR SOME REASON.
I'M SORRY...
YOUR MAJESTY?
GRAND MARSHAL!

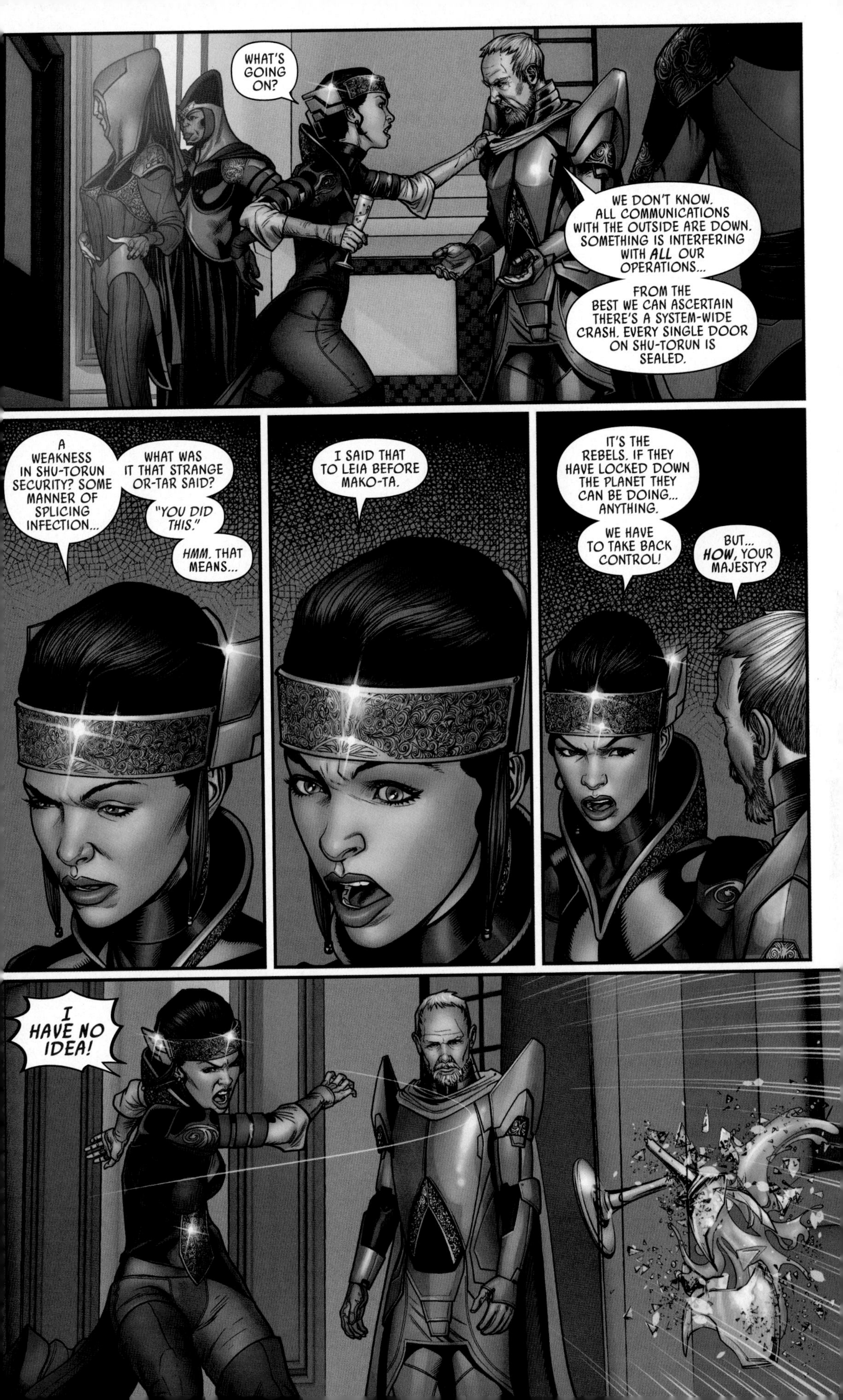
WHAT'S GOING ON?
WE DON'T KNOW. ALL COMMUNICATIONS WITH THE OUTSIDE ARE DOWN. SOMETHING IS INTERFERING WITH ALL OUR OPERATIONS...
FROM THE BEST WE CAN ASCERTAIN THERE'S A SYSTEM-WIDE CRASH. EVERY SINGLE DOOR ON SHU-TORUN IS SEALED.
A WEAKNESS IN SHU-TORUN SECURITY? SOME MANNER OF SPLICING INFECTION...
WHAT WAS IT THAT STRANGE OR-TAR SAID?
"YOU DID THIS."
HMM. THAT MEANS...
I SAID THAT TO LEIA BEFORE MAKO-TA.
IT'S THE REBELS. IF THEY HAVE LOCKED DOWN THE PLANET THEY CAN BE DOING... ANYTHING.
WE HAVE TO TAKE BACK CONTROL!
BUT... HOW, YOUR MAJESTY?
I HAVE NO IDEA!

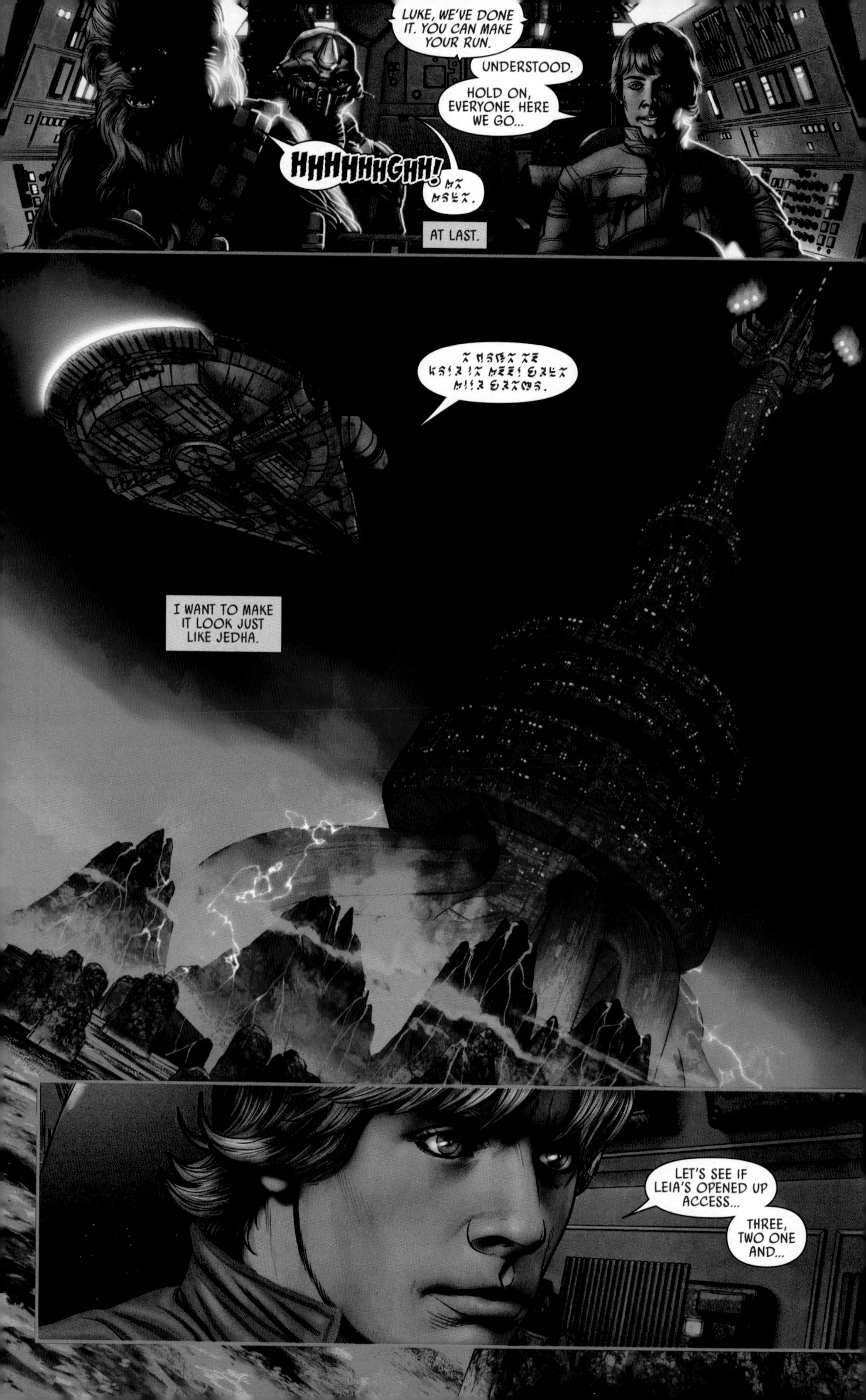
LUKE, WE'VE DONE IT. YOU CAN MAKE YOUR RUN.
UNDERSTOOD.
HOLD ON, EVERYONE. HERE WE GO...
HHHHHHGHH!
AT LAST.
I WANT TO MAKE IT LOOK JUST LIKE JEDHA.
LET'S SEE IF LEIA'S OPENED UP ACCESS...
THREE, TWO ONE AND...

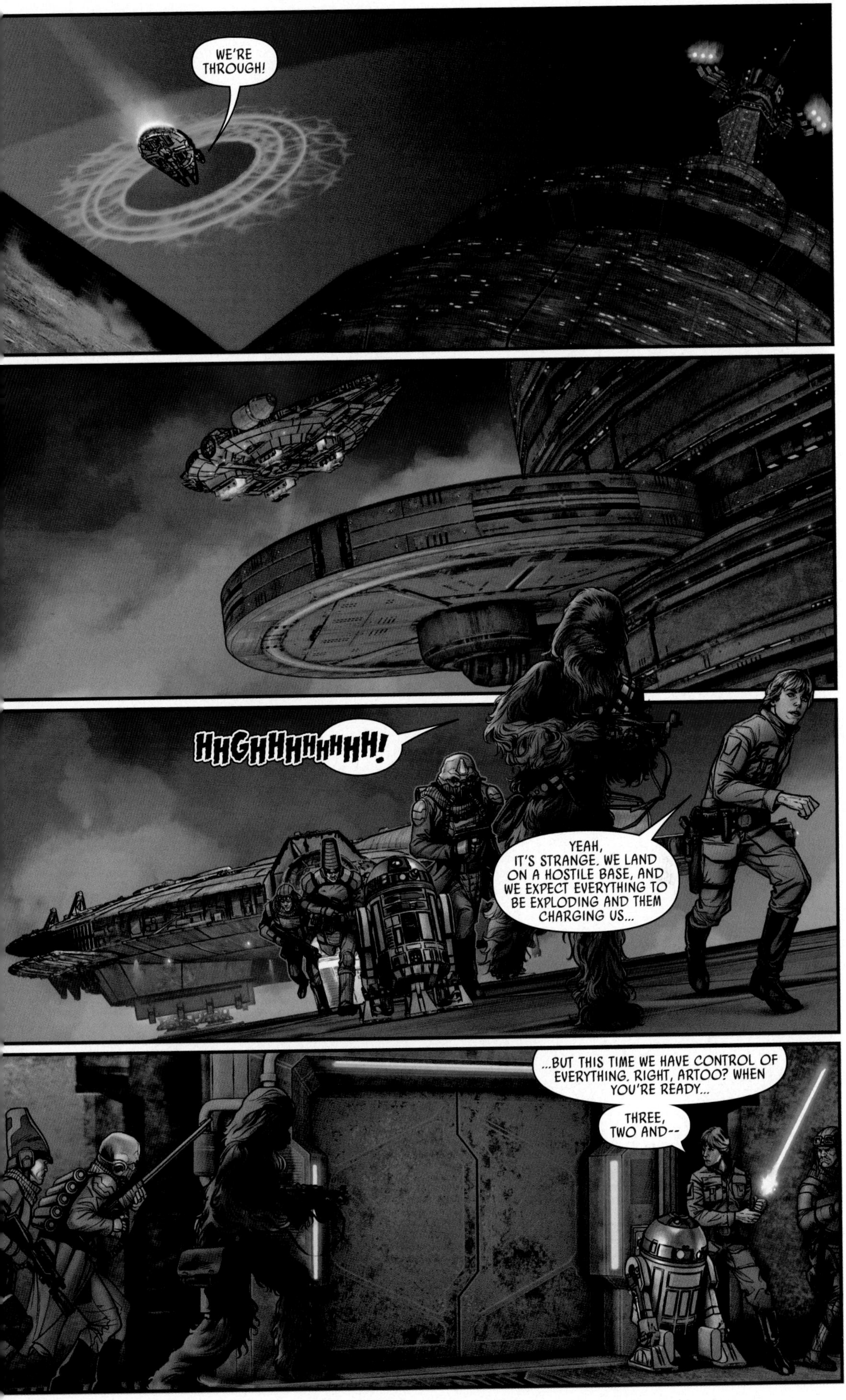
WE'RE THROUGH!
HHGHHHHHHHH!
YEAH, IT'S STRANGE. WE LAND ON A HOSTILE BASE, AND WE EXPECT EVERYTHING TO BE EXPLODING AND THEM CHARGING US...
...BUT THIS TIME WE HAVE CONTROL OF EVERYTHING. RIGHT, ARTOO? WHEN YOU'RE READY...
THREE, TWO AND--

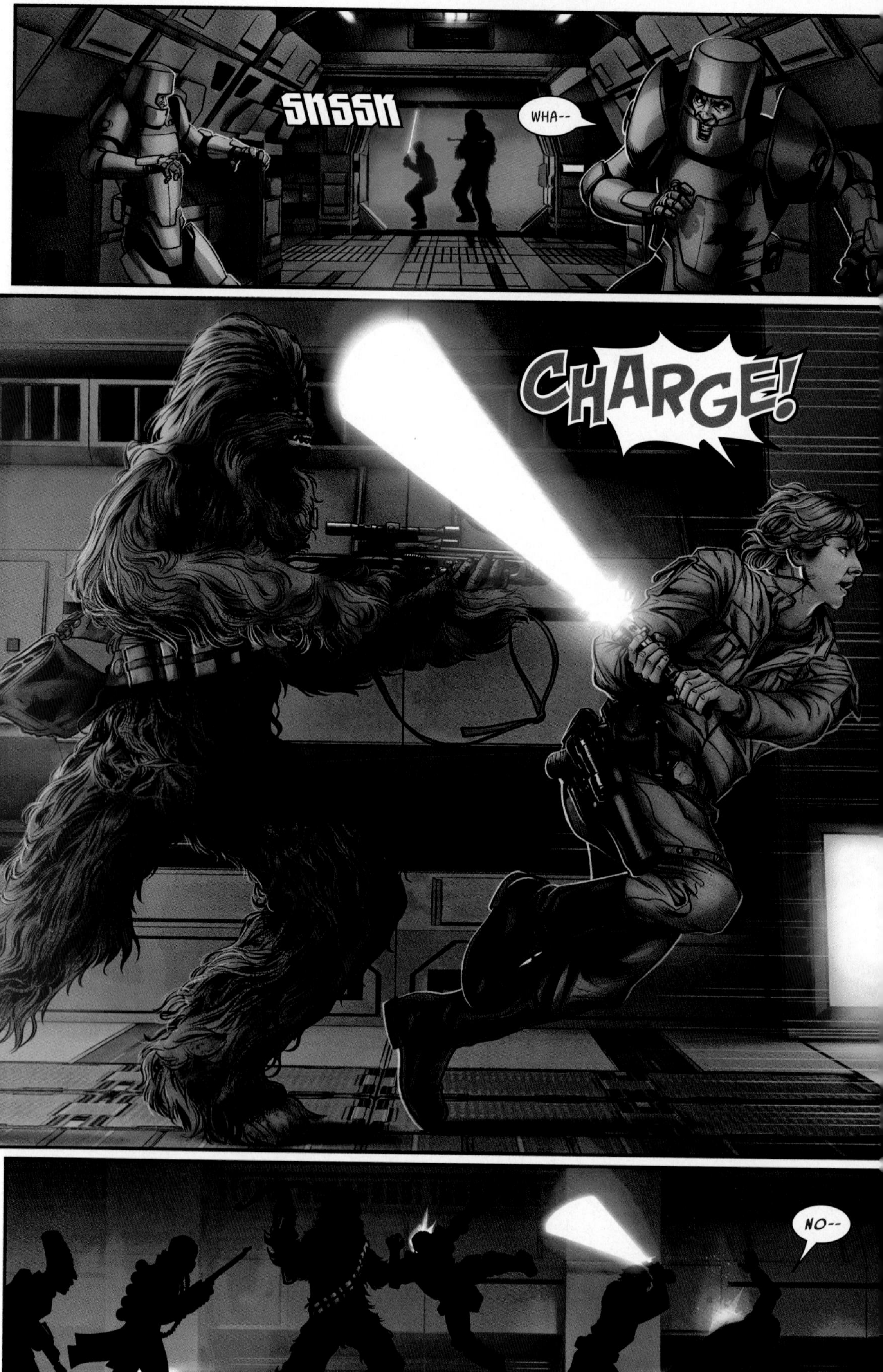
SKSSK
WHA--
CHARGE!
NO--

WE'RE FINISHED HERE. SECURE THE PRISONERS AND--

BENTHIC!

VEZ BEIZT ZOZ ZBGZIESBE ZE BEIE MEZ. ZE MEZ GZ EZGGGIEZZ MGZE ZOZA BEZ MIIZ ZOZ ZBGZIESBE.

YOU ASKED THE PARTISANS TO JOIN YOU. DO NOT BE SURPRISED WHEN THEY ACT LIKE THE PARTISANS.

MEZ GZEIZZGMMMZ EZBBEZ GIEI MZGGIEN ZBMMEZ ZE ZZG GZZG.

AND BESIDES-- WE CANNOT RISK LEAVING ANYONE TO OUR REAR.

I... JUST DON'T PUSH IT. WE HAVE **ALL** THE ADVANTAGES HERE.

ONLY **WE** CAN OPEN DOORS. WE MAKE OUR WAY TO EACH OF THE CORES, BLOW THEM UP AND BRING THE SPIKE DOWN.

THIS WAY!

ALL WE HAVE TO DO IS STICK TOGETHER.

CHEWIE--
GET BACK TO
THE SHIP AND KEEP
CONTACT WITH THE
PRINCESS.

RGGGGHHH!

BENTHIC,
AS REQUESTED, I
HAVE BEEN STUDYING
THE SYSTEMS.

ᏇᎮᎮᏆᏕ
ᎮᎬᏇᏆᏕ WILL IT
WORK?

YES. THE SPIKE WILL
BE DESTROYED. IT WILL
RUIN THE SHU-TORUN
ECONOMY...

...BUT THERE IS AN
OPPORTUNITY.

WE CAN
HYPER-CHARGE THE FINAL
CORE AND INCREASE ITS
SHIELDING. THE SPIKE WILL
NOT TEAR APART.

INSTEAD, IT
WILL PIVOT AND
TEAR OPEN THE WHOLE
PLANET, LIKE A
SHIELDED
KNIFE...

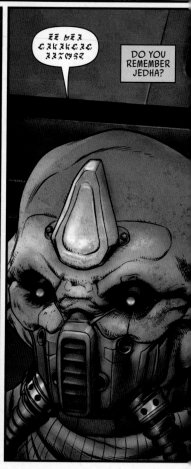

ᏕᏕ ᎮᏕᏕ
ᏣᎦᏗᏂᎦᏣᏣᏗ
ᏗᏗᏂᏟᎦᏣᏕ DO YOU
REMEMBER
JEDHA?

OF COURSE, BENTHIC.

ᏃᏔᏃᏔᏃᏔ

ᏃᏔᏃᏔᏃ

A PLANET TORN APART BY THEIR TECHNOLOGICAL HUBRIS.

ALL WHO SERVE THE EMPIRE ARE COMPLICIT IN THAT SIN.

ᏃᏔᏃᏔᏃ

I THINK SHU-TORUN MAY HAVE FORGOTTEN THEIR GUILT.

ᏃᏔᏃᏔᏃ

ᏃᏔᏃᏔᏃ

LET US REMIND THEM IN FIRE.

LET US MAKE SURE THEY CAN *NEVER* FORGET.

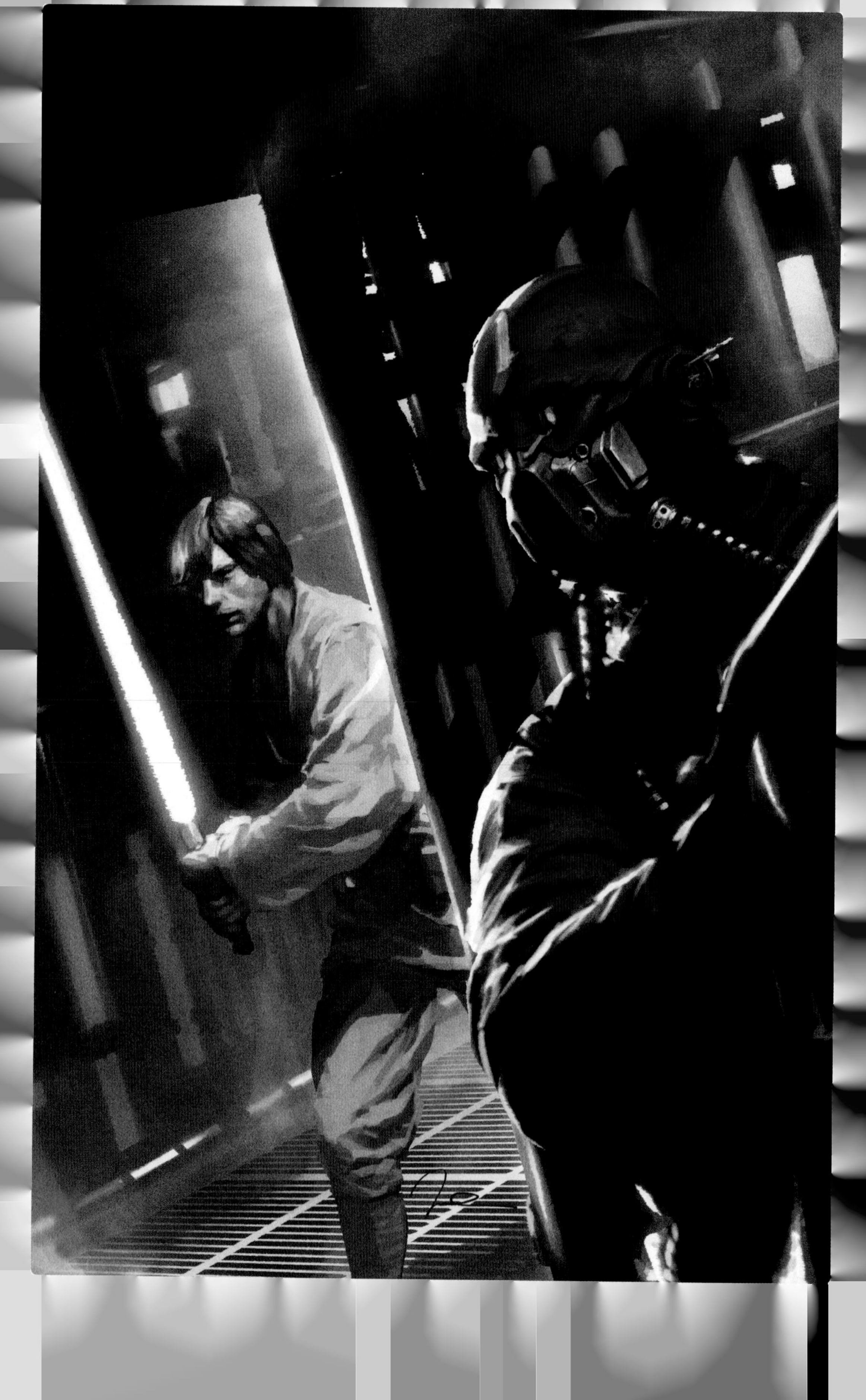

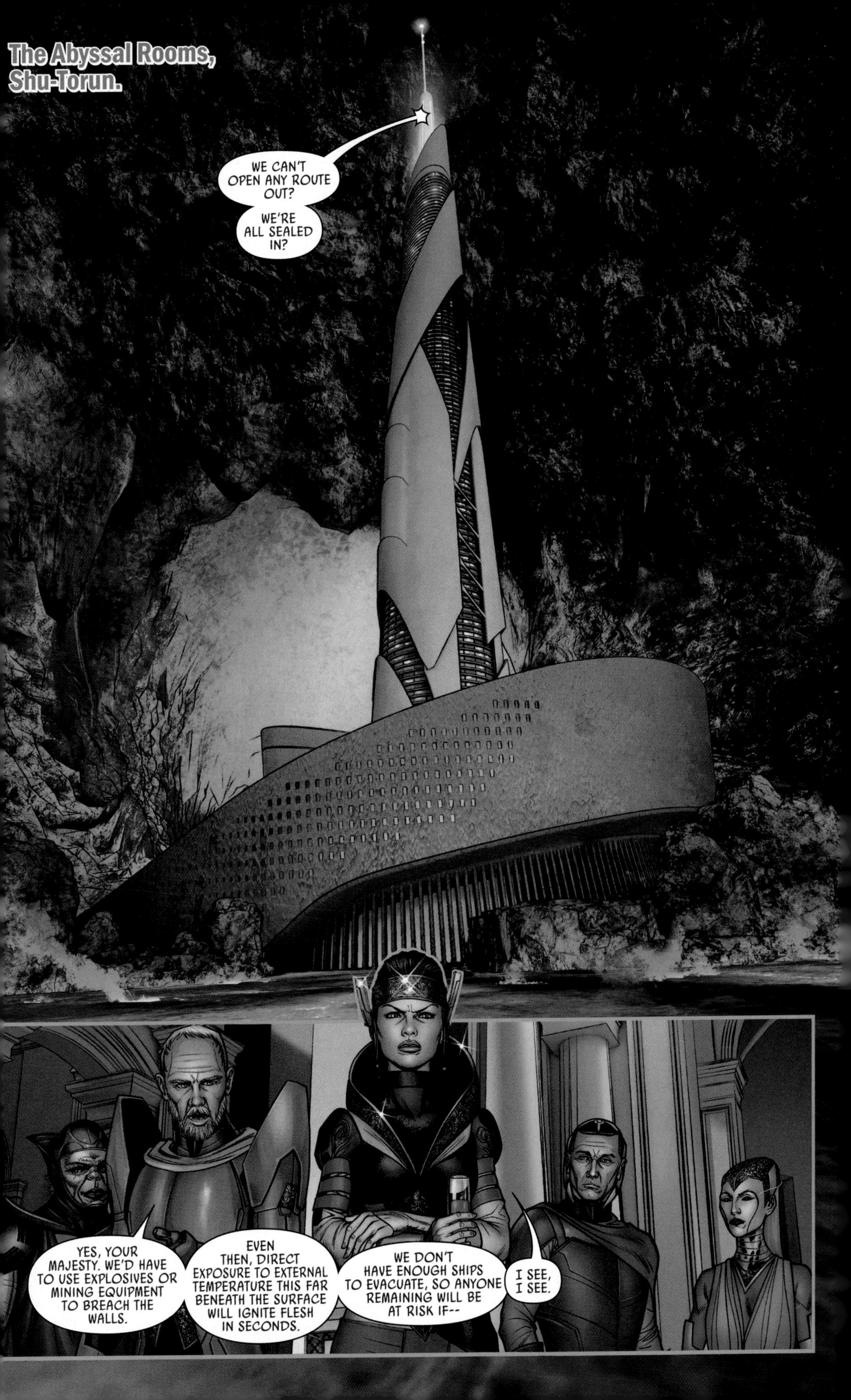
The Abyssal Rooms, Shu-Torun.
WE CAN'T OPEN ANY ROUTE OUT?
WE'RE ALL SEALED IN?
YES, YOUR MAJESTY. WE'D HAVE TO USE EXPLOSIVES OR MINING EQUIPMENT TO BREACH THE WALLS.
EVEN THEN, DIRECT EXPOSURE TO EXTERNAL TEMPERATURE THIS FAR BENEATH THE SURFACE WILL IGNITE FLESH IN SECONDS.
WE DON'T HAVE ENOUGH SHIPS TO EVACUATE, SO ANYONE REMAINING WILL BE AT RISK IF--
I SEE, I SEE.

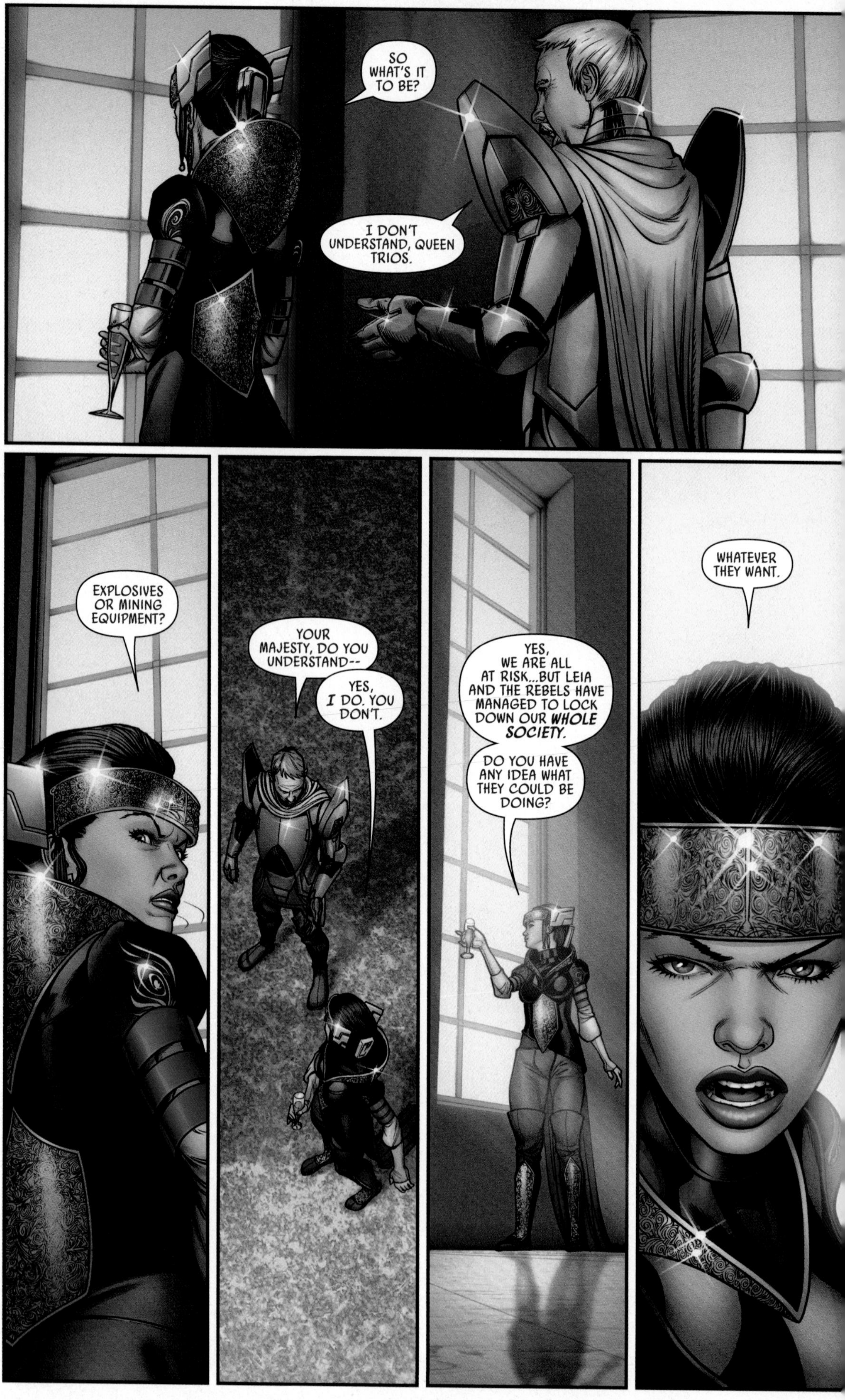
SO WHAT'S IT TO BE?
I DON'T UNDERSTAND, QUEEN TRIOS.
EXPLOSIVES OR MINING EQUIPMENT?
YOUR MAJESTY, DO YOU UNDERSTAND--
YES, I DO. YOU DON'T.
YES, WE ARE ALL AT RISK...BUT LEIA AND THE REBELS HAVE MANAGED TO LOCK DOWN OUR WHOLE SOCIETY.
DO YOU HAVE ANY IDEA WHAT THEY COULD BE DOING?
WHATEVER THEY WANT.

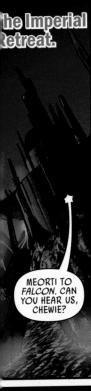

MEORTI TO FALCON. CAN YOU HEAR US, CHEWIE?

ANY REPORT FROM LUKE? WE'RE DEFENDING THE THRONE ROOM, BUT WE'D REALLY RATHER BE GONE...

OH. THE STRUCTURE'S BLOCKING COMMS. THAT MAKES SENSE. I...I'LL PASS IT ON.

SEE YOU SOON.

HHHHSHFHHH!

GGGGHHHHHHHHH!

THE SPIKE'S TOO BIG, LEIA. TOO MUCH INTERFERENCE. SIGNALS ARE ALL LOST.

WE'VE SEEN THE EXPLOSIONS OF THREE OF ITS GENERATORS THOUGH--SO TWO TO GO! THAT MEANS ITS DEFENDERS ARE STILL TRAPPED. LUKE AND HIS TEAM ARE STILL THE ONLY PEOPLE ABLE TO OPEN DOORS...

OH, I HOPE ARTOO IS DOING WELL. THAT BRAVE LITTLE DROID TAKES SUCH RISKS!

SO WHAT DO WE DO NOW? I KNOW A FEW CONVERSATIONAL GAMES OF IMPROVISATION THAT ARE PASSABLY AMUSING.

NO, TUNGA. STAY HERE. WE'LL SET UP DEFENSES IN CASE WE GET COMPANY. THOSE GUARDS YOU LOCKED UP WILL HAVE HEAVY WEAPONRY. WE CAN SET IT UP...

IF IT COMES TO IT, WE NEED TO GIVE LUKE AND THE PARTISANS EVERY SECOND THEY NEED...

CARTING GUNS AROUND?

WELL, WE KNOW THE ALTERNATIVE...

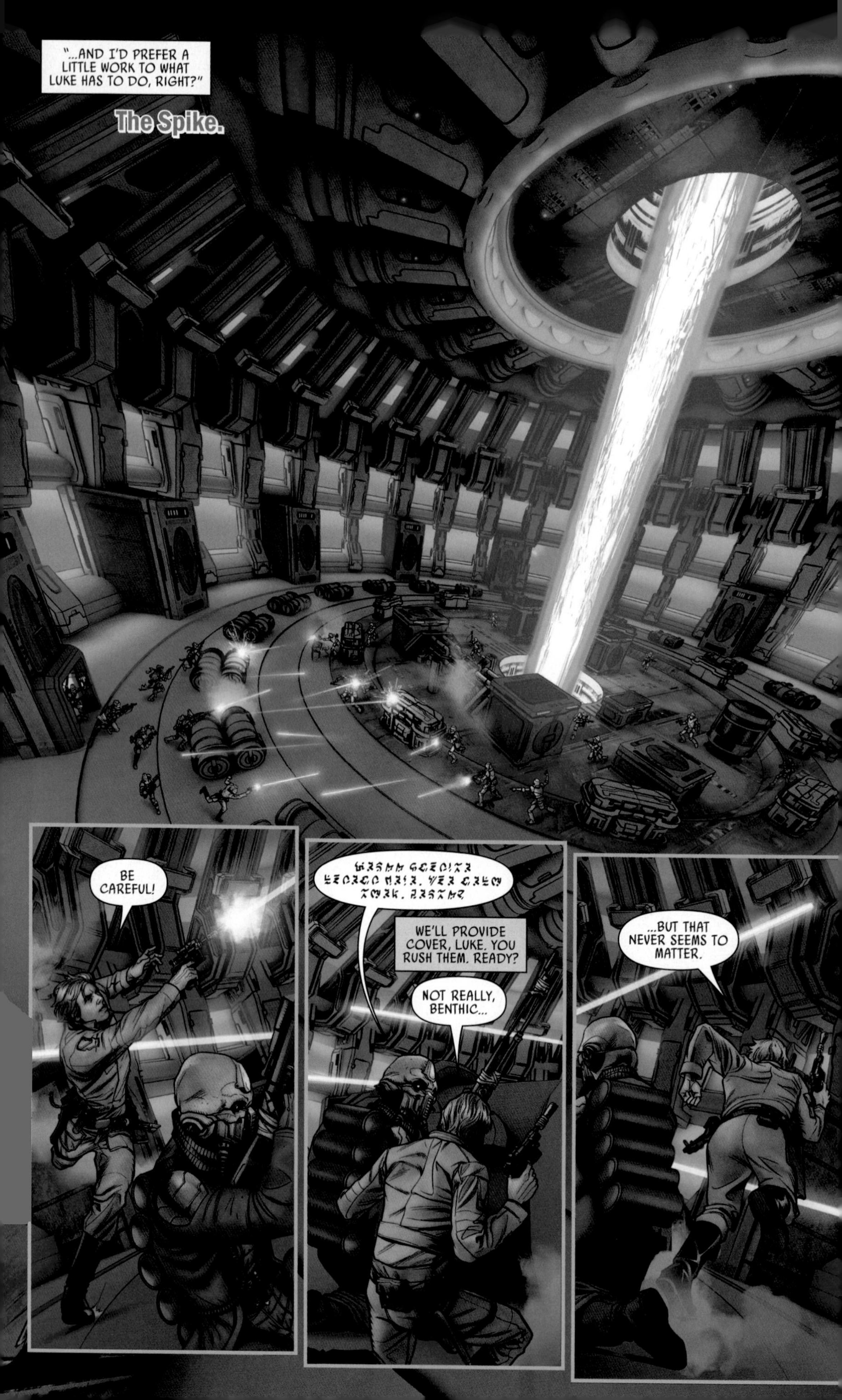
"...AND I'D PREFER A LITTLE WORK TO WHAT LUKE HAS TO DO, RIGHT?"
The Spike.
BE CAREFUL!
WE'LL PROVIDE COVER, LUKE. YOU RUSH THEM. READY?
NOT REALLY, BENTHIC...
...BUT THAT NEVER SEEMS TO MATTER.

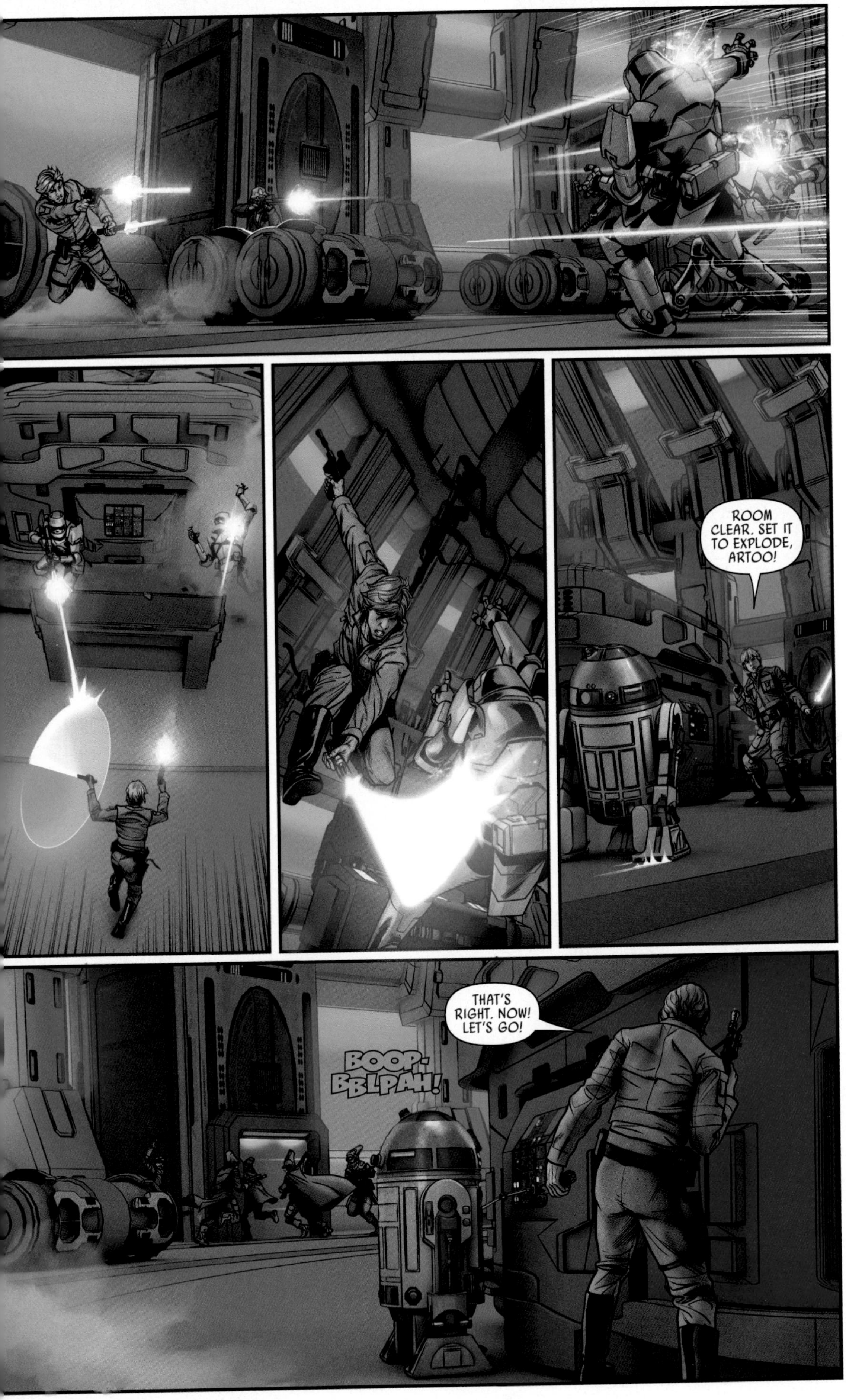
ROOM CLEAR. SET IT TO EXPLODE, ARTOO!
THAT'S RIGHT. NOW! LET'S GO!
BOOP-BBLPAH!

BLLOOOOIOOP! **KKRRAKKOOM**

OKAY. THAT'S FOUR DOWN. ONE MORE TO GO AND WE CAN GET BACK TO THE FALCON.

STILL NO CONTACT?

BIOOP!

ⁱ ᵗᵉˣᵗ ⁱⁿ ᵃᵘʳᵉᵇᵉˢʰ

I WOULDN'T EXPECT ANY. WE'RE JUST TOO DEEP. WE'RE ON OUR OWN.

THEN LET'S MAKE THIS QUICK AND GET BACK!

BENTHIC...

IF WE HYPERCHARGE THE FINAL CORE, WE'LL DESTROY THE WHOLE PLANET RATHER THAN THIS DEVICE.

ARE WE TO PROCEED?

ⁱ ᵗᵉˣᵗ ⁱⁿ ᵃᵘʳᵉᵇᵉˢʰ

I ASK YOU, MY FRIEND...

ⁱ ᵗᵉˣᵗ ⁱⁿ ᵃᵘʳᵉᵇᵉˢʰ

...WHEN HAVE WE EVER TURNED BACK FROM PUNISHING THE GUILTY?

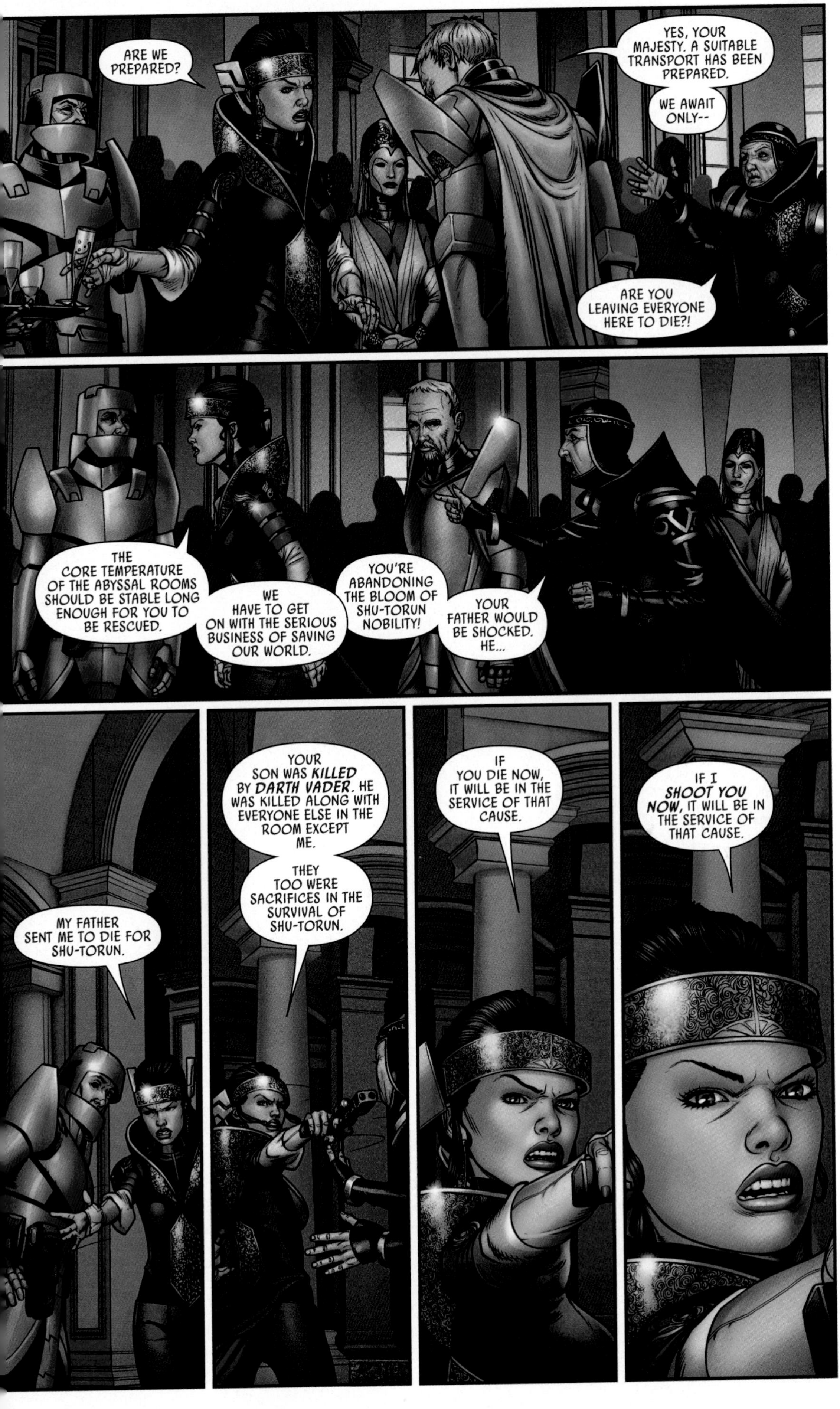

ARE WE PREPARED?
YES, YOUR MAJESTY. A SUITABLE TRANSPORT HAS BEEN PREPARED.
WE AWAIT ONLY--
ARE YOU LEAVING EVERYONE HERE TO DIE?!
THE CORE TEMPERATURE OF THE ABYSSAL ROOMS SHOULD BE STABLE LONG ENOUGH FOR YOU TO BE RESCUED.
WE HAVE TO GET ON WITH THE SERIOUS BUSINESS OF SAVING OUR WORLD.
YOU'RE ABANDONING THE BLOOM OF SHU-TORUN NOBILITY!
YOUR FATHER WOULD BE SHOCKED. HE...
MY FATHER SENT ME TO DIE FOR SHU-TORUN.
YOUR SON WAS KILLED BY DARTH VADER. HE WAS KILLED ALONG WITH EVERYONE ELSE IN THE ROOM EXCEPT ME.
THEY TOO WERE SACRIFICES IN THE SURVIVAL OF SHU-TORUN.
IF YOU DIE NOW, IT WILL BE IN THE SERVICE OF THAT CAUSE.
IF I SHOOT YOU NOW, IT WILL BE IN THE SERVICE OF THAT CAUSE.

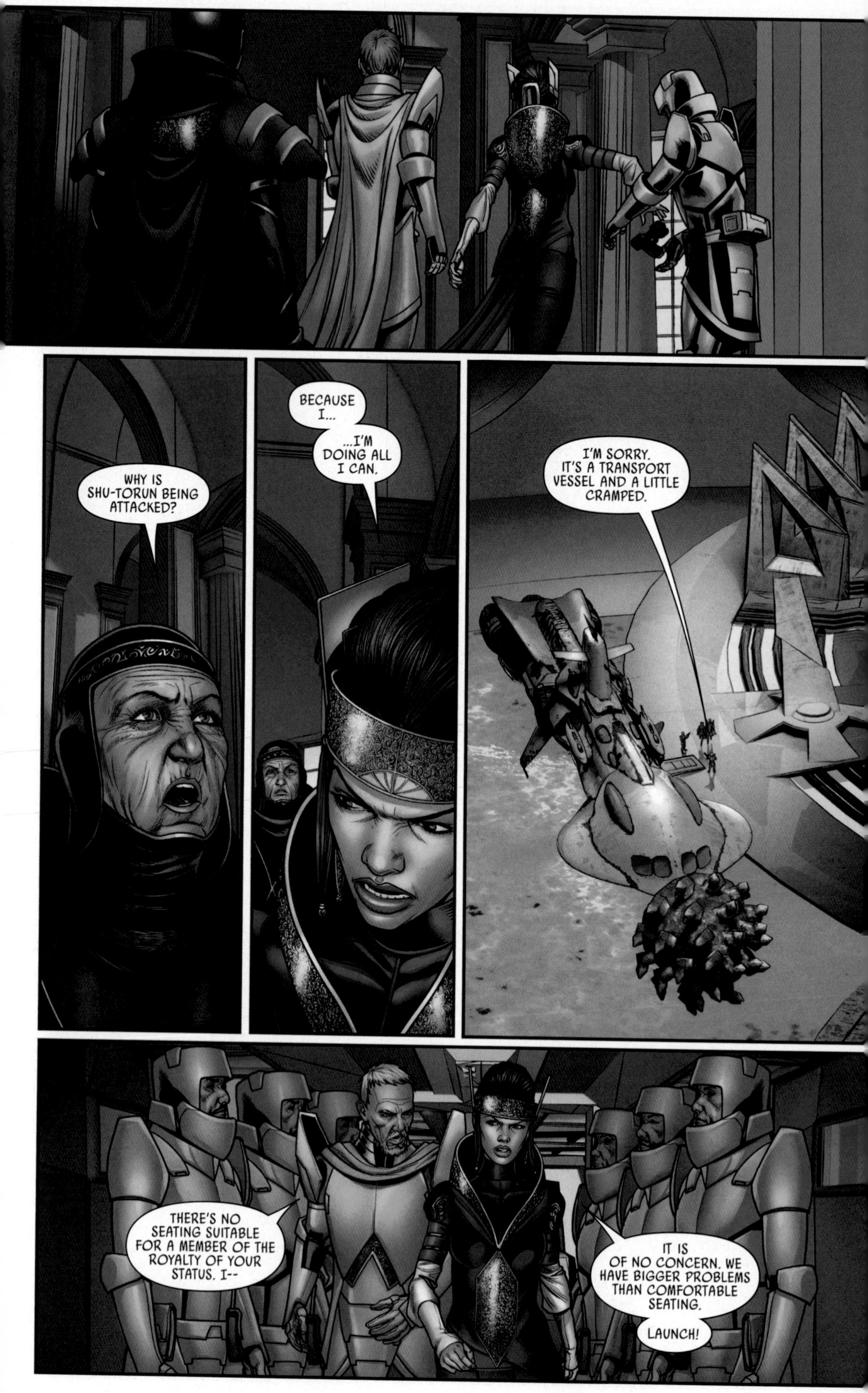
WHY IS SHU-TORUN BEING ATTACKED?
BECAUSE I...
...I'M DOING ALL I CAN.
I'M SORRY. IT'S A TRANSPORT VESSEL AND A LITTLE CRAMPED.
THERE'S NO SEATING SUITABLE FOR A MEMBER OF THE ROYALTY OF YOUR STATUS. I--
IT IS OF NO CONCERN. WE HAVE BIGGER PROBLEMS THAN COMFORTABLE SEATING.
LAUNCH!

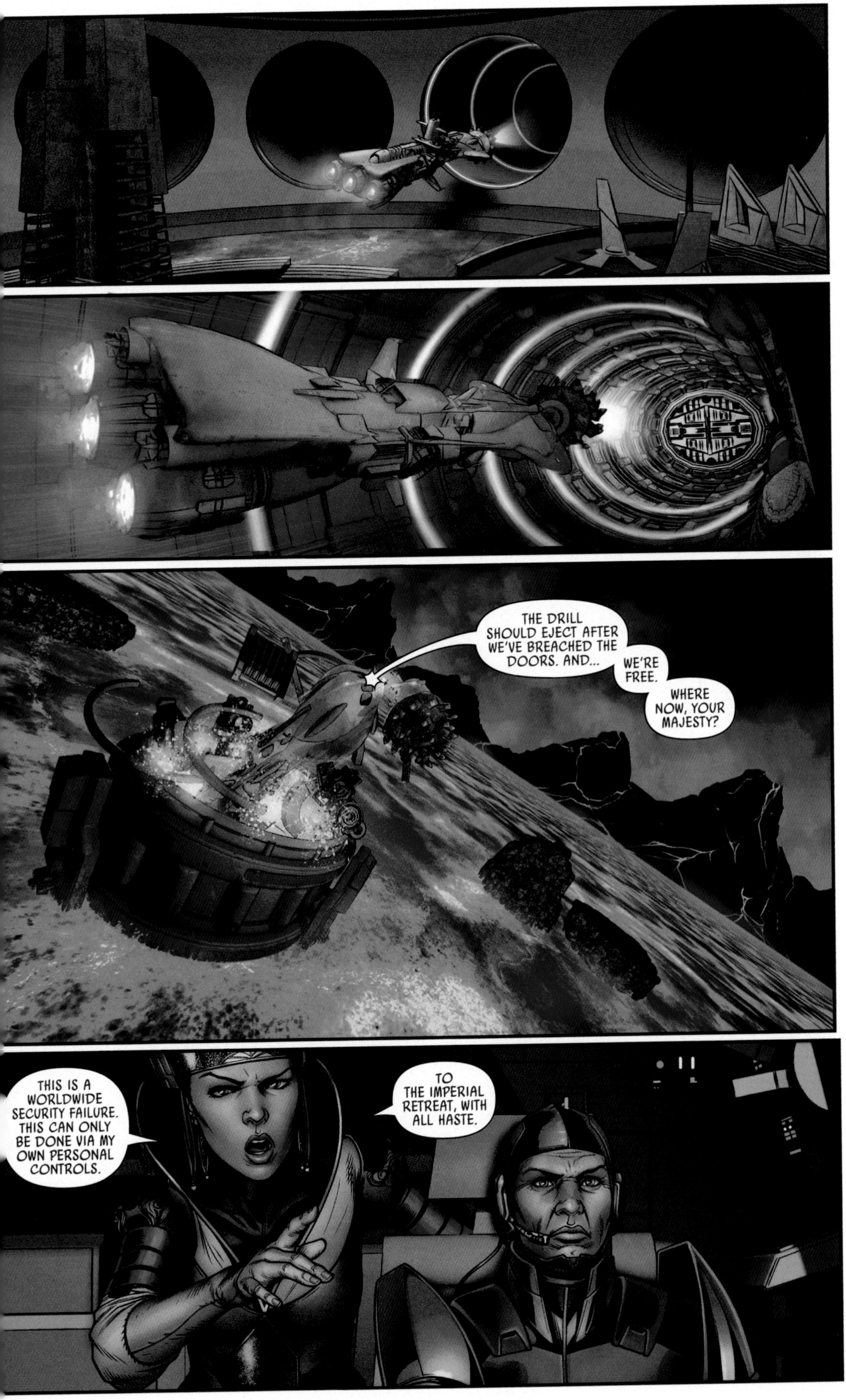
THE DRILL SHOULD EJECT AFTER WE'VE BREACHED THE DOORS. AND...
WE'RE FREE.
WHERE NOW, YOUR MAJESTY?
THIS IS A WORLDWIDE SECURITY FAILURE. THIS CAN ONLY BE DONE VIA MY OWN PERSONAL CONTROLS.
TO THE IMPERIAL RETREAT, WITH ALL HASTE.

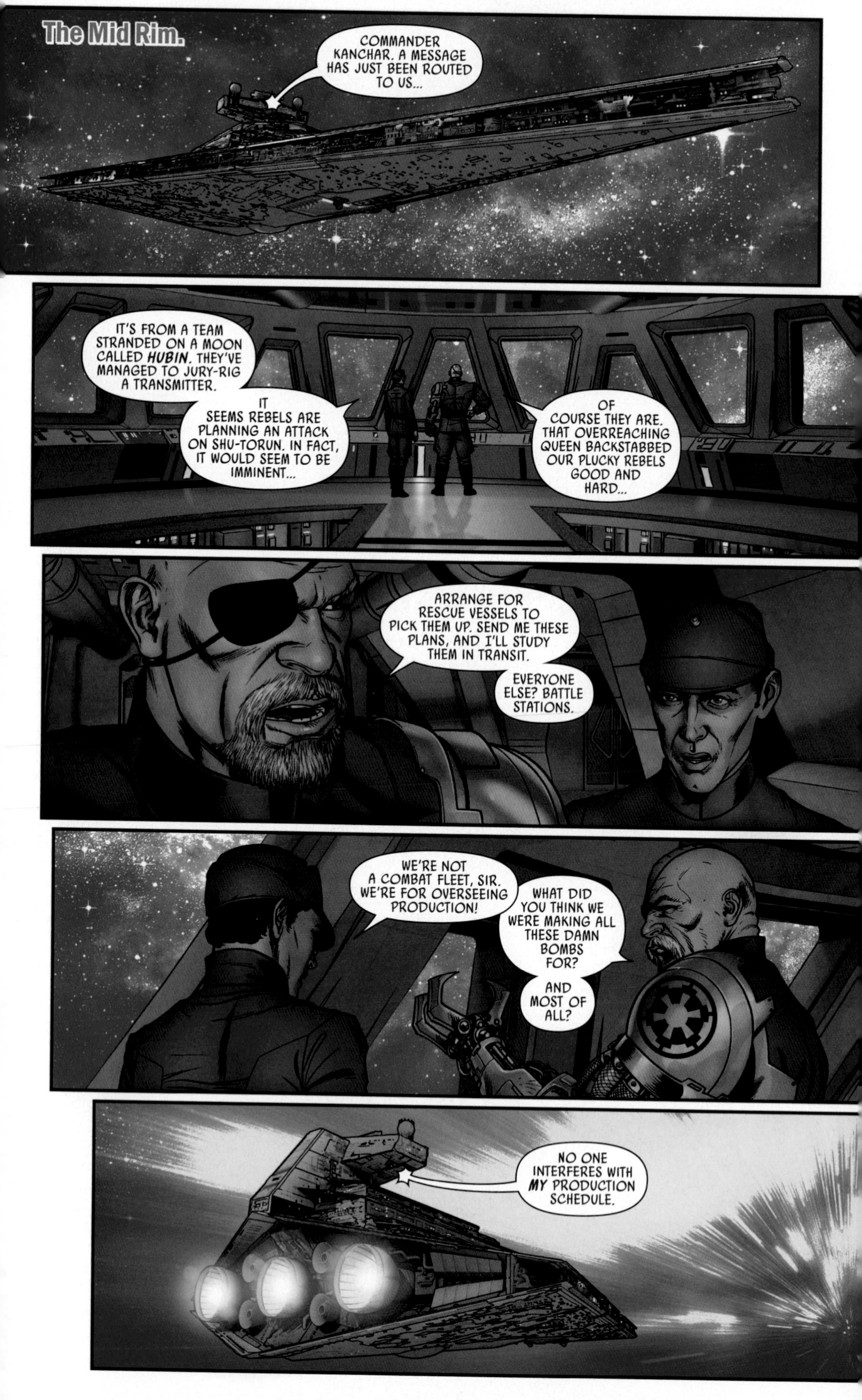
The Mid Rim.
COMMANDER KANCHAR. A MESSAGE HAS JUST BEEN ROUTED TO US...
IT'S FROM A TEAM STRANDED ON A MOON CALLED HUBIN. THEY'VE MANAGED TO JURY-RIG A TRANSMITTER.
IT SEEMS REBELS ARE PLANNING AN ATTACK ON SHU-TORUN. IN FACT, IT WOULD SEEM TO BE IMMINENT...
OF COURSE THEY ARE. THAT OVERREACHING QUEEN BACKSTABBED OUR PLUCKY REBELS GOOD AND HARD...
ARRANGE FOR RESCUE VESSELS TO PICK THEM UP. SEND ME THESE PLANS, AND I'LL STUDY THEM IN TRANSIT.
EVERYONE ELSE? BATTLE STATIONS.
WE'RE NOT A COMBAT FLEET, SIR. WE'RE FOR OVERSEEING PRODUCTION!
WHAT DID YOU THINK WE WERE MAKING ALL THESE DAMN BOMBS FOR?
AND MOST OF ALL?
NO ONE INTERFERES WITH MY PRODUCTION SCHEDULE.

WE'VE GOT THEM!

ROOM SECURE!

LAST CHARGE TO SET, THEN OUT.

ARTOO? GET TO WORK.

AOOOOOPP?

ᚱᛖᛉ ᛉᚨᚱ ᛉᚱᛖᛏᚱᚨᛉᛏᛖᚱ ᛖᛉᛉᛉᚱ. ᛖᛗᛉᚱᛉᛖᛗᛉᚱᛉᛏᚱᛖ ᛉᛉᛖᛉᛉ.

NOT THE DESTRUCTION CODES. HYPERCHARGE IT, DROID.

VHHHMM

HUH?

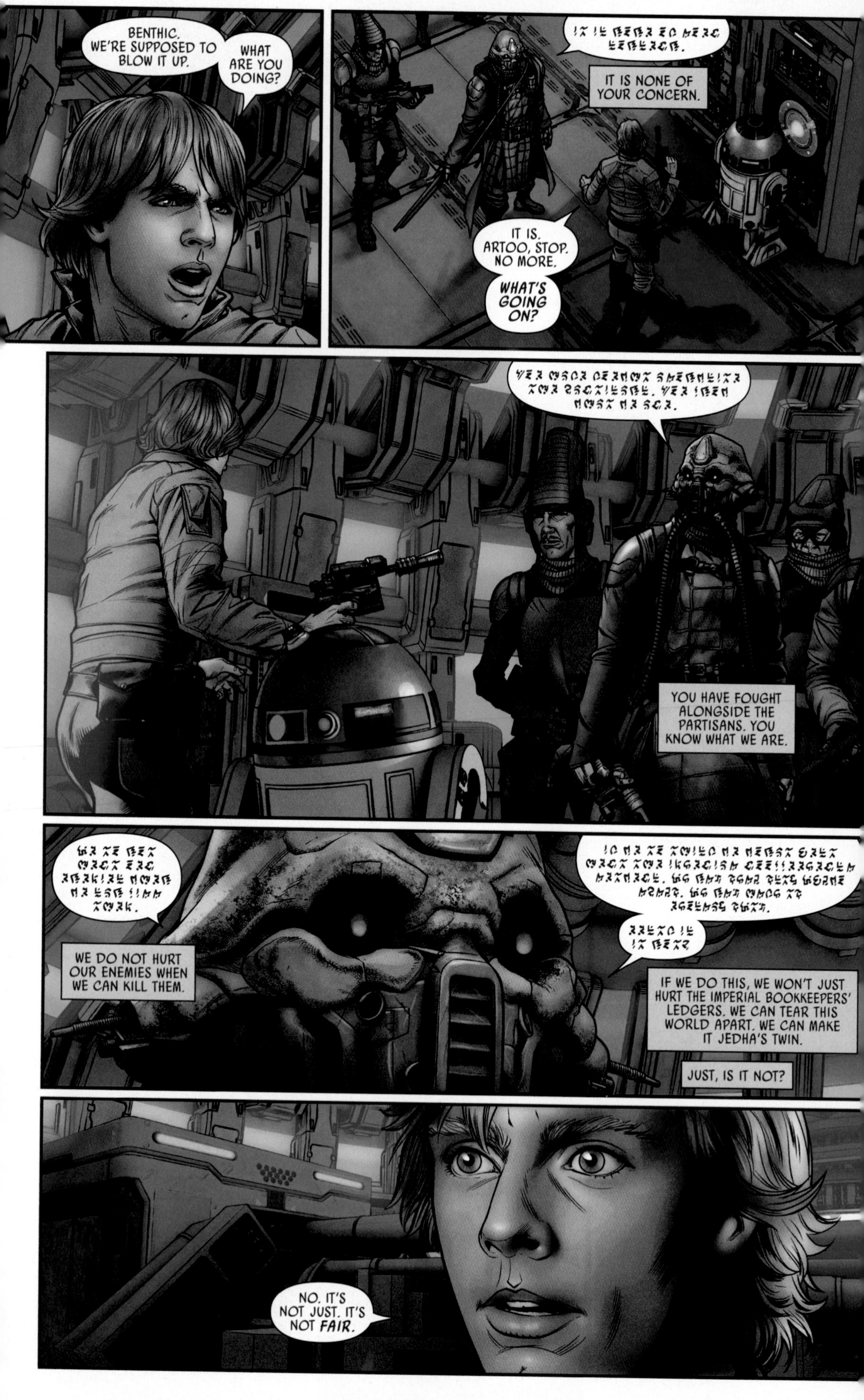
BENTHIC. WE'RE SUPPOSED TO BLOW IT UP.
WHAT ARE YOU DOING?
IT IS NONE OF YOUR CONCERN.
IT IS. ARTOO, STOP. NO MORE.
WHAT'S GOING ON?
YOU HAVE FOUGHT ALONGSIDE THE PARTISANS. YOU KNOW WHAT WE ARE.
WE DO NOT HURT OUR ENEMIES WHEN WE CAN KILL THEM.
IF WE DO THIS, WE WON'T JUST HURT THE IMPERIAL BOOKKEEPERS' LEDGERS. WE CAN TEAR THIS WORLD APART. WE CAN MAKE IT JEDHA'S TWIN.
JUST, IS IT NOT?
NO. IT'S NOT JUST. IT'S NOT FAIR.

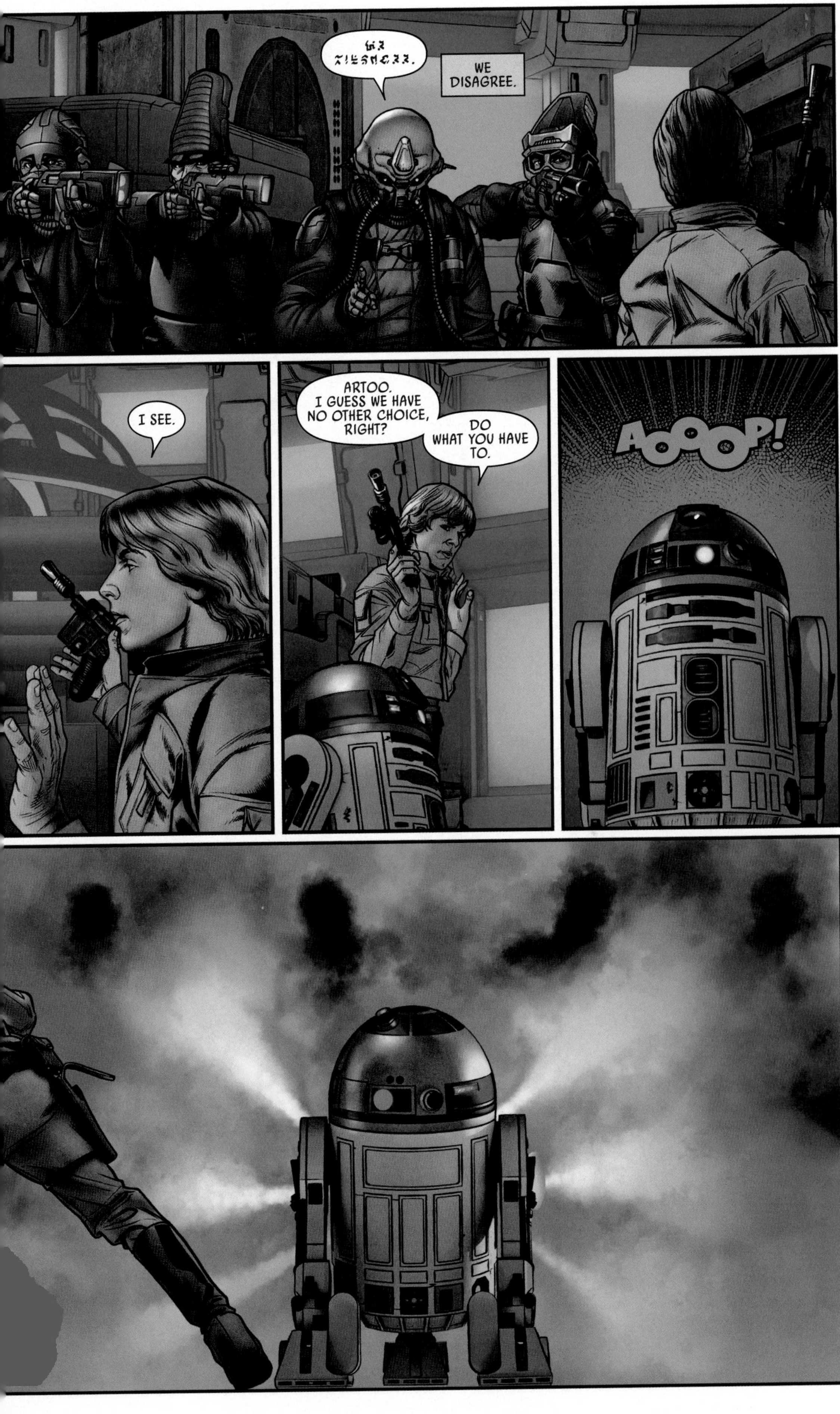
WE DISAGREE.
I SEE.
ARTOO. I GUESS WE HAVE NO OTHER CHOICE, RIGHT?
DO WHAT YOU HAVE TO.
AOOOP!

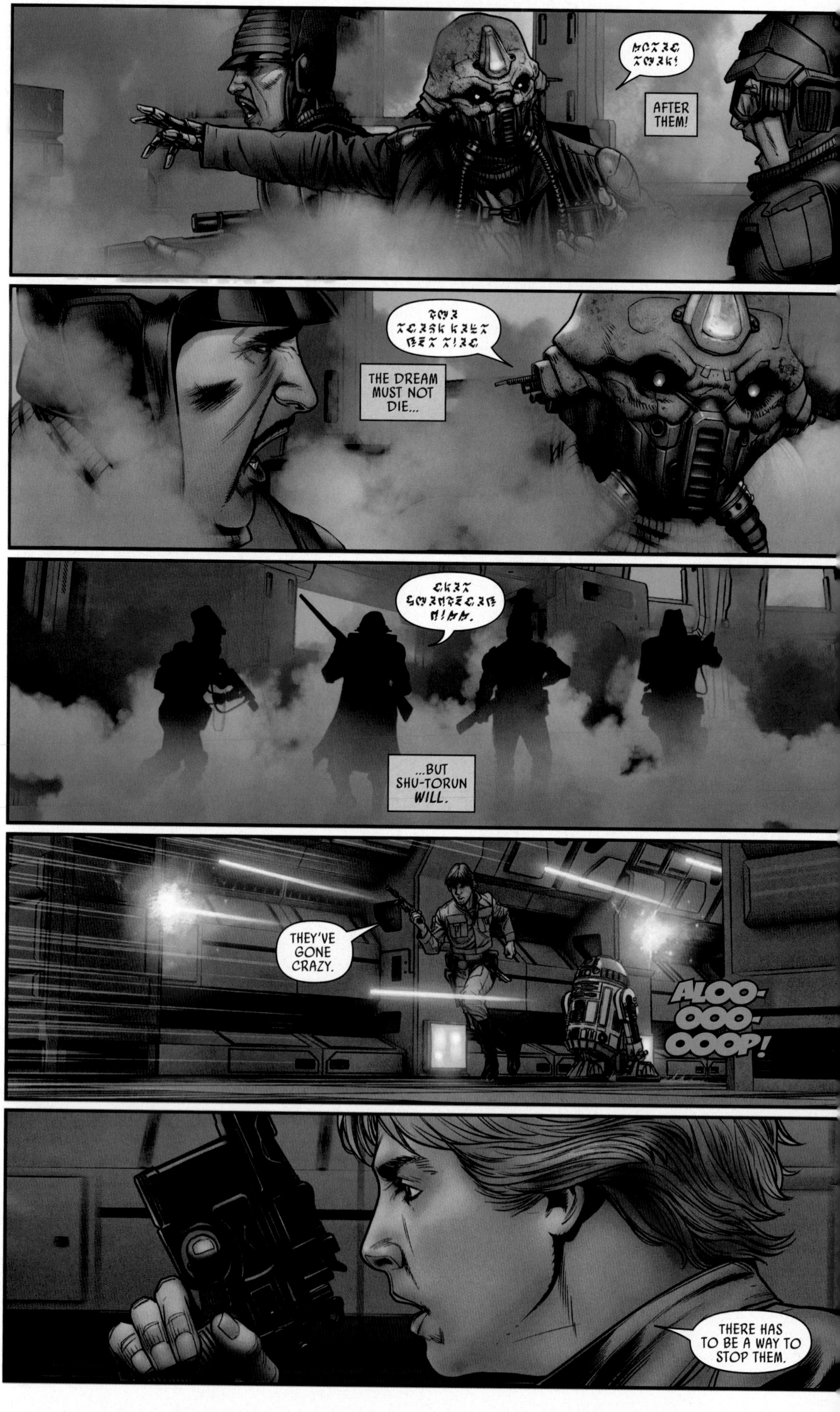

AFTER THEM!
THE DREAM MUST NOT DIE...
...BUT SHU-TORUN WILL.
THEY'VE GONE CRAZY.
ALOO-OOO-OOOP!
THERE HAS TO BE A WAY TO STOP THEM.

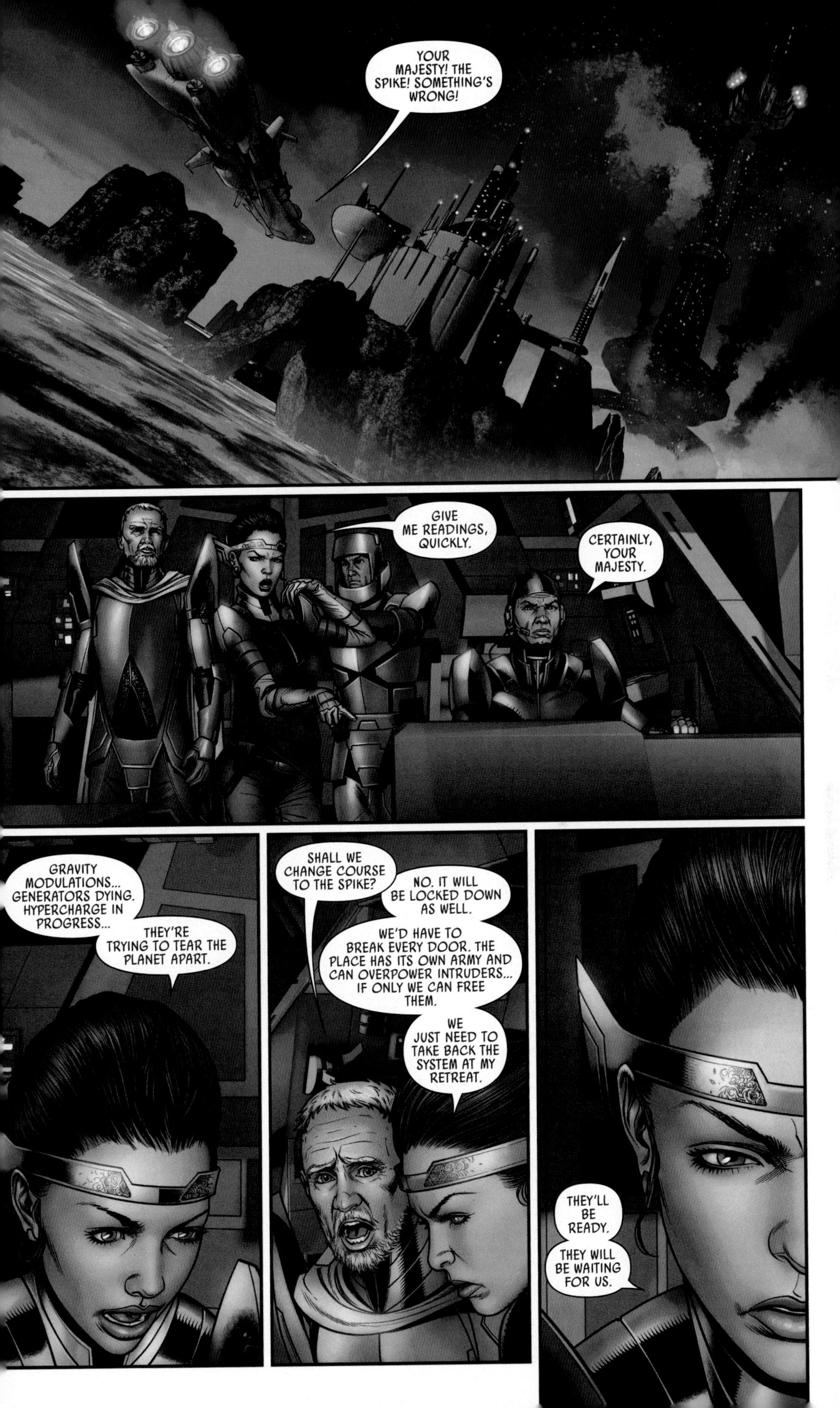

YOUR MAJESTY! THE SPIKE! SOMETHING'S WRONG!
GIVE ME READINGS, QUICKLY.
CERTAINLY, YOUR MAJESTY.
GRAVITY MODULATIONS... GENERATORS DYING. HYPERCHARGE IN PROGRESS...
THEY'RE TRYING TO TEAR THE PLANET APART.
SHALL WE CHANGE COURSE TO THE SPIKE?
NO. IT WILL BE LOCKED DOWN AS WELL.
WE'D HAVE TO BREAK EVERY DOOR. THE PLACE HAS ITS OWN ARMY AND CAN OVERPOWER INTRUDERS... IF ONLY WE CAN FREE THEM.
WE JUST NEED TO TAKE BACK THE SYSTEM AT MY RETREAT.
THEY'LL BE READY.
THEY WILL BE WAITING FOR US.

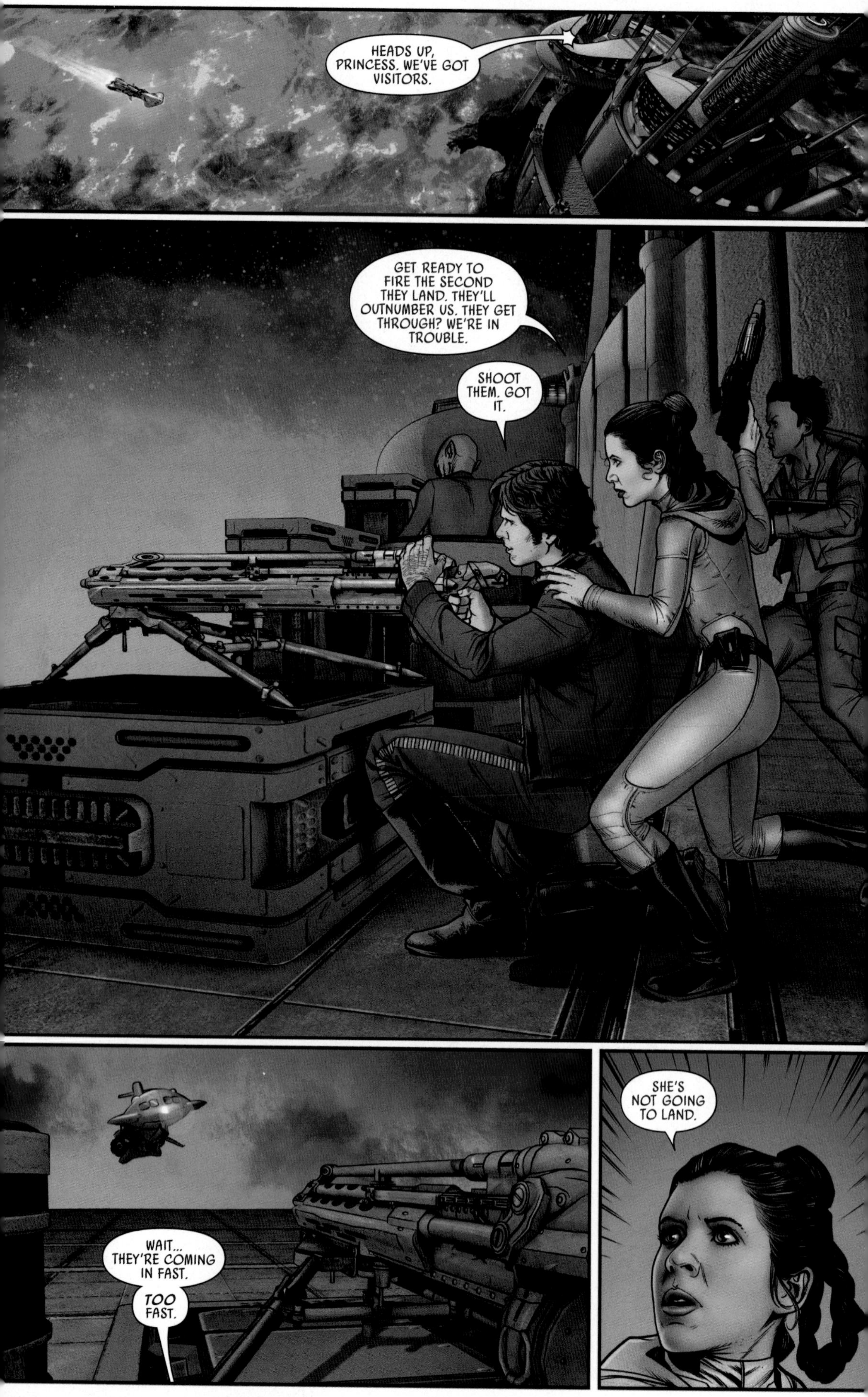
HEADS UP, PRINCESS. WE'VE GOT VISITORS.
GET READY TO FIRE THE SECOND THEY LAND. THEY'LL OUTNUMBER US. THEY GET THROUGH? WE'RE IN TROUBLE.
SHOOT THEM. GOT IT.
WAIT... THEY'RE COMING IN FAST.
TOO FAST.
SHE'S NOT GOING TO LAND.

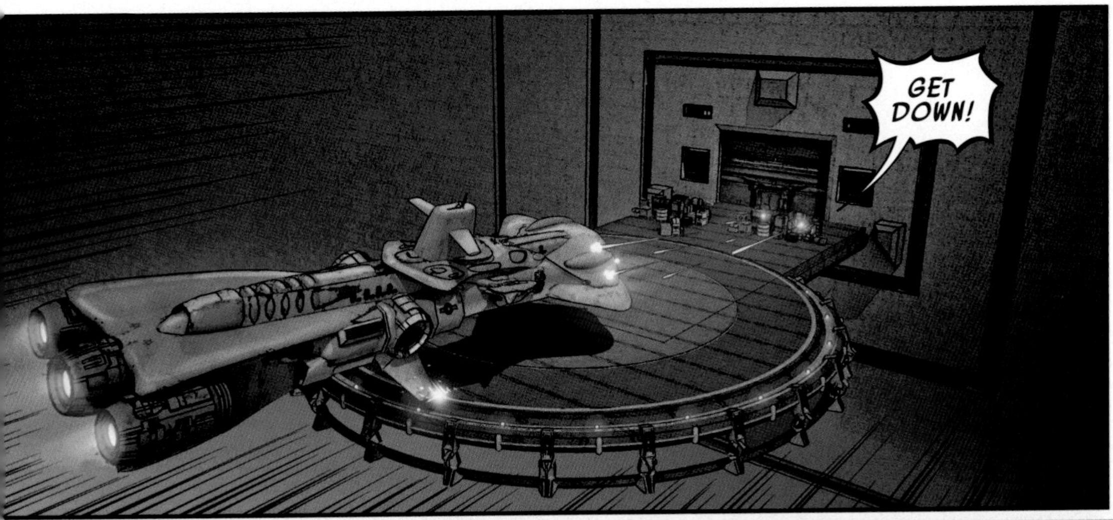
GET DOWN!

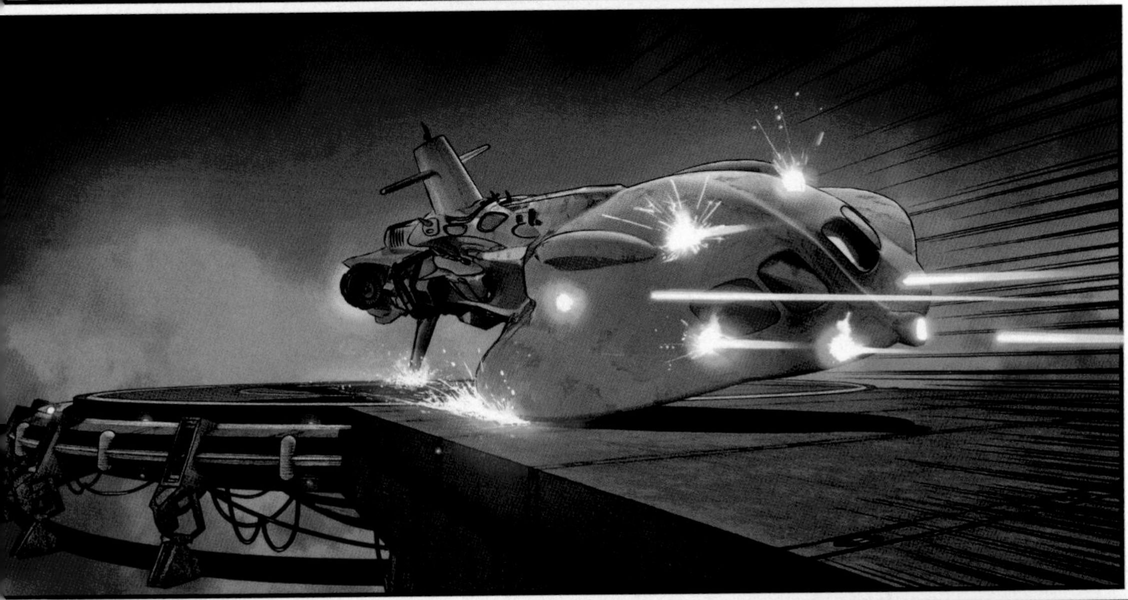

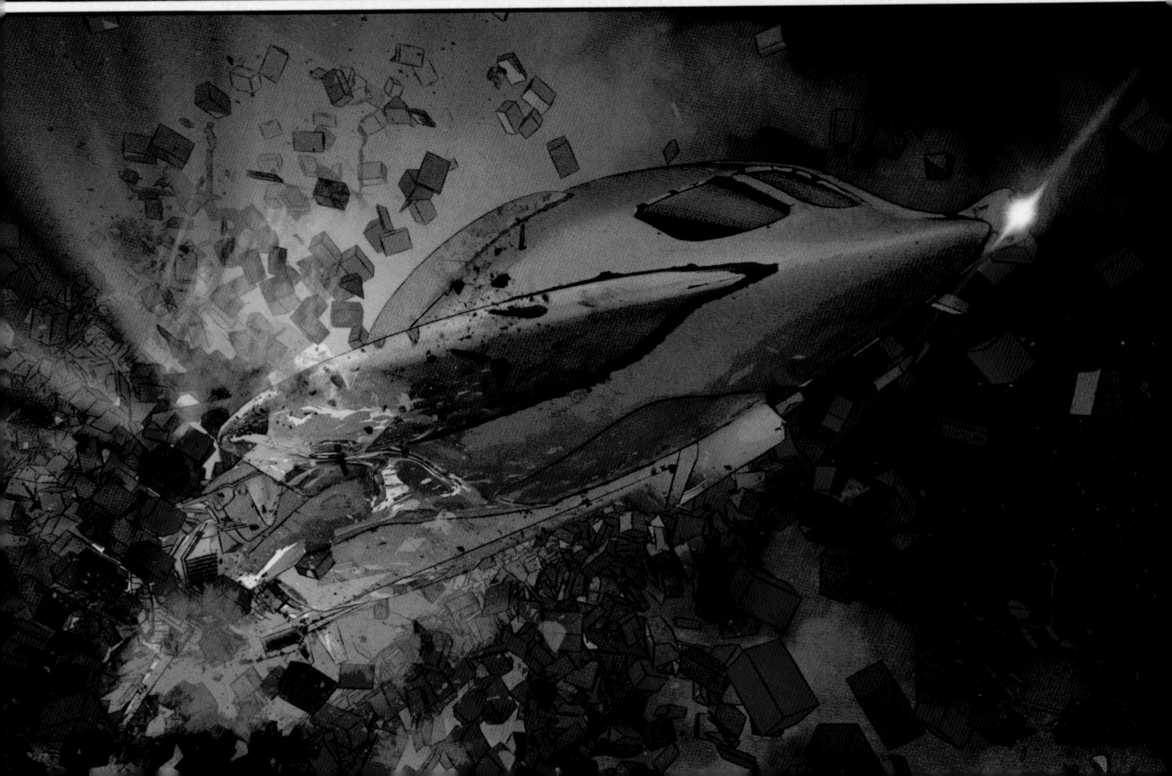

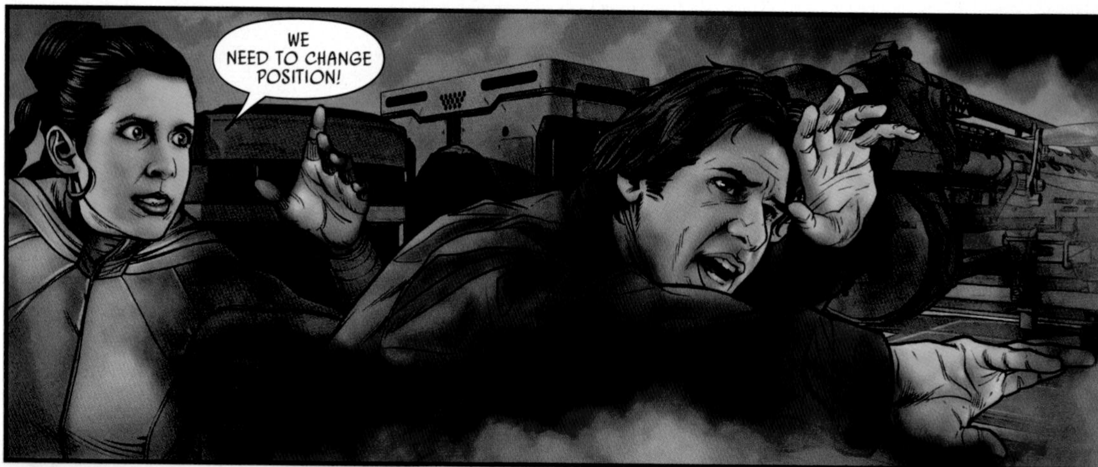
WE NEED TO CHANGE POSITION!

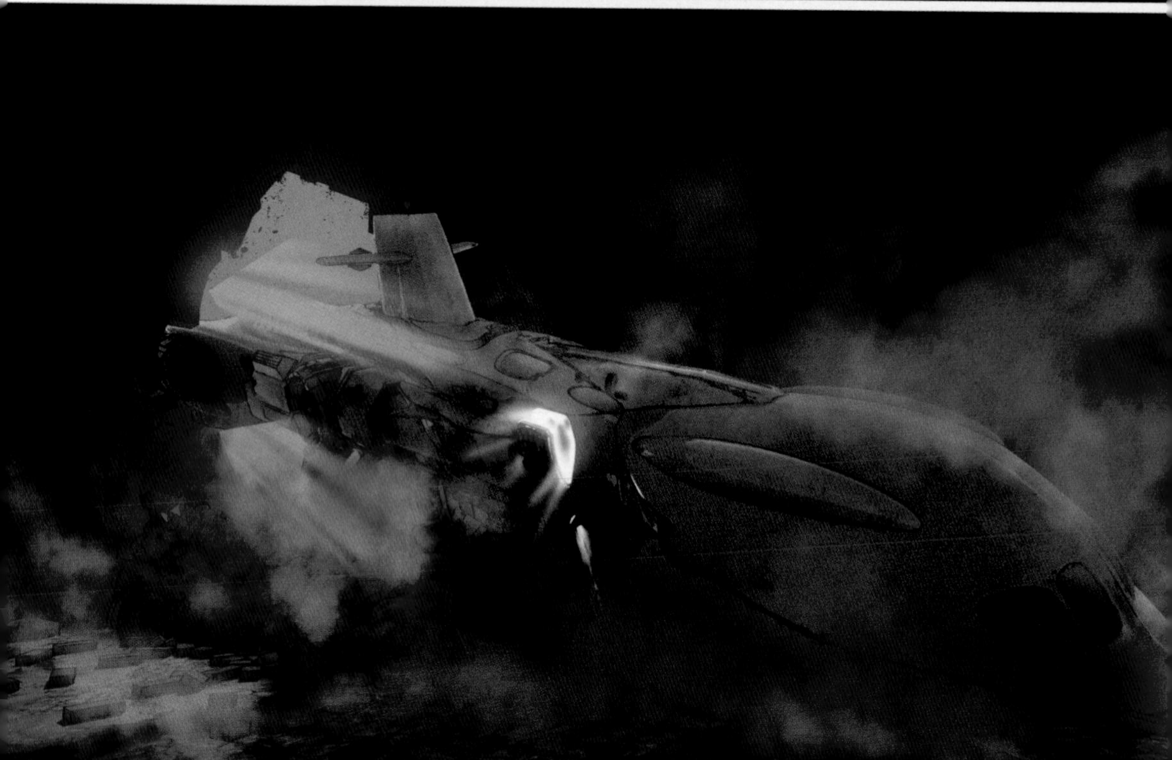

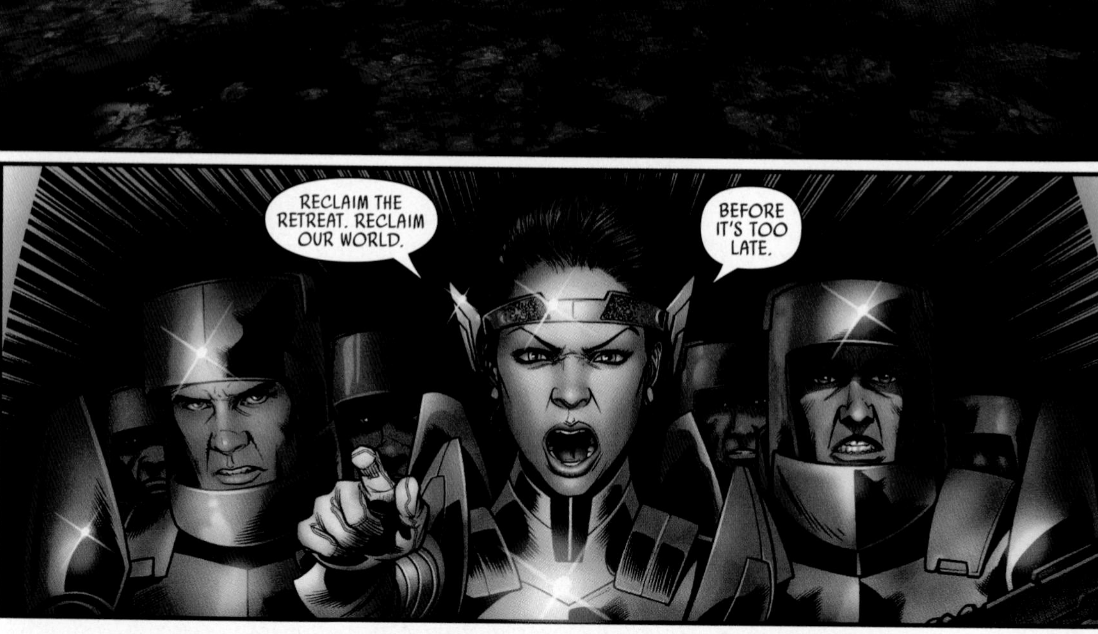
RECLAIM THE RETREAT. RECLAIM OUR WORLD.
BEFORE IT'S TOO LATE.

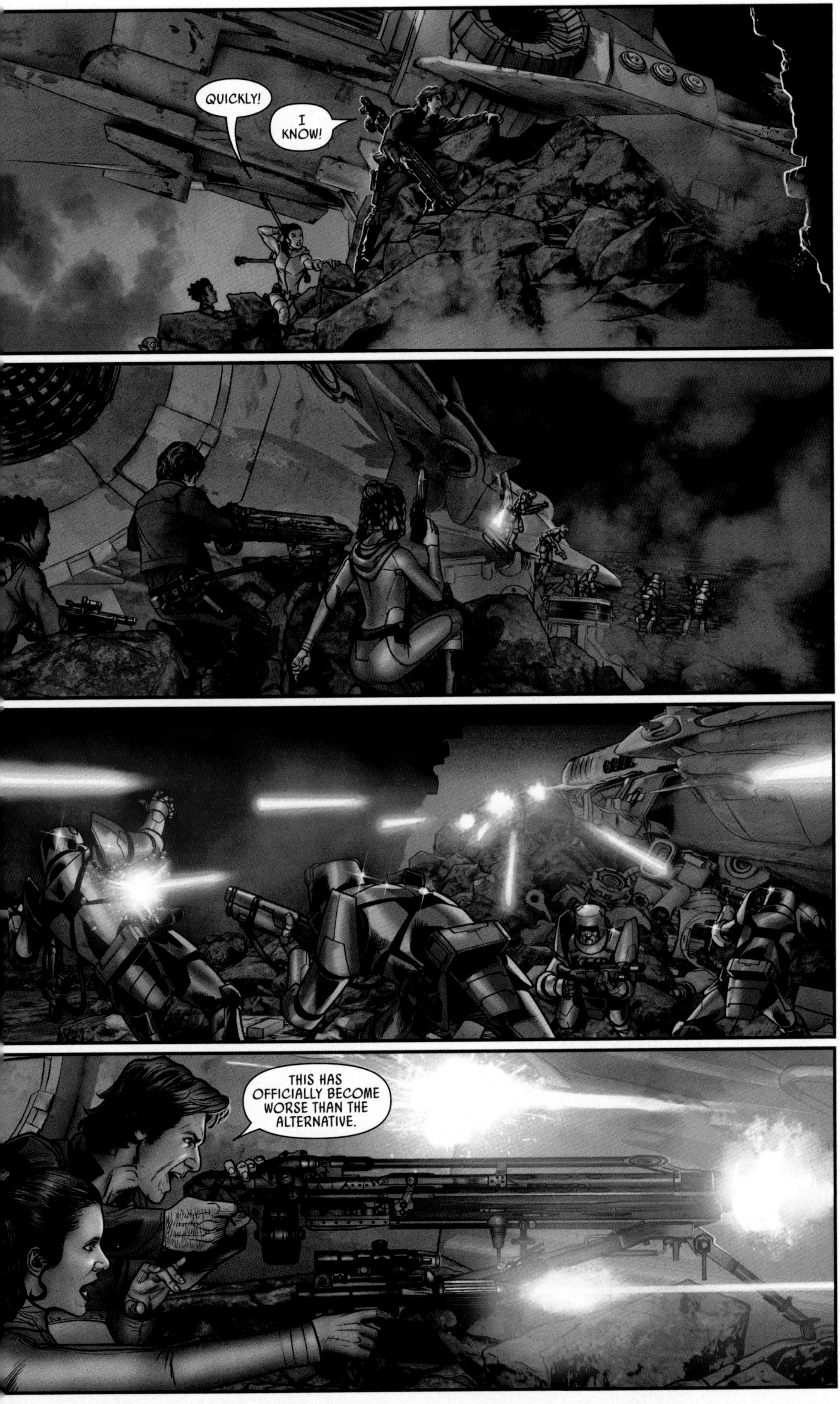
QUICKLY!
I KNOW!
THIS HAS OFFICIALLY BECOME WORSE THAN THE ALTERNATIVE.

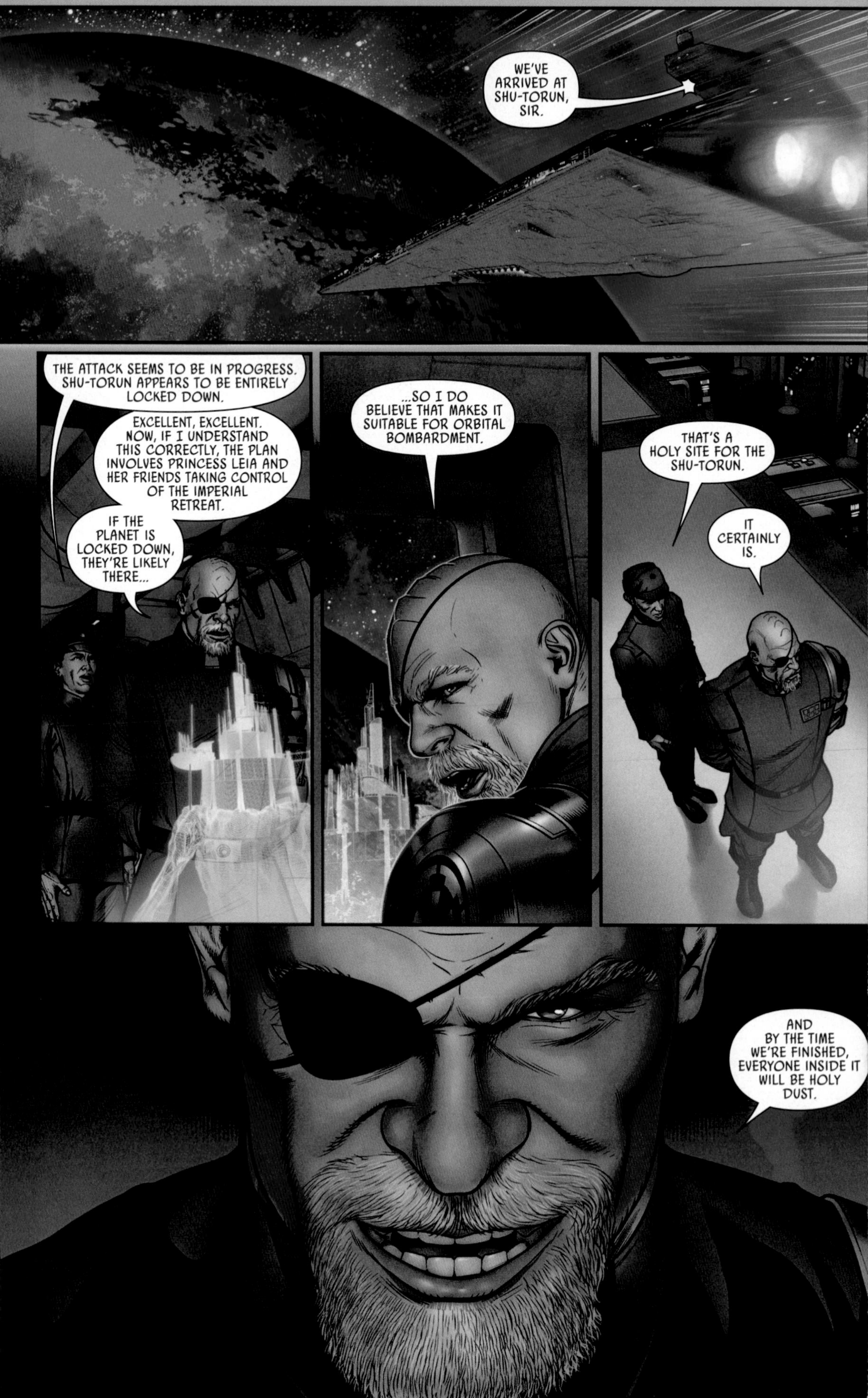
WE'VE ARRIVED AT SHU-TORUN, SIR.
THE ATTACK SEEMS TO BE IN PROGRESS. SHU-TORUN APPEARS TO BE ENTIRELY LOCKED DOWN.
EXCELLENT, EXCELLENT. NOW, IF I UNDERSTAND THIS CORRECTLY, THE PLAN INVOLVES PRINCESS LEIA AND HER FRIENDS TAKING CONTROL OF THE IMPERIAL RETREAT.
IF THE PLANET IS LOCKED DOWN, THEY'RE LIKELY THERE...
...SO I DO BELIEVE THAT MAKES IT SUITABLE FOR ORBITAL BOMBARDMENT.
THAT'S A HOLY SITE FOR THE SHU-TORUN.
IT CERTAINLY IS.
AND BY THE TIME WE'RE FINISHED, EVERYONE INSIDE IT WILL BE HOLY DUST.

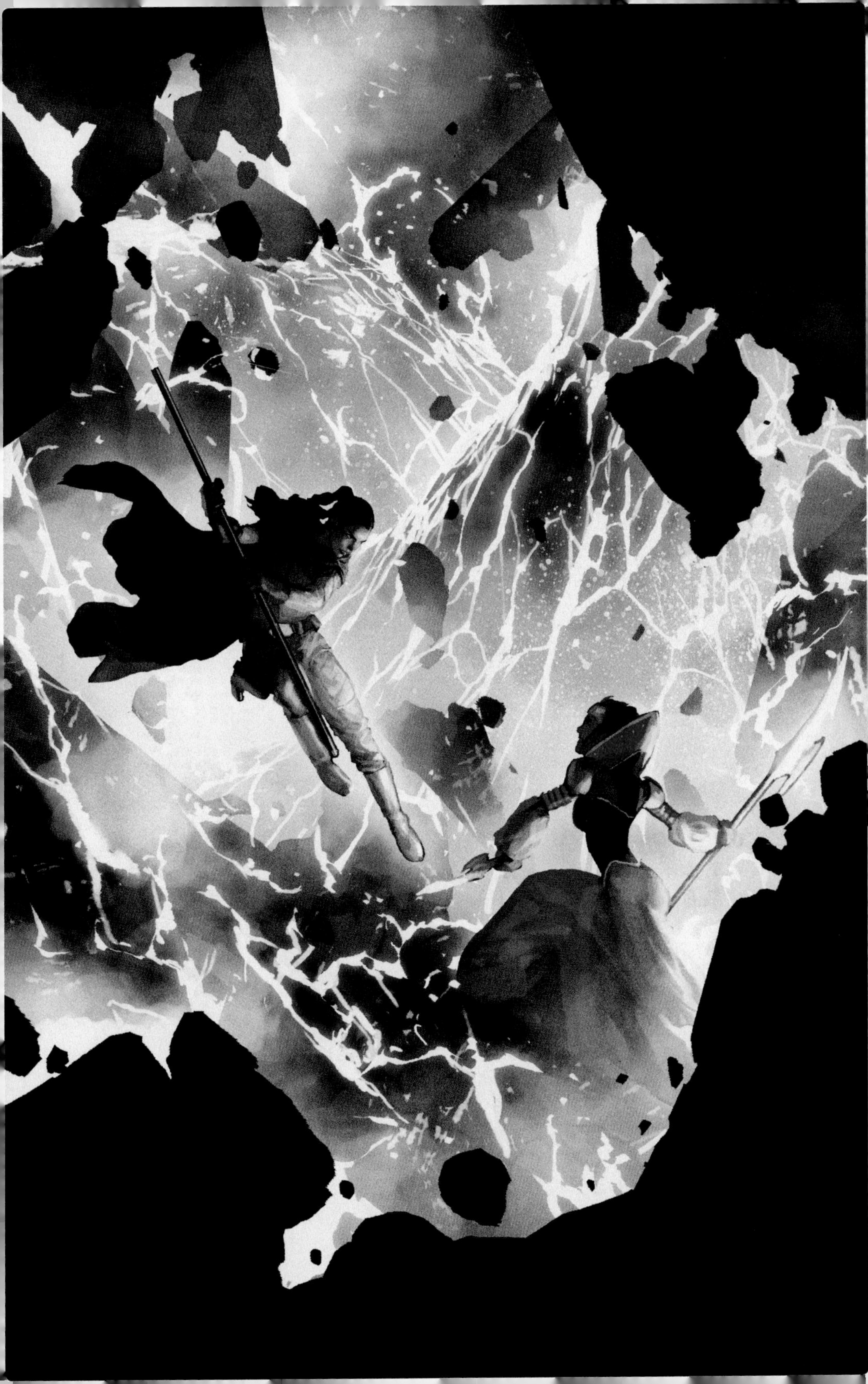

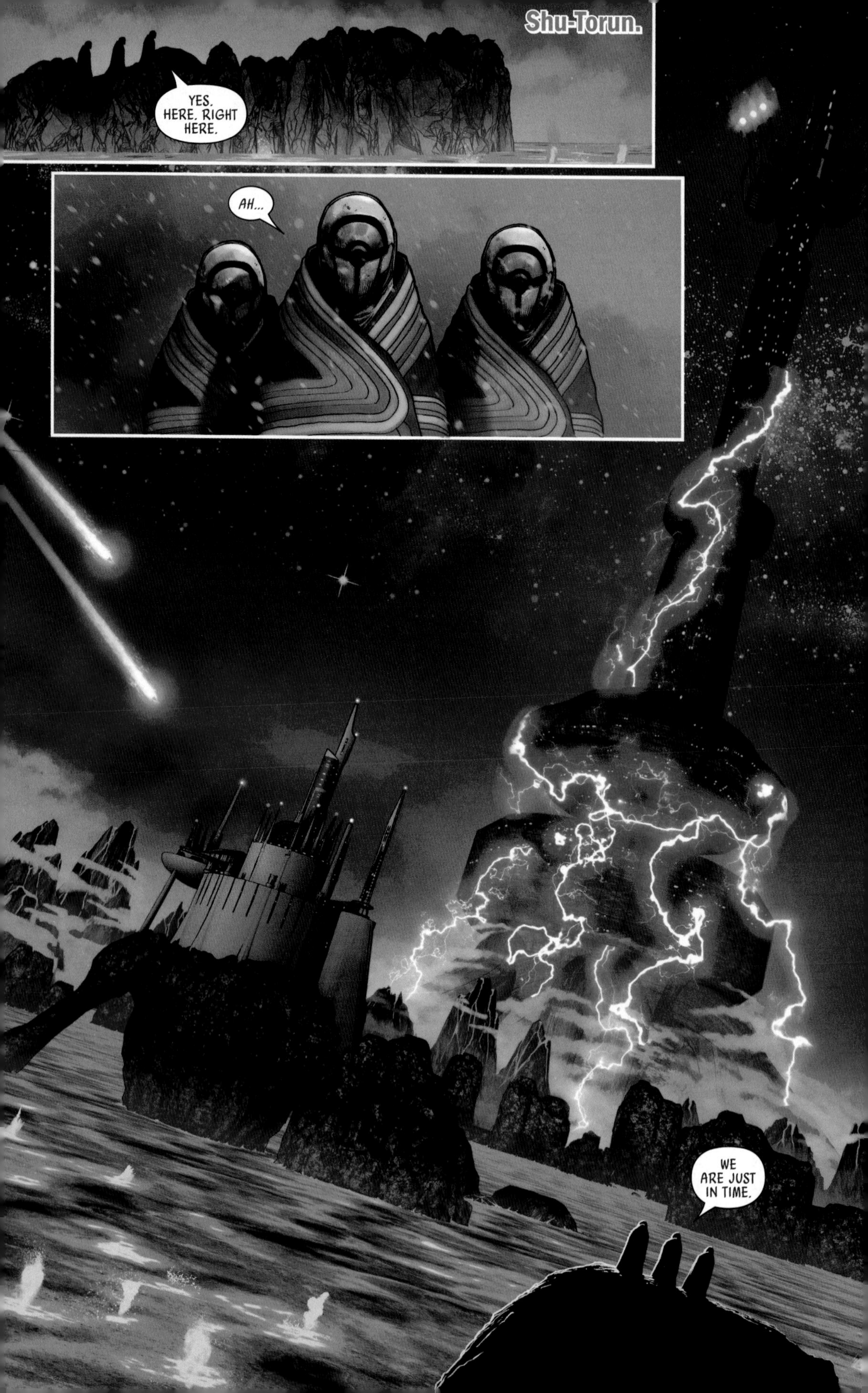
Shu-Torun.
YES. HERE. RIGHT HERE.
AH...
WE ARE JUST IN TIME.

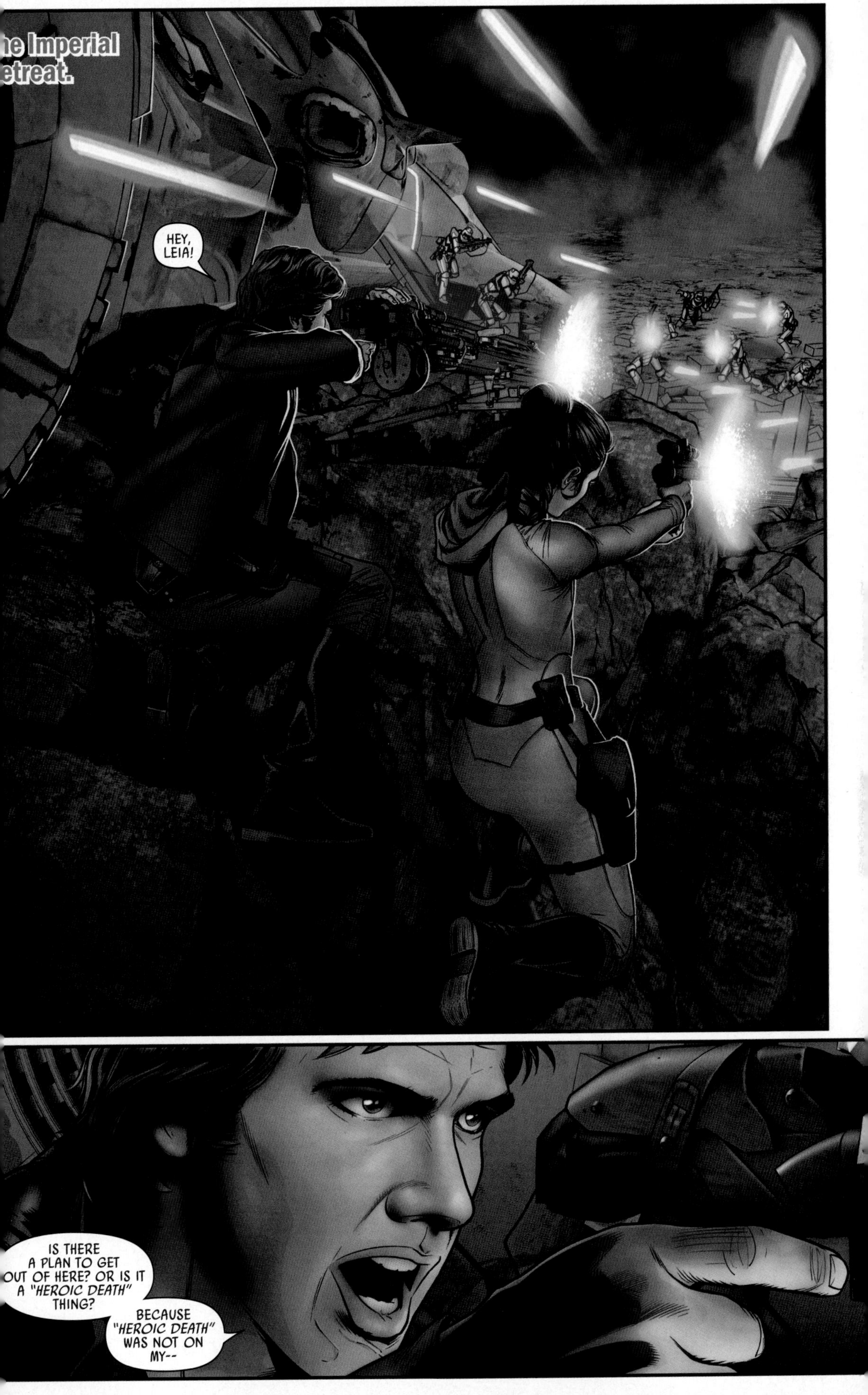
he Imperial
etreat.
HEY, LEIA!
IS THERE A PLAN TO GET OUT OF HERE? OR IS IT A "HEROIC DEATH" THING?
BECAUSE "HEROIC DEATH" WAS NOT ON MY--

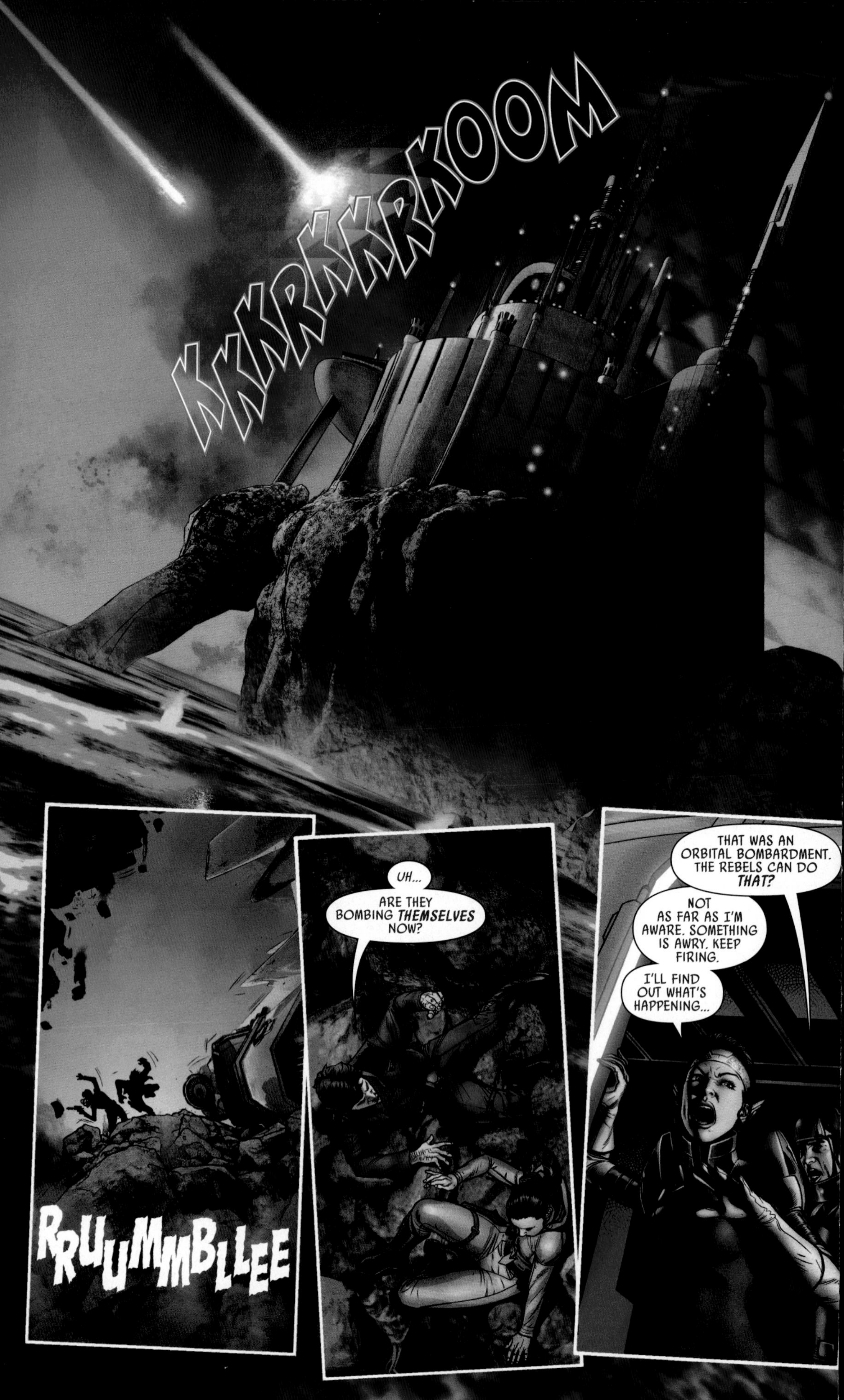
KKKRKKRKOOM
RRUUMMBLLEE
UH...
ARE THEY BOMBING THEMSELVES NOW?
THAT WAS AN ORBITAL BOMBARDMENT. THE REBELS CAN DO THAT?
NOT AS FAR AS I'M AWARE. SOMETHING IS AWRY. KEEP FIRING.
I'LL FIND OUT WHAT'S HAPPENING...

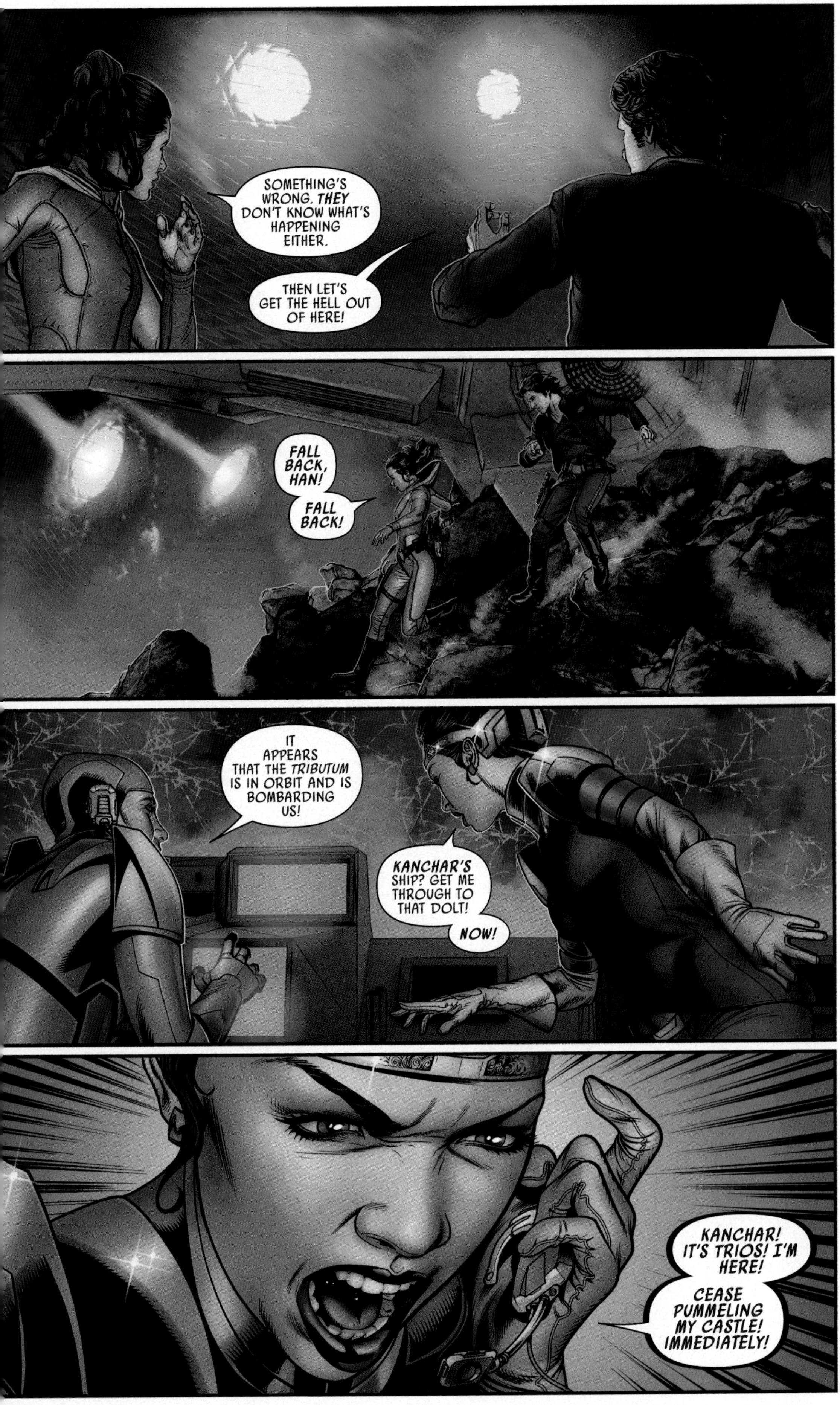
SOMETHING'S WRONG. THEY DON'T KNOW WHAT'S HAPPENING EITHER.
THEN LET'S GET THE HELL OUT OF HERE!
FALL BACK, HAN!
FALL BACK!
IT APPEARS THAT THE TRIBUTUM IS IN ORBIT AND IS BOMBARDING US!
KANCHAR'S SHIP? GET ME THROUGH TO THAT DOLT!
NOW!
KANCHAR! IT'S TRIOS! I'M HERE!
CEASE PUMMELING MY CASTLE! IMMEDIATELY!

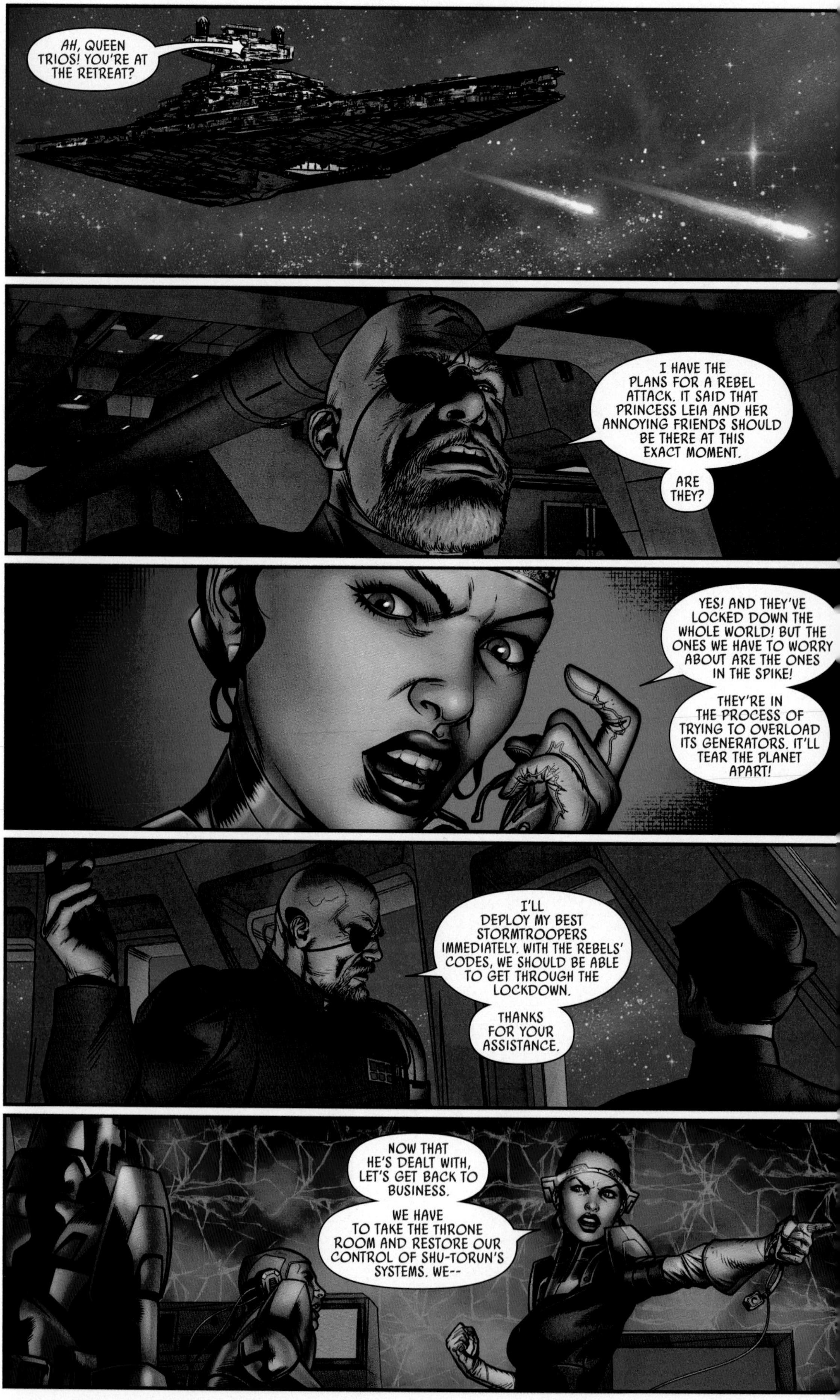
AH, QUEEN TRIOS! YOU'RE AT THE RETREAT?
I HAVE THE PLANS FOR A REBEL ATTACK. IT SAID THAT PRINCESS LEIA AND HER ANNOYING FRIENDS SHOULD BE THERE AT THIS EXACT MOMENT.
ARE THEY?
YES! AND THEY'VE LOCKED DOWN THE WHOLE WORLD! BUT THE ONES WE HAVE TO WORRY ABOUT ARE THE ONES IN THE SPIKE!
THEY'RE IN THE PROCESS OF TRYING TO OVERLOAD ITS GENERATORS. IT'LL TEAR THE PLANET APART!
I'LL DEPLOY MY BEST STORMTROOPERS IMMEDIATELY. WITH THE REBELS' CODES, WE SHOULD BE ABLE TO GET THROUGH THE LOCKDOWN.
THANKS FOR YOUR ASSISTANCE.
NOW THAT HE'S DEALT WITH, LET'S GET BACK TO BUSINESS.
WE HAVE TO TAKE THE THRONE ROOM AND RESTORE OUR CONTROL OF SHU-TORUN'S SYSTEMS. WE--

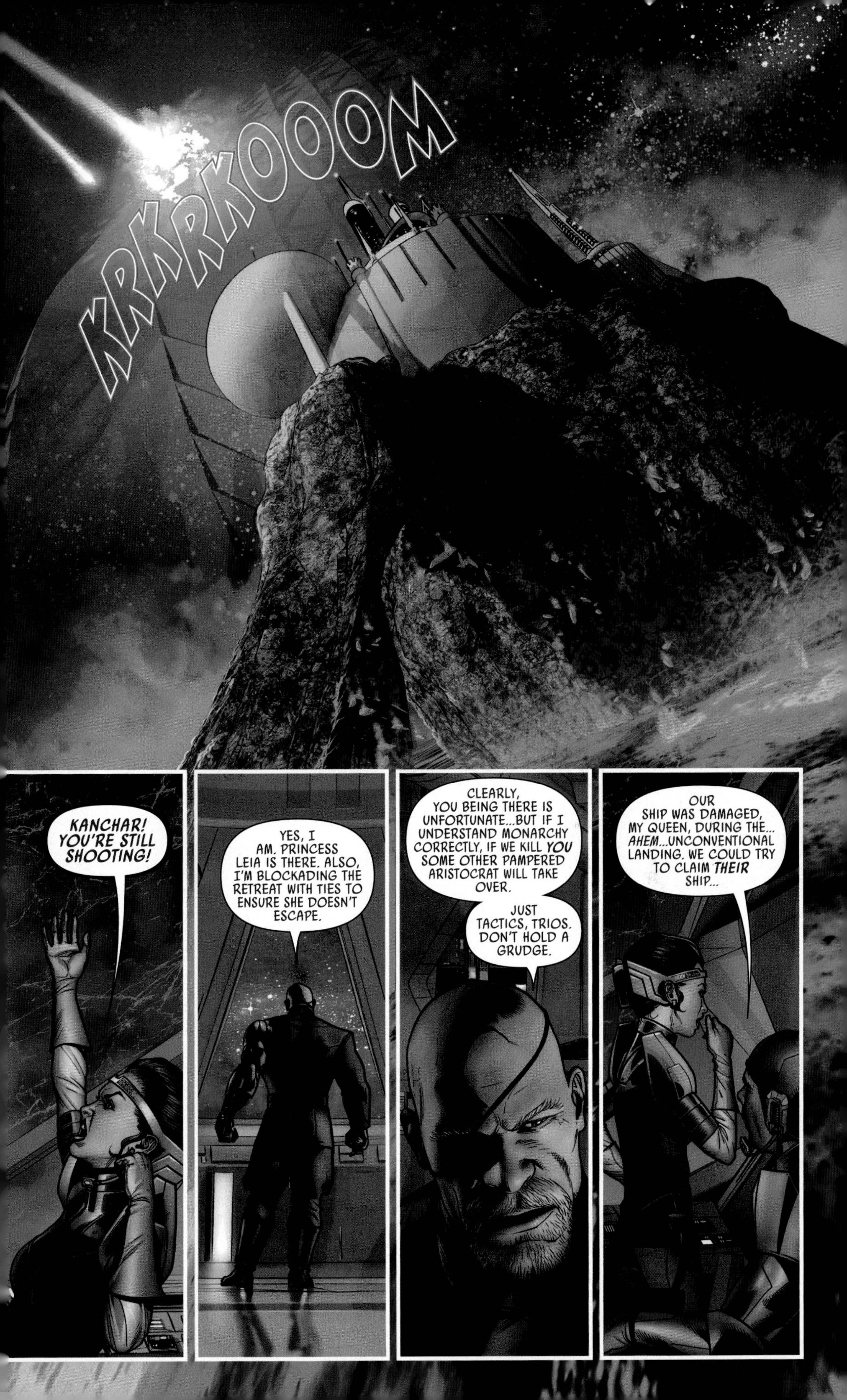
KRKRKOOOM
KANCHAR! YOU'RE STILL SHOOTING!
YES, I AM. PRINCESS LEIA IS THERE. ALSO, I'M BLOCKADING THE RETREAT WITH TIES TO ENSURE SHE DOESN'T ESCAPE.
CLEARLY, YOU BEING THERE IS UNFORTUNATE...BUT IF I UNDERSTAND MONARCHY CORRECTLY, IF WE KILL *YOU* SOME OTHER PAMPERED ARISTOCRAT WILL TAKE OVER.
JUST TACTICS, TRIOS. DON'T HOLD A GRUDGE.
OUR SHIP WAS DAMAGED, MY QUEEN, DURING THE... *AHEM*...UNCONVENTIONAL LANDING. WE COULD TRY TO CLAIM *THEIR* SHIP...

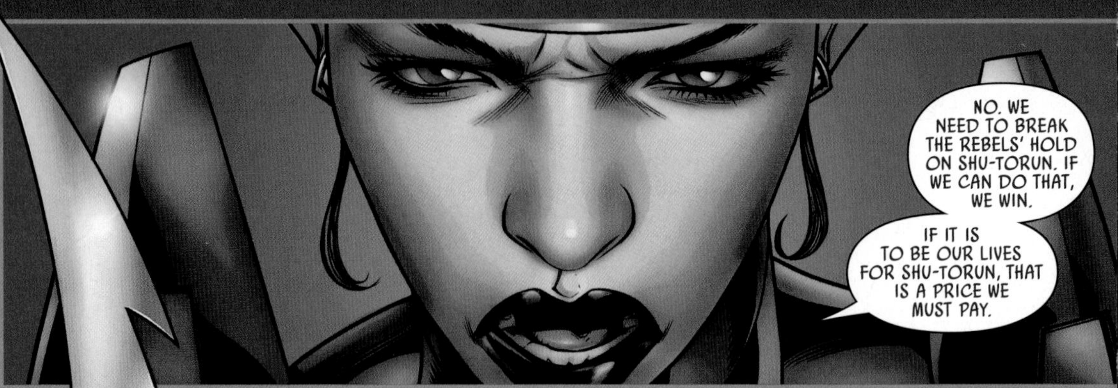
NO. WE NEED TO BREAK THE REBELS' HOLD ON SHU-TORUN. IF WE CAN DO THAT, WE WIN.
IF IT IS TO BE OUR LIVES FOR SHU-TORUN, THAT IS A PRICE WE MUST PAY.

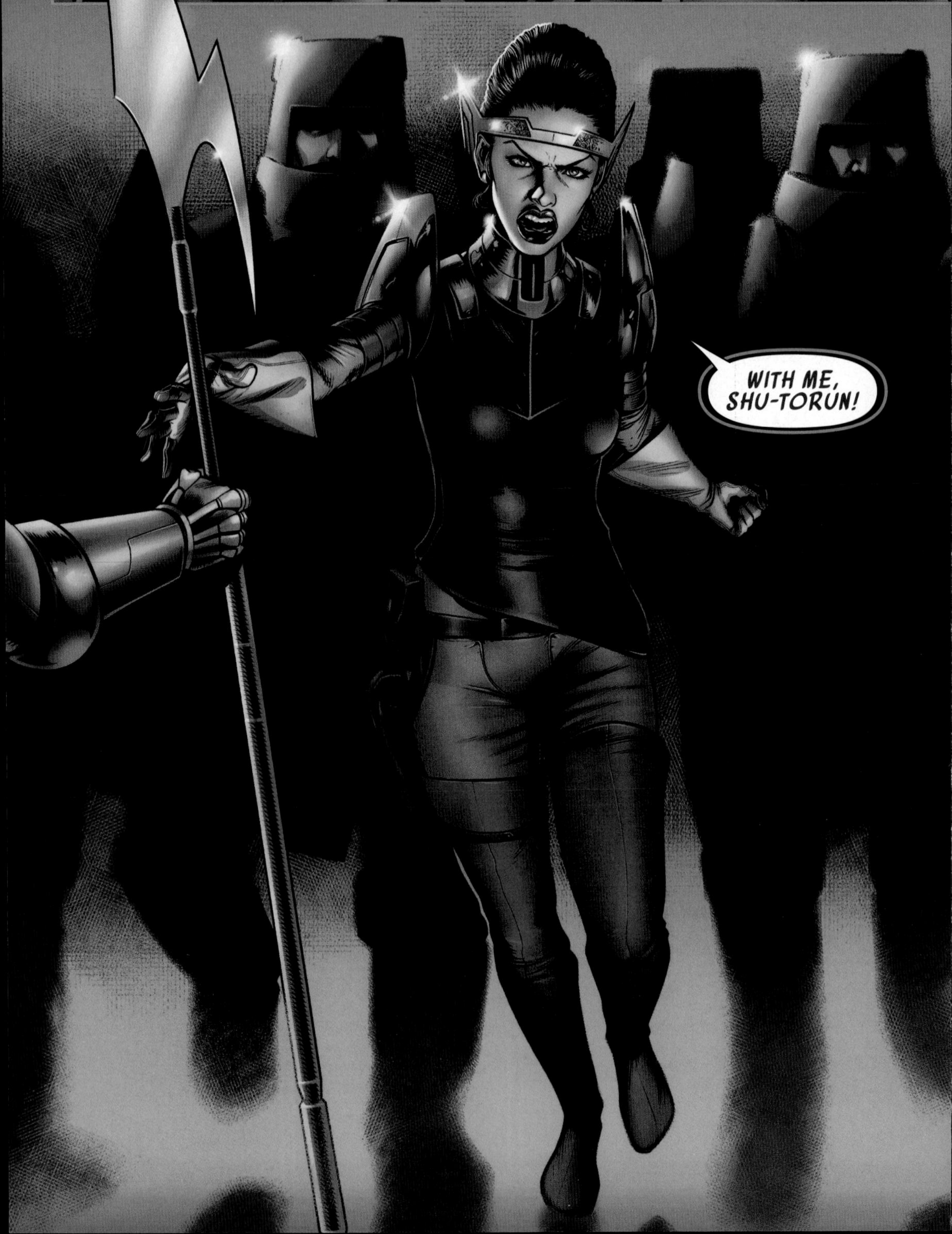
WITH ME, SHU-TORUN!

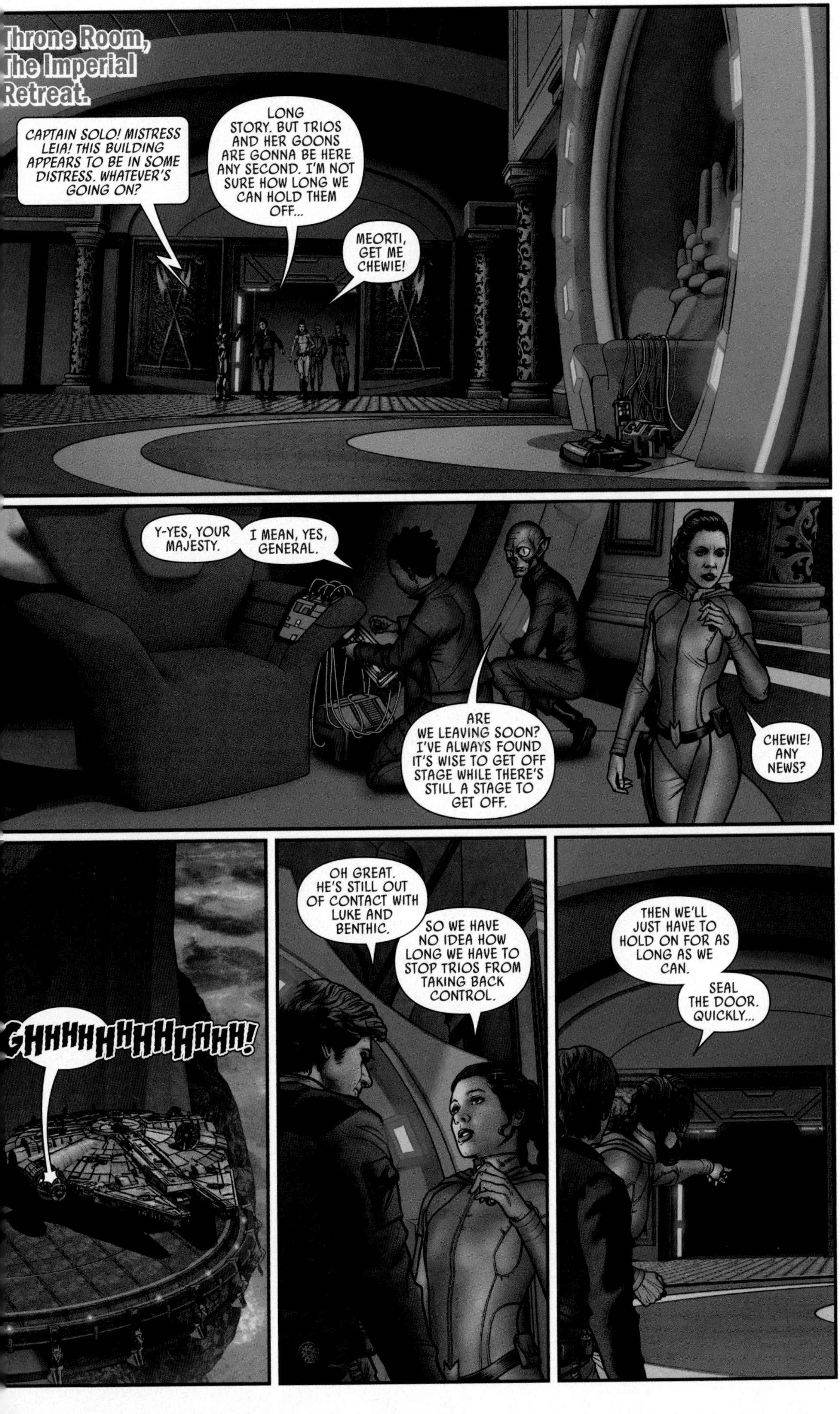
Throne Room, The Imperial Retreat.
CAPTAIN SOLO! MISTRESS LEIA! THIS BUILDING APPEARS TO BE IN SOME DISTRESS. WHATEVER'S GOING ON?
LONG STORY. BUT TRIOS AND HER GOONS ARE GONNA BE HERE ANY SECOND. I'M NOT SURE HOW LONG WE CAN HOLD THEM OFF...
MEORTI, GET ME CHEWIE!
Y-YES, YOUR MAJESTY.
I MEAN, YES, GENERAL.
ARE WE LEAVING SOON? I'VE ALWAYS FOUND IT'S WISE TO GET OFF STAGE WHILE THERE'S STILL A STAGE TO GET OFF.
CHEWIE! ANY NEWS?
GHHHHHHHHHHHH!
OH GREAT. HE'S STILL OUT OF CONTACT WITH LUKE AND BENTHIC.
SO WE HAVE NO IDEA HOW LONG WE HAVE TO STOP TRIOS FROM TAKING BACK CONTROL.
THEN WE'LL JUST HAVE TO HOLD ON FOR AS LONG AS WE CAN.
SEAL THE DOOR. QUICKLY...

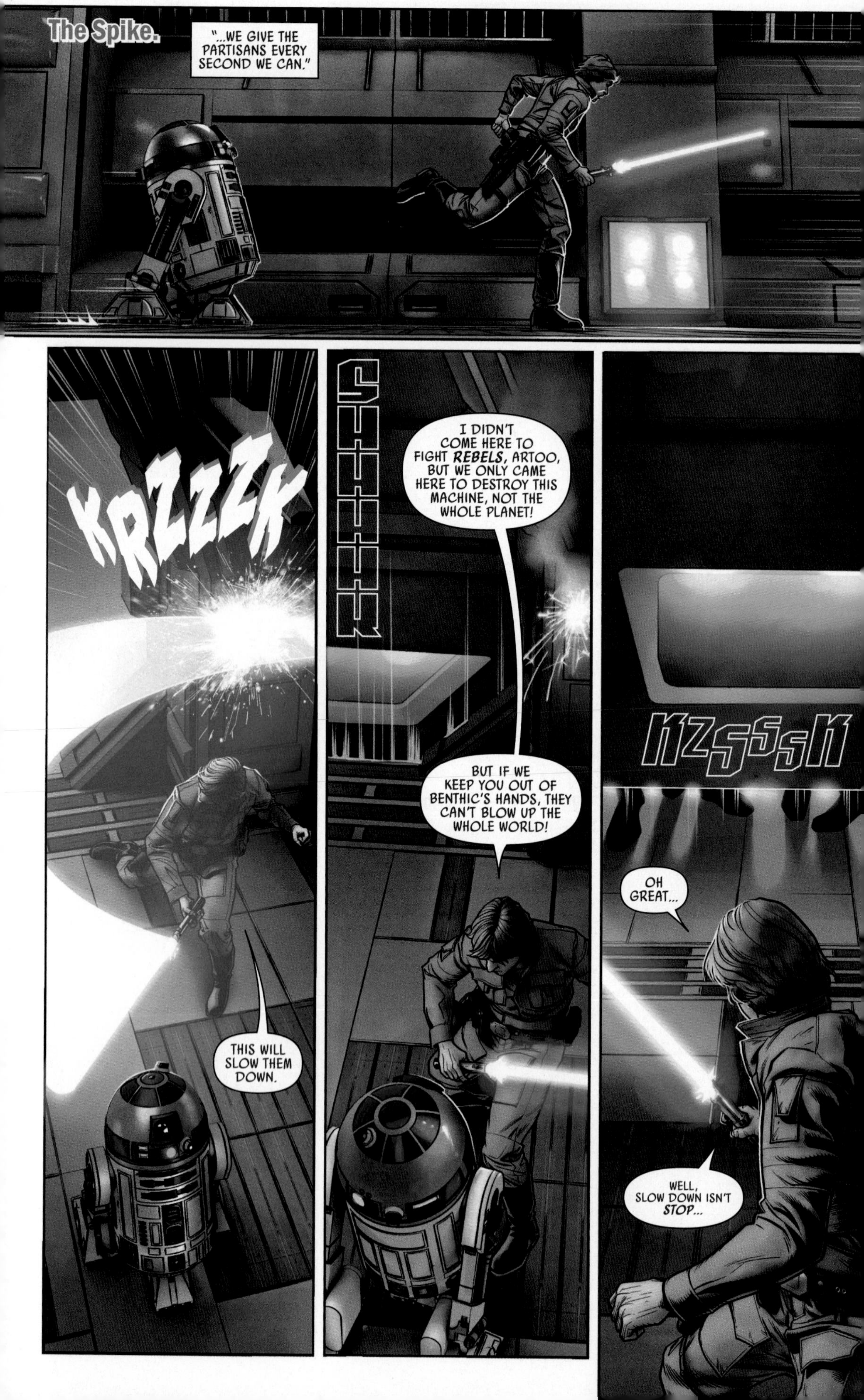

The Spike.
"...WE GIVE THE PARTISANS EVERY SECOND WE CAN."
KRZZZK
THIS WILL SLOW THEM DOWN.
SHHHHHR
I DIDN'T COME HERE TO FIGHT REBELS, ARTOO, BUT WE ONLY CAME HERE TO DESTROY THIS MACHINE, NOT THE WHOLE PLANET!
BUT IF WE KEEP YOU OUT OF BENTHIC'S HANDS, THEY CAN'T BLOW UP THE WHOLE WORLD!
KZSSSH
OH GREAT...
WELL, SLOW DOWN ISN'T STOP...

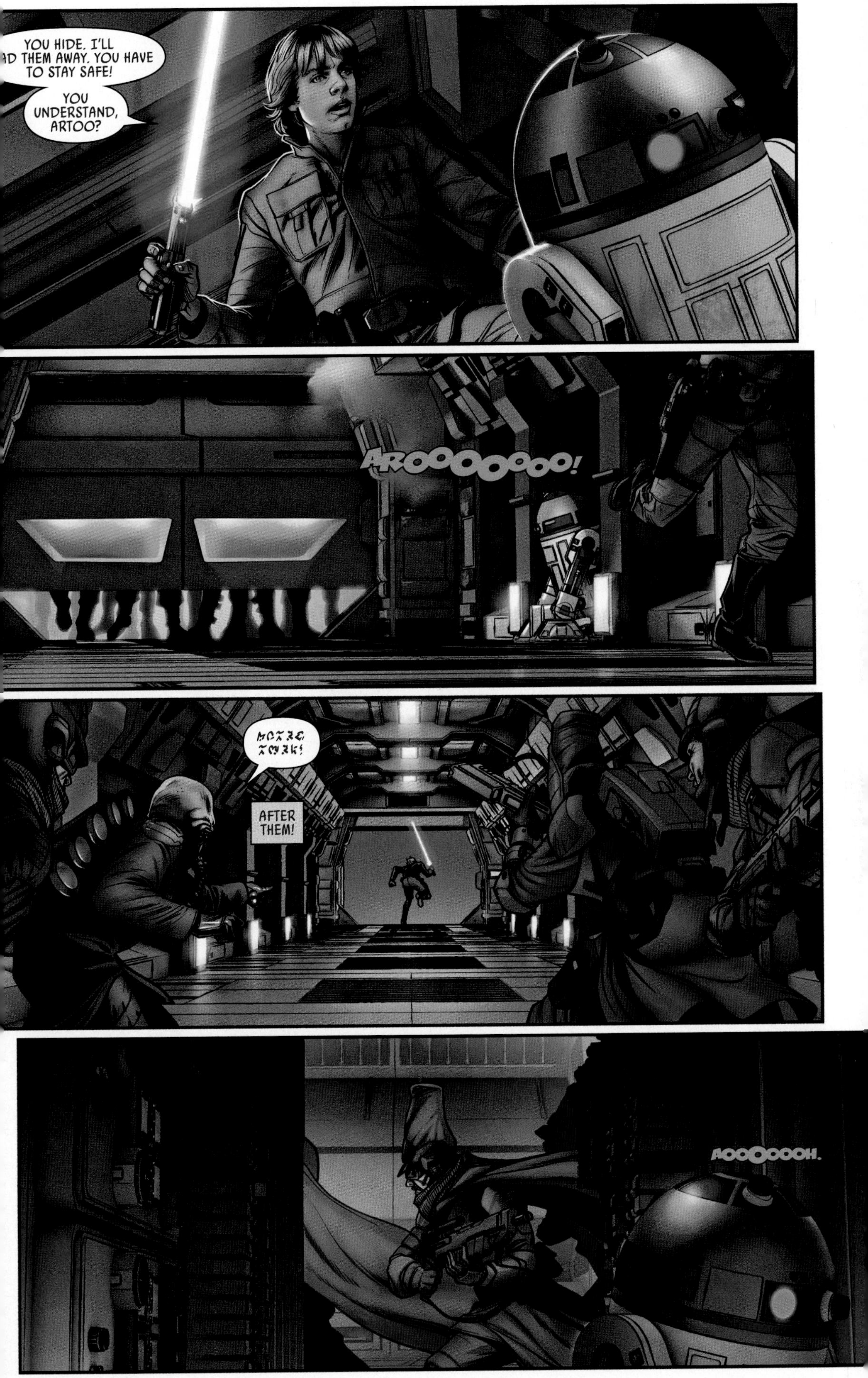
YOU HIDE. I'LL
AD THEM AWAY. YOU HAVE
TO STAY SAFE!
YOU UNDERSTAND, ARTOO?
AROOOOOOOO!
AFTER THEM!
AOOOOOOH.

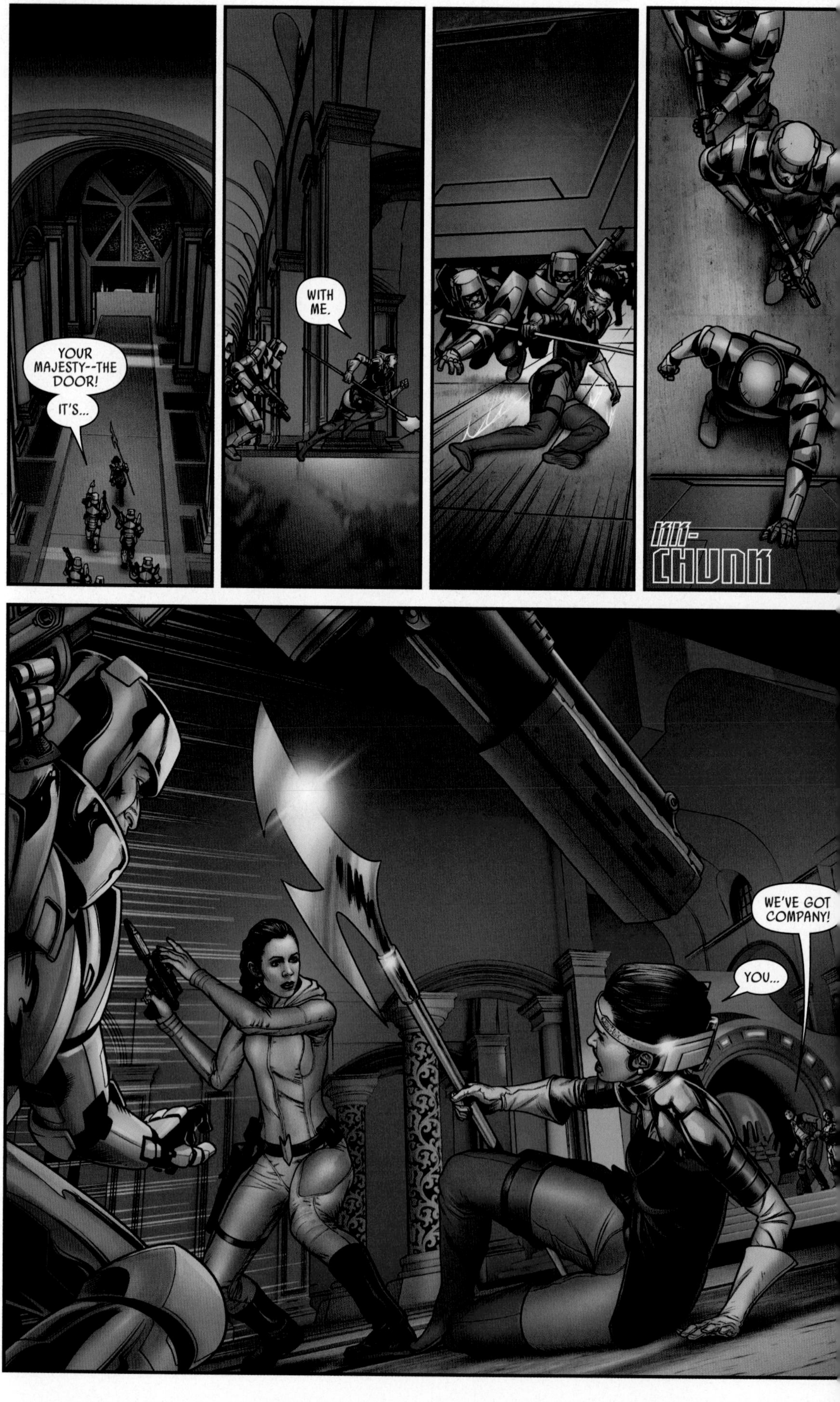
YOUR MAJESTY--THE DOOR!
IT'S...
WITH ME.
KK-CHUNK
WE'VE GOT COMPANY!
YOU...

...MONSTER!

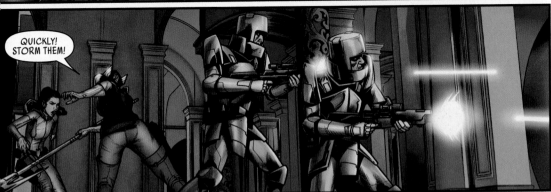

QUICKLY! STORM THEM!

OH MY!

KZZZRRK

OH NO.

NO WAY THROUGH.

ᔕᓭᑎᑎᏆ ᑎᎥᕼᕼ Ꮖ ᒣᑎᎥᒣ. ᔕᕼᎥᒣᎥᕼᔕ ᒣᎥᕼᕼ Ꮿᕼᑎᑎᕼᑎ ᏯᕼᏯᔕᑎᕼ ᎥᏯᔕ ᏯᎥᕼᏯᎥ ᕼᕼᏚ ᕼᔕᕼᏯᎥ ᑎᎥᏯᏚ

ᕼᏯᏯᔕᎥ ᔕᏯᎥ ᕼᏚᏯᏯ ᑎᎥᎥᏚᏚ

SO--IT WILL BE THIS. SLICING DOWN FELLOW REBELS IN A FIGHT YOU CAN'T WIN?

WHAT *ARE* YOU, LUKE?

WHAT ARE *YOU*, BENTHIC?

CAPTURING ME DOESN'T MAKE A DIFFERENCE ANYWAY! YOU NEED ARTOO.

ᏦᏯᏯᏚᎥᕼᏚᏯᎥ ᏦᏚ.

BROADCAST ME.

YES, BENTHIC. CHANNEL OPEN.

ᏚᏯᏚᎥᏚᎥ ᏯᏚᏚ ᏚᏚᕼ ᏯᏯᏚᏯ ᏚᏯᎥᎥᏚ

DROID! YOU CAN HEAR THIS...

ᏯᏚᏚ ᏚᏚᏦᏚ ᏯᎥᏯᏚᏚ ᏚᏚ ᏯᏚ ᏇᎥᕼᕼ ᕼᏚᏚᏚ ᏦᏚᏚᏚᏚᏚ.

YOU COME HERE, OR WE KILL YOUR MASTER.

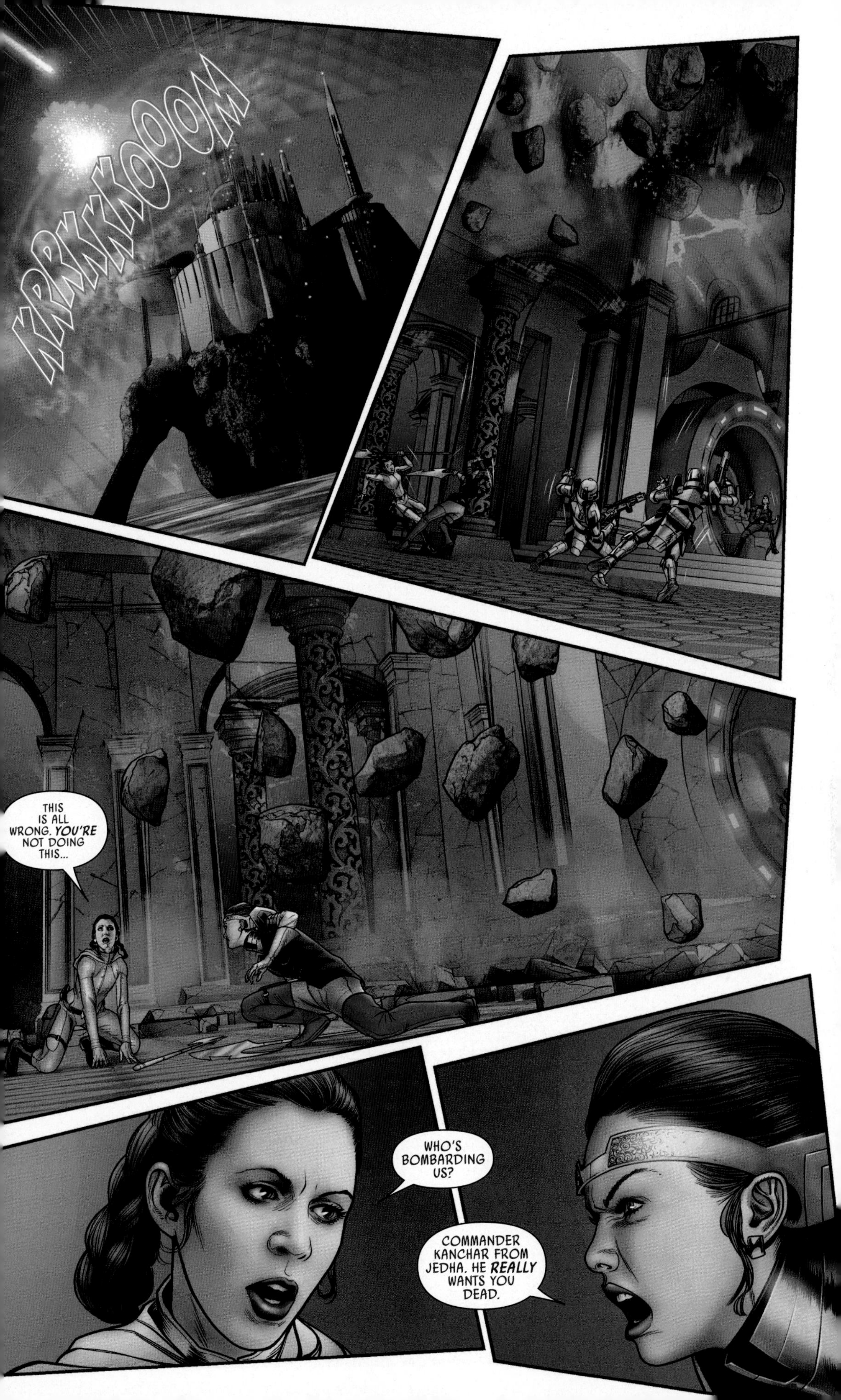
KRRKKOOOM
THIS IS ALL WRONG. YOU'RE NOT DOING THIS...
WHO'S BOMBARDING US?
COMMANDER KANCHAR FROM JEDHA. HE REALLY WANTS YOU DEAD.

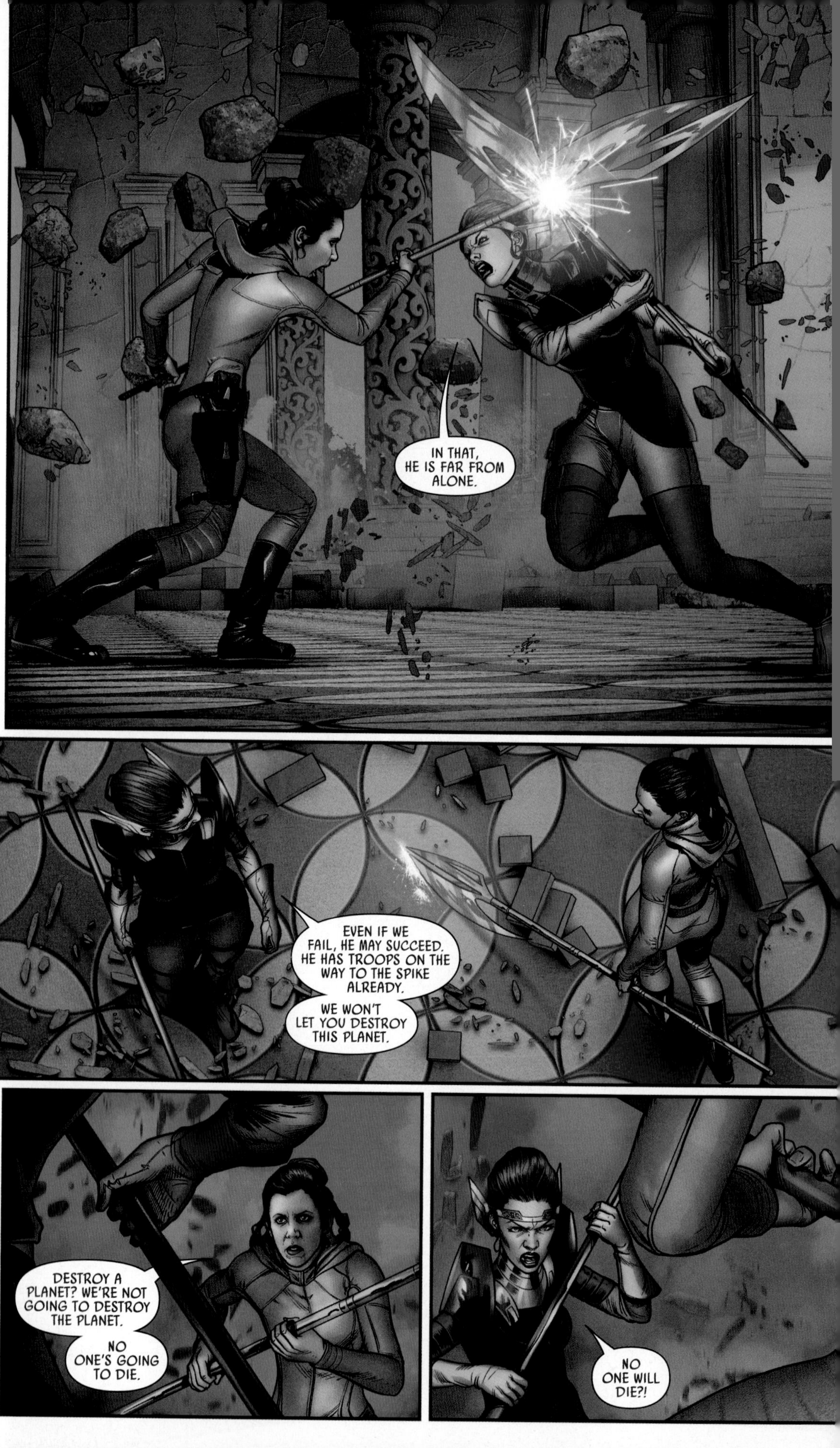
IN THAT, HE IS FAR FROM ALONE.
EVEN IF WE FAIL, HE MAY SUCCEED. HE HAS TROOPS ON THE WAY TO THE SPIKE ALREADY.
WE WON'T LET YOU DESTROY THIS PLANET.
DESTROY A PLANET? WE'RE NOT GOING TO DESTROY THE PLANET.
NO ONE'S GOING TO DIE.
NO ONE WILL DIE?!

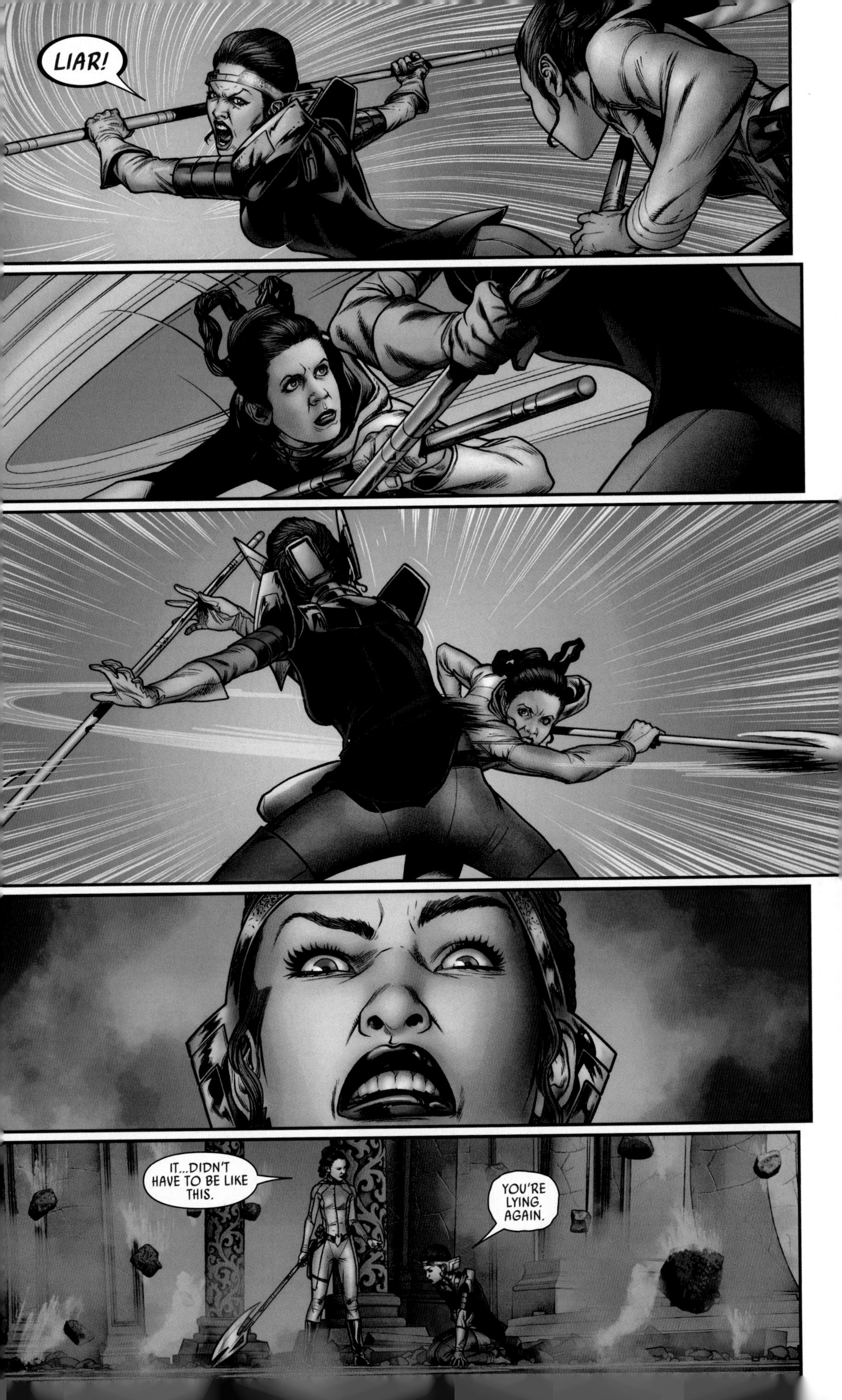
LIAR!
IT...DIDN'T HAVE TO BE LIKE THIS.
YOU'RE LYING. AGAIN.

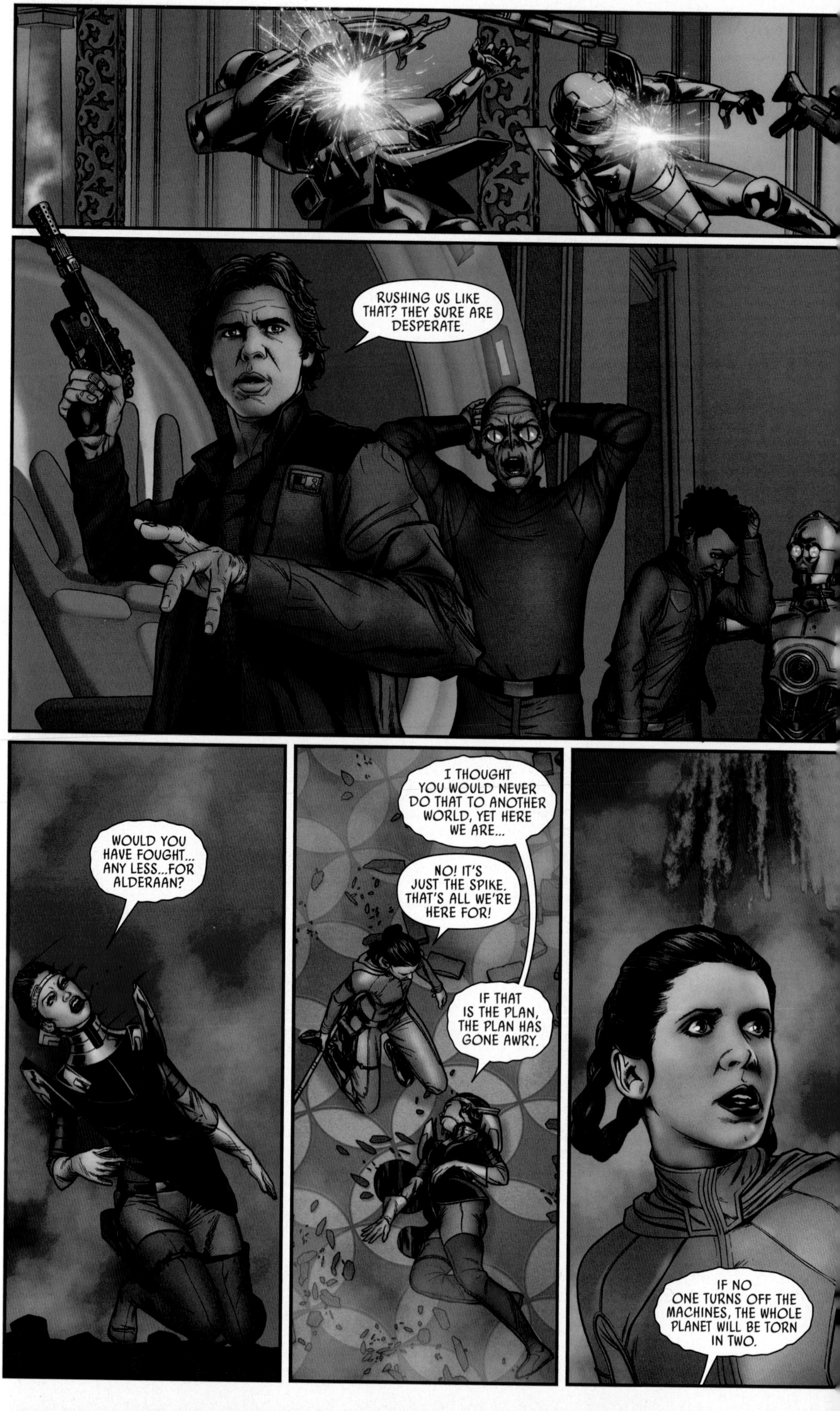
RUSHING US LIKE THAT? THEY SURE ARE DESPERATE.
WOULD YOU HAVE FOUGHT... ANY LESS...FOR ALDERAAN?
I THOUGHT YOU WOULD NEVER DO THAT TO ANOTHER WORLD, YET HERE WE ARE...
NO! IT'S JUST THE SPIKE. THAT'S ALL WE'RE HERE FOR!
IF THAT IS THE PLAN, THE PLAN HAS GONE AWRY.
IF NO ONE TURNS OFF THE MACHINES, THE WHOLE PLANET WILL BE TORN IN TWO.

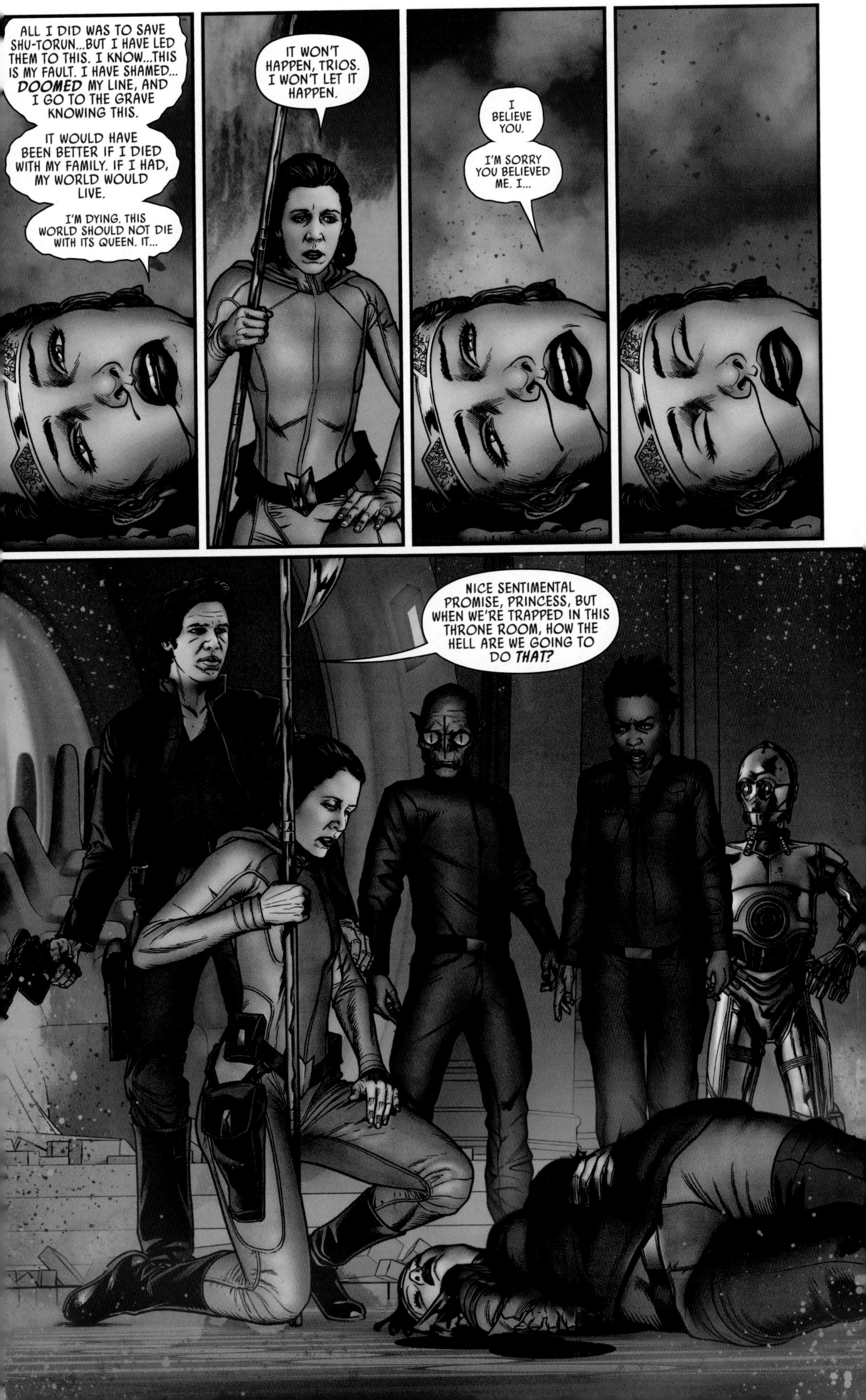
ALL I DID WAS TO SAVE SHU-TORUN...BUT I HAVE LED THEM TO THIS. I KNOW...THIS IS MY FAULT. I HAVE SHAMED... ***DOOMED*** MY LINE, AND I GO TO THE GRAVE KNOWING THIS.
IT WOULD HAVE BEEN BETTER IF I DIED WITH MY FAMILY. IF I HAD, MY WORLD WOULD LIVE.
I'M DYING. THIS WORLD SHOULD NOT DIE WITH ITS QUEEN. IT...
IT WON'T HAPPEN, TRIOS. I WON'T LET IT HAPPEN.
I BELIEVE YOU.
I'M SORRY YOU BELIEVED ME. I...
NICE SENTIMENTAL PROMISE, PRINCESS, BUT WHEN WE'RE TRAPPED IN THIS THRONE ROOM, HOW THE HELL ARE WE GOING TO DO ***THAT?***

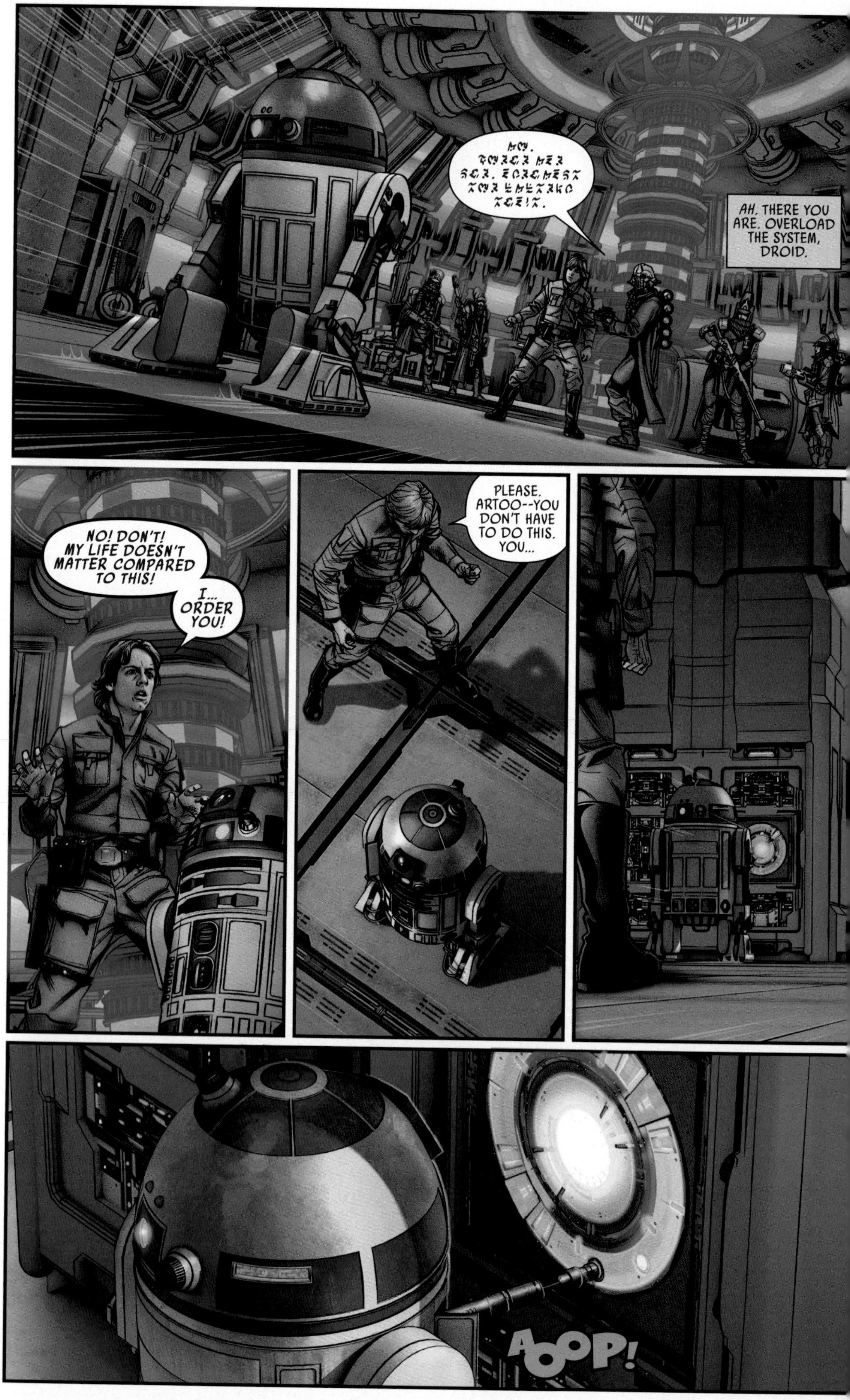
AH. THERE YOU ARE. OVERLOAD THE SYSTEM, DROID.
NO! DON'T! MY LIFE DOESN'T MATTER COMPARED TO THIS!
I... ORDER YOU!
PLEASE. ARTOO--YOU DON'T HAVE TO DO THIS. YOU...
AOOP!

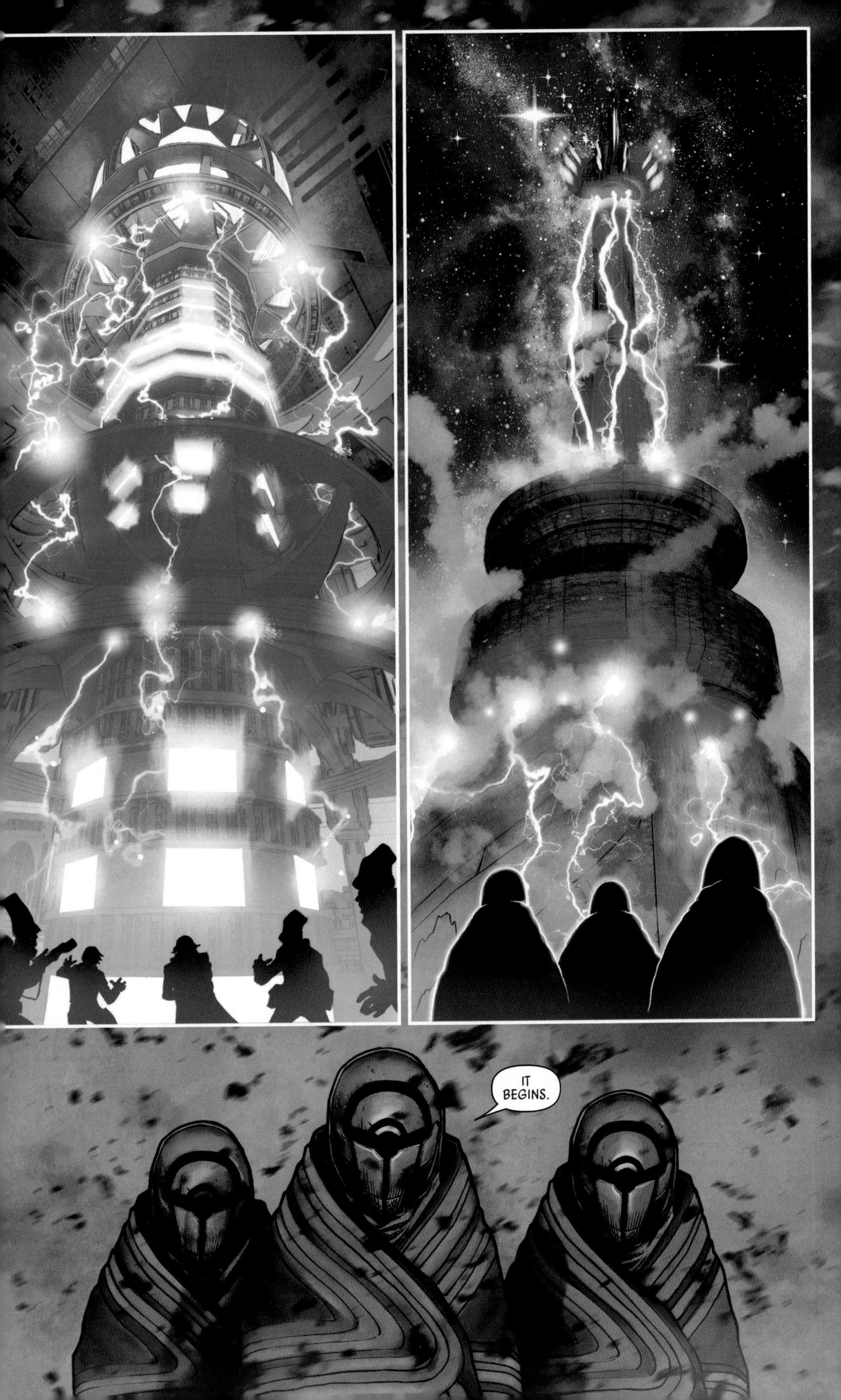
IT BEGINS.

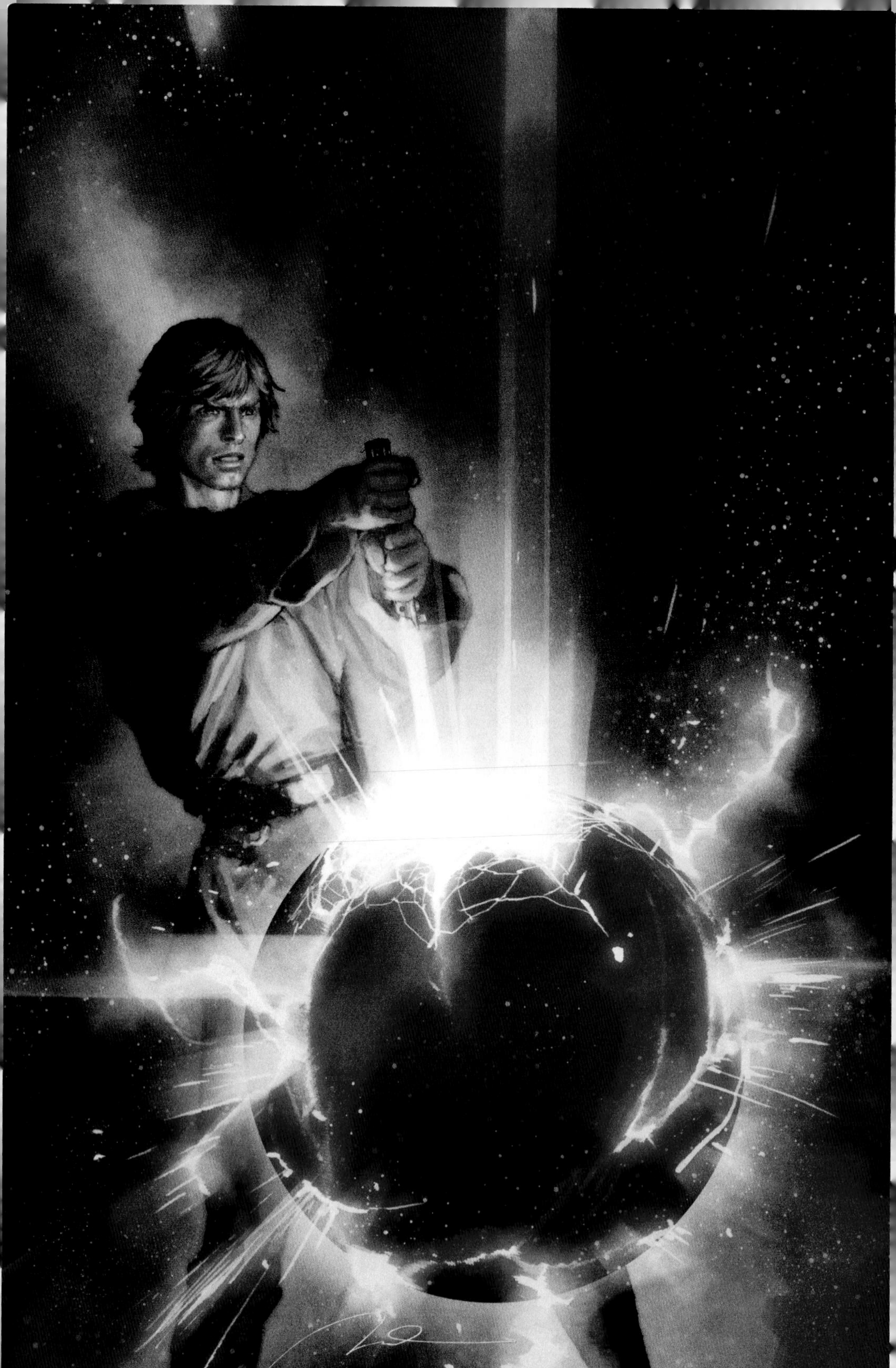

BENTHIC! STOP! YOU'RE GOING TO KILL EVERYONE ON THIS PLANET!

ᔕᔦᒪ. ᓭᔑᒷᔑᔑᐢ ᔑᒷ. ᔑᒷᔑᔑᐢᔑᐢ ᔦᒷ ᔑᔦᒷᒷᔑᔦ ᔦᐢᔑᒷ ᔦᔑᔦᔑᐢᔦᒷ ᐢᔑᔦᒷᔑ ᔦᔦᔑᒷ.

YES. INCLUDING US. ANYTHING TO ENSURE THIS HELLISH PLANET DIES.

ᔕᔑᔦ ᔦᔦᔑᔦᔦᔑᔦᔑᔦ. ᔦᔑᔑᔦᔑᔑᐢ ᒷᒷᔦᑕ ᔦᒷᐢ. ᒷᔑ ᔦᒷᔦ ᔑᔑ ᐢᔑᐢᐢᔑᔑᐢ ᔦᒷ ᔦᔑᔑᒷᔑᐢ ᔦᔑᔦᔦ ᔦᒷᒷᔦᔦ.

ᔑᒷᔦ ᔦᔑᔑ ᔑᔦ ᔦᔑᔦ ᔦᒷᔦ. ᒷᔑ ᔦᒷ ᔦᔦᒷᒷᔑᒷᔦᔕ ᔦᔦᒷᔦᔦᔑᔦᔦᒷᔦ.

SET PERIMETER. THEY'LL COME NOW. WE MUST BE WILLING TO DEFEND THE DREAM.

AND TIE UP THE BOY. HE IS PROVING A DISTRACTION.

ARTOO! YOU SHOULD HAVE JUST LET ME DIE RATHER THAN SLICE THE REACTOR! THERE'S JUST TOO MUCH AT STAKE!

AROOOOOO PAHPAH!

I DON'T UNDERSTAND YOU AT ALL.

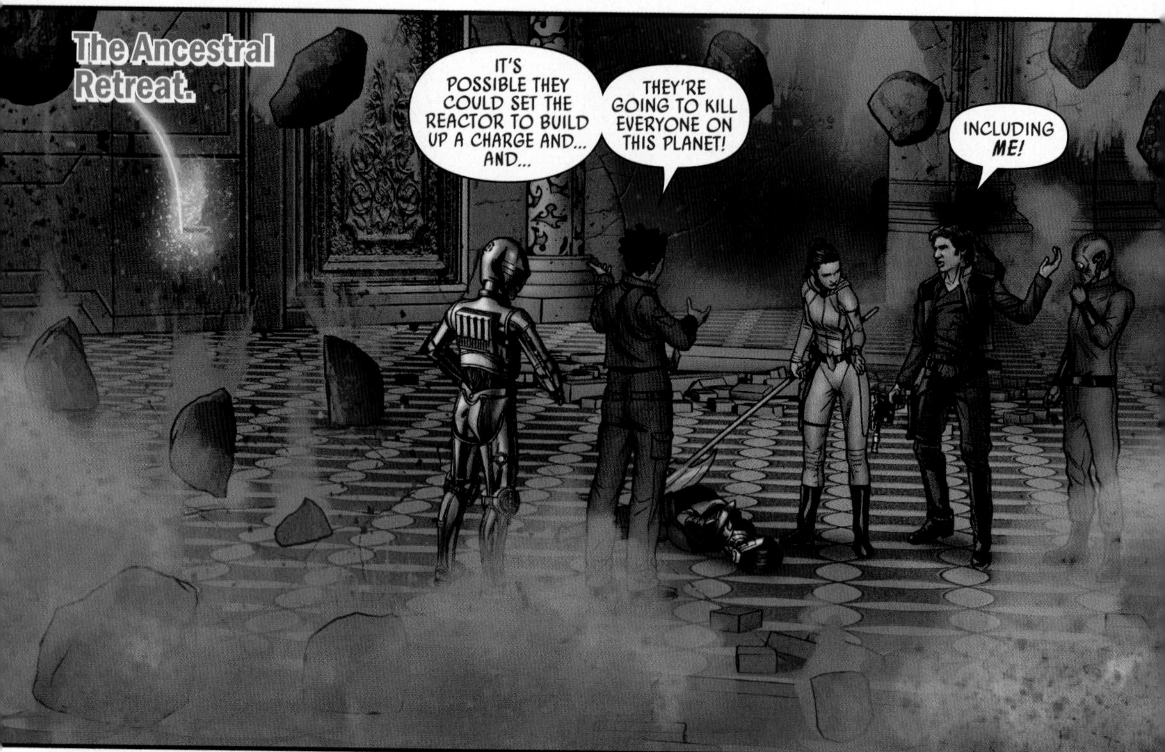
The Ancestral Retreat.
IT'S POSSIBLE THEY COULD SET THE REACTOR TO BUILD UP A CHARGE AND... AND...
THEY'RE GOING TO KILL EVERYONE ON THIS PLANET!
INCLUDING *ME!*

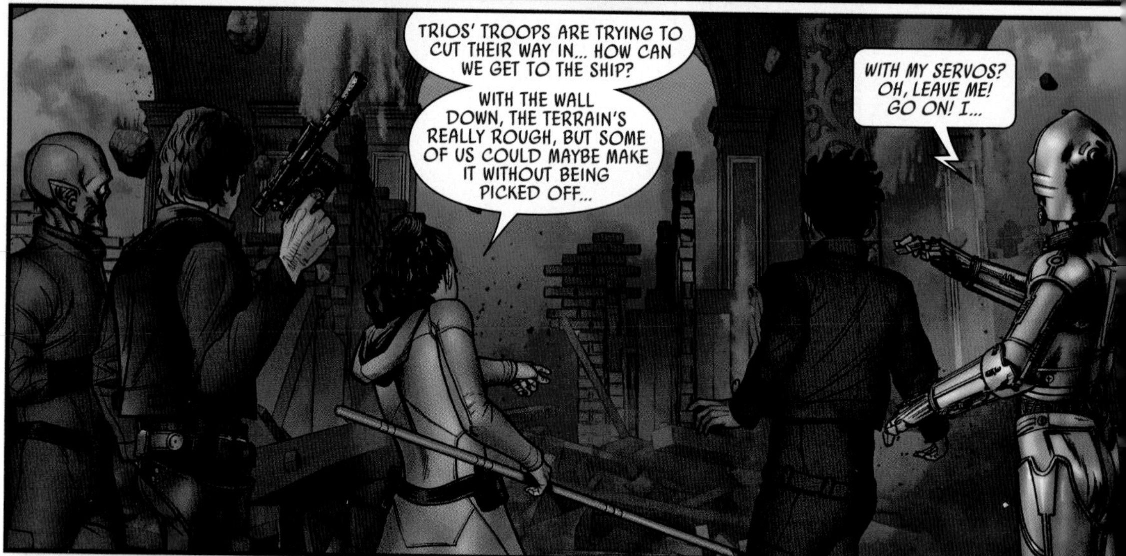
TRIOS' TROOPS ARE TRYING TO CUT THEIR WAY IN... HOW CAN WE GET TO THE SHIP?
WITH THE WALL DOWN, THE TERRAIN'S REALLY ROUGH, BUT SOME OF US COULD MAYBE MAKE IT WITHOUT BEING PICKED OFF...
WITH MY SERVOS? OH, LEAVE ME! GO ON! I...

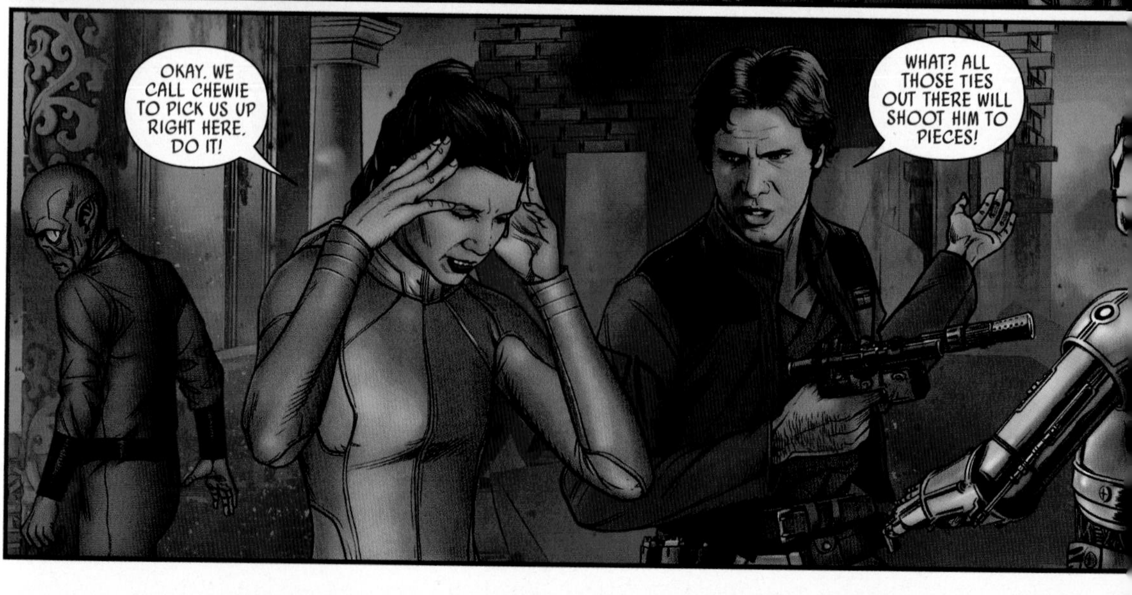
OKAY. WE CALL CHEWIE TO PICK US UP RIGHT HERE. DO IT!
WHAT? ALL THOSE TIES OUT THERE WILL SHOOT HIM TO PIECES!

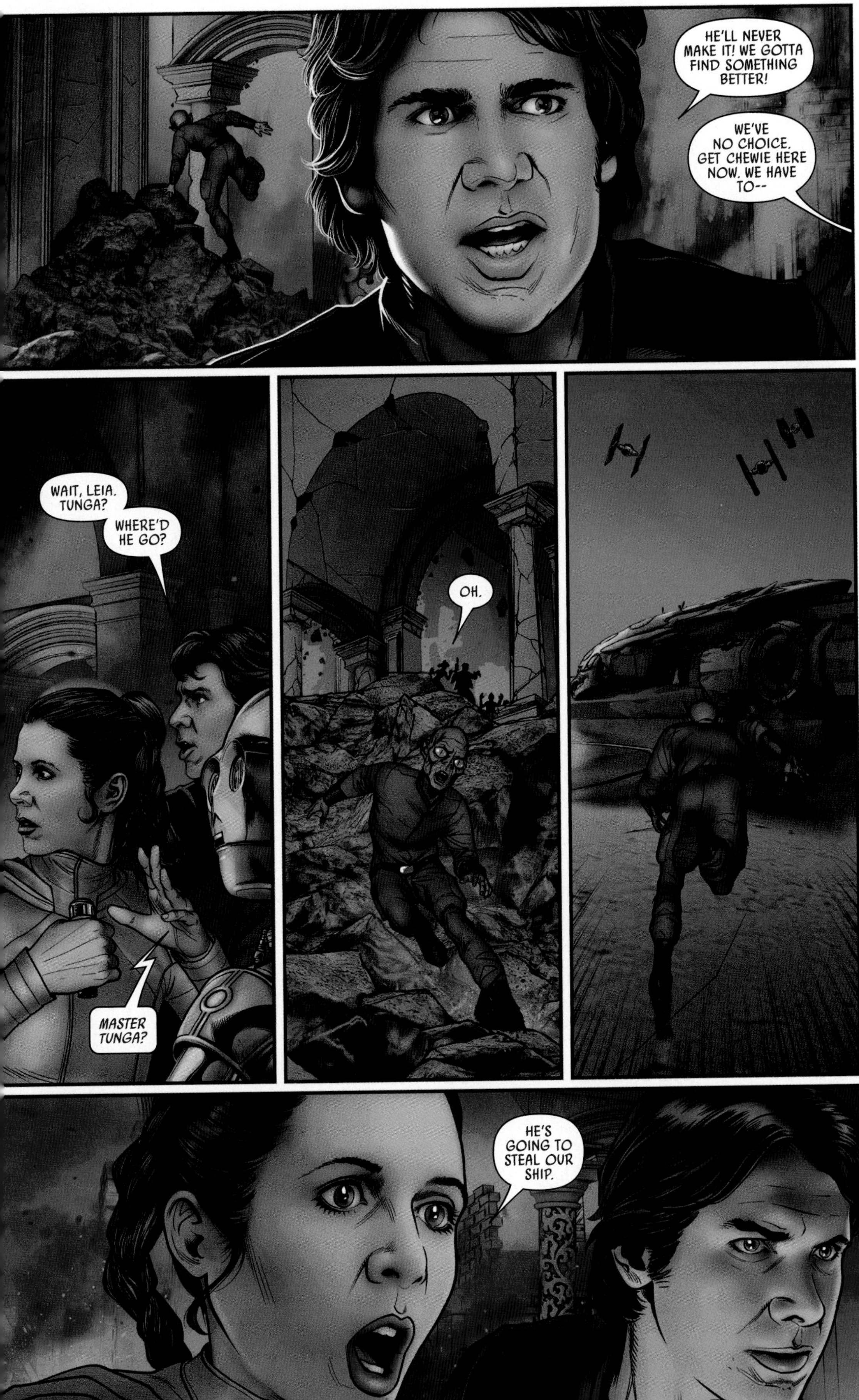
HE'LL NEVER MAKE IT! WE GOTTA FIND SOMETHING BETTER!
WE'VE NO CHOICE. GET CHEWIE HERE NOW. WE HAVE TO--
WAIT, LEIA. TUNGA?
WHERE'D HE GO?
MASTER TUNGA?
OH.
HE'S GOING TO STEAL OUR SHIP.

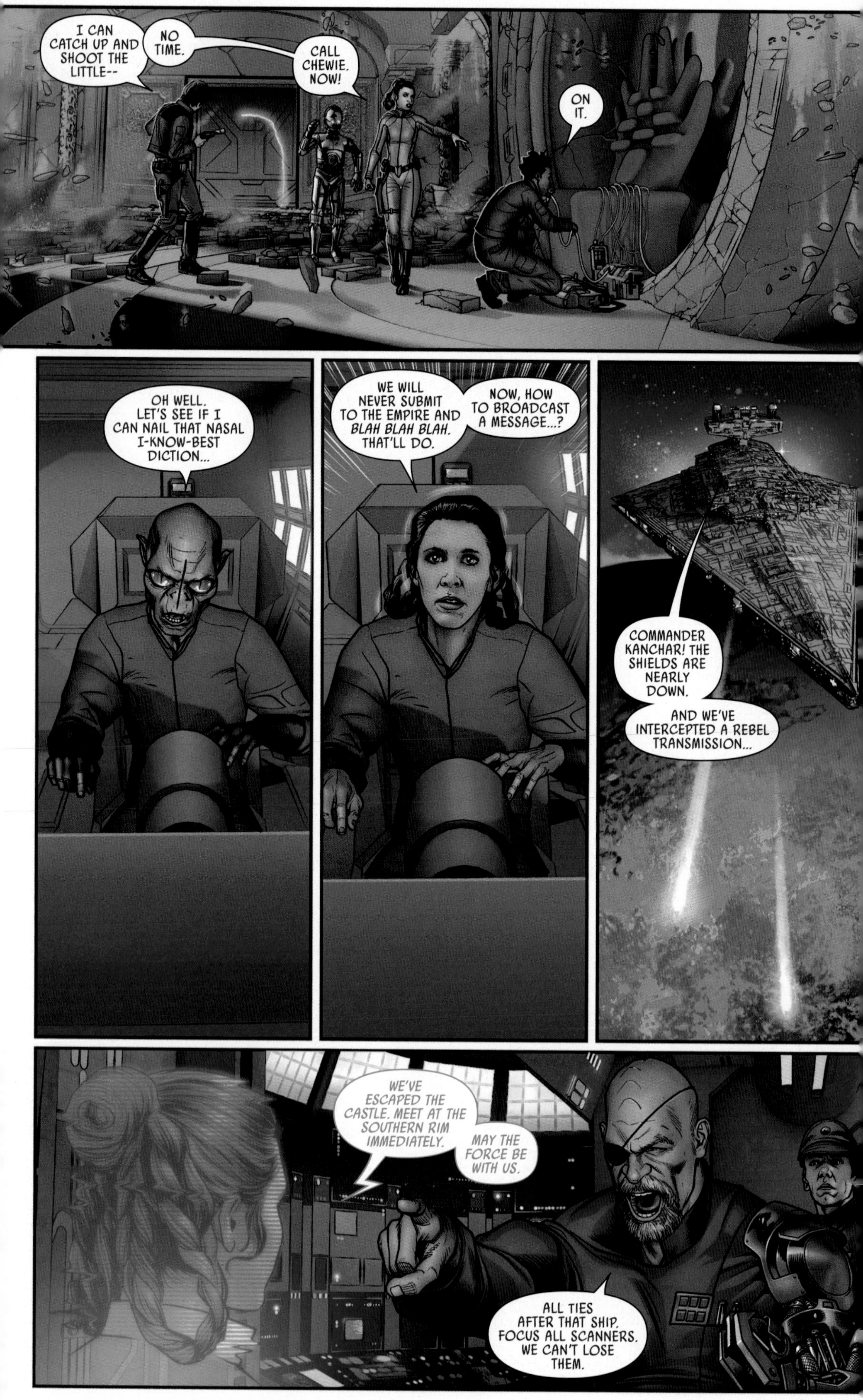
I CAN CATCH UP AND SHOOT THE LITTLE--
NO TIME.
CALL CHEWIE. NOW!
ON IT.
OH WELL. LET'S SEE IF I CAN NAIL THAT NASAL I-KNOW-BEST DICTION...
WE WILL NEVER SUBMIT TO THE EMPIRE AND *BLAH BLAH BLAH.* THAT'LL DO.
NOW, HOW TO BROADCAST A MESSAGE...?
COMMANDER KANCHAR! THE SHIELDS ARE NEARLY DOWN.
AND WE'VE INTERCEPTED A REBEL TRANSMISSION...
WE'VE ESCAPED THE CASTLE. MEET AT THE SOUTHERN RIM IMMEDIATELY.
MAY THE FORCE BE WITH US.
ALL TIES AFTER THAT SHIP. FOCUS ALL SCANNERS. WE CAN'T LOSE THEM.

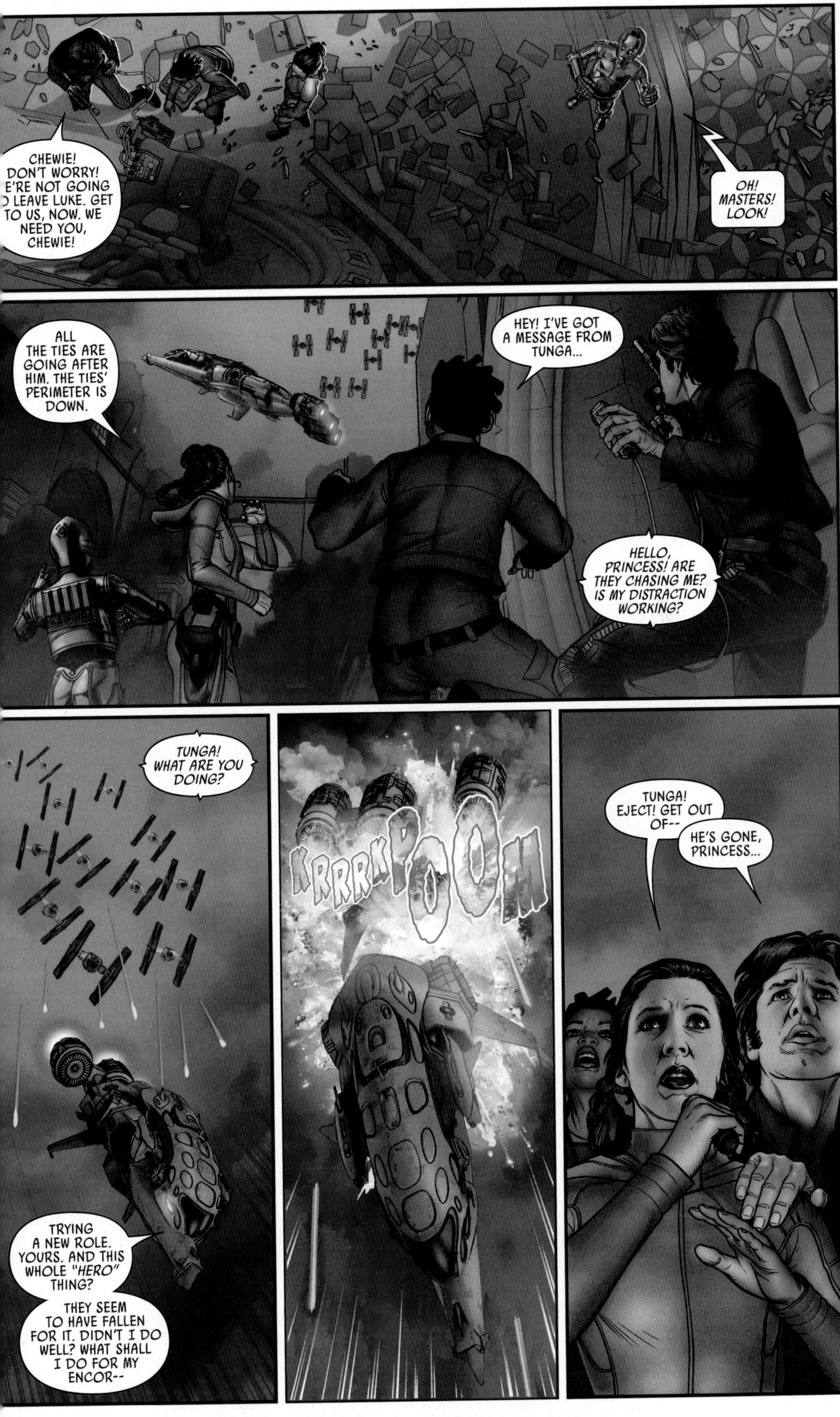

CHEWIE! DON'T WORRY! E'RE NOT GOING D LEAVE LUKE. GET TO US, NOW. WE NEED YOU, CHEWIE!
OH! MASTERS! LOOK!
ALL THE TIES ARE GOING AFTER HIM. THE TIES' PERIMETER IS DOWN.
HEY! I'VE GOT A MESSAGE FROM TUNGA...
HELLO, PRINCESS! ARE THEY CHASING ME? IS MY DISTRACTION WORKING?
TUNGA! WHAT ARE YOU DOING?
TRYING A NEW ROLE. YOURS. AND THIS WHOLE "HERO" THING?
THEY SEEM TO HAVE FALLEN FOR IT. DIDN'T I DO WELL? WHAT SHALL I DO FOR MY ENCOR--
KRRRKPOOOM
TUNGA! EJECT! GET OUT OF--
HE'S GONE, PRINCESS...

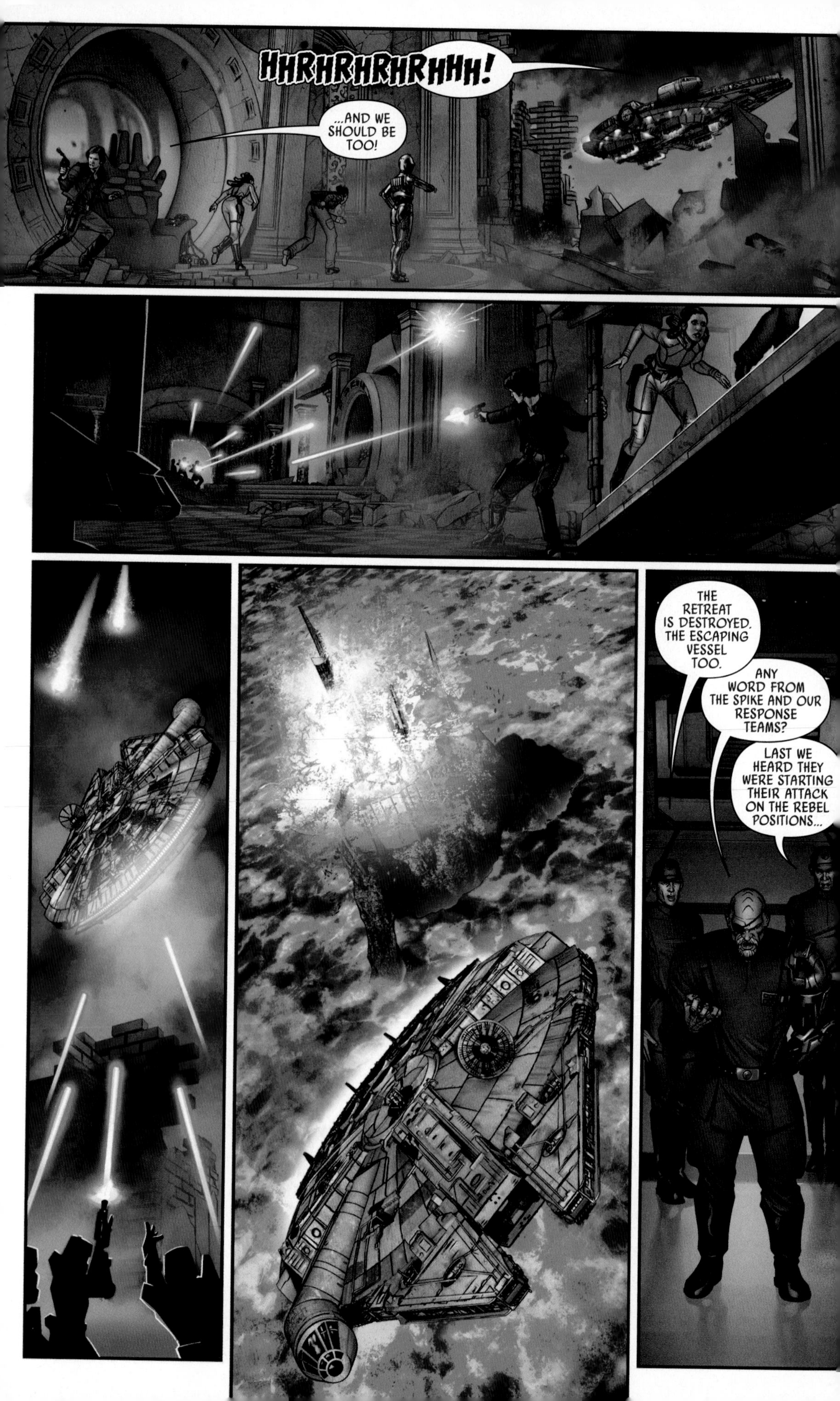
HHRHRHRHRHHH!
...AND WE SHOULD BE TOO!
THE RETREAT IS DESTROYED. THE ESCAPING VESSEL TOO.
ANY WORD FROM THE SPIKE AND OUR RESPONSE TEAMS?
LAST WE HEARD THEY WERE STARTING THEIR ATTACK ON THE REBEL POSITIONS...

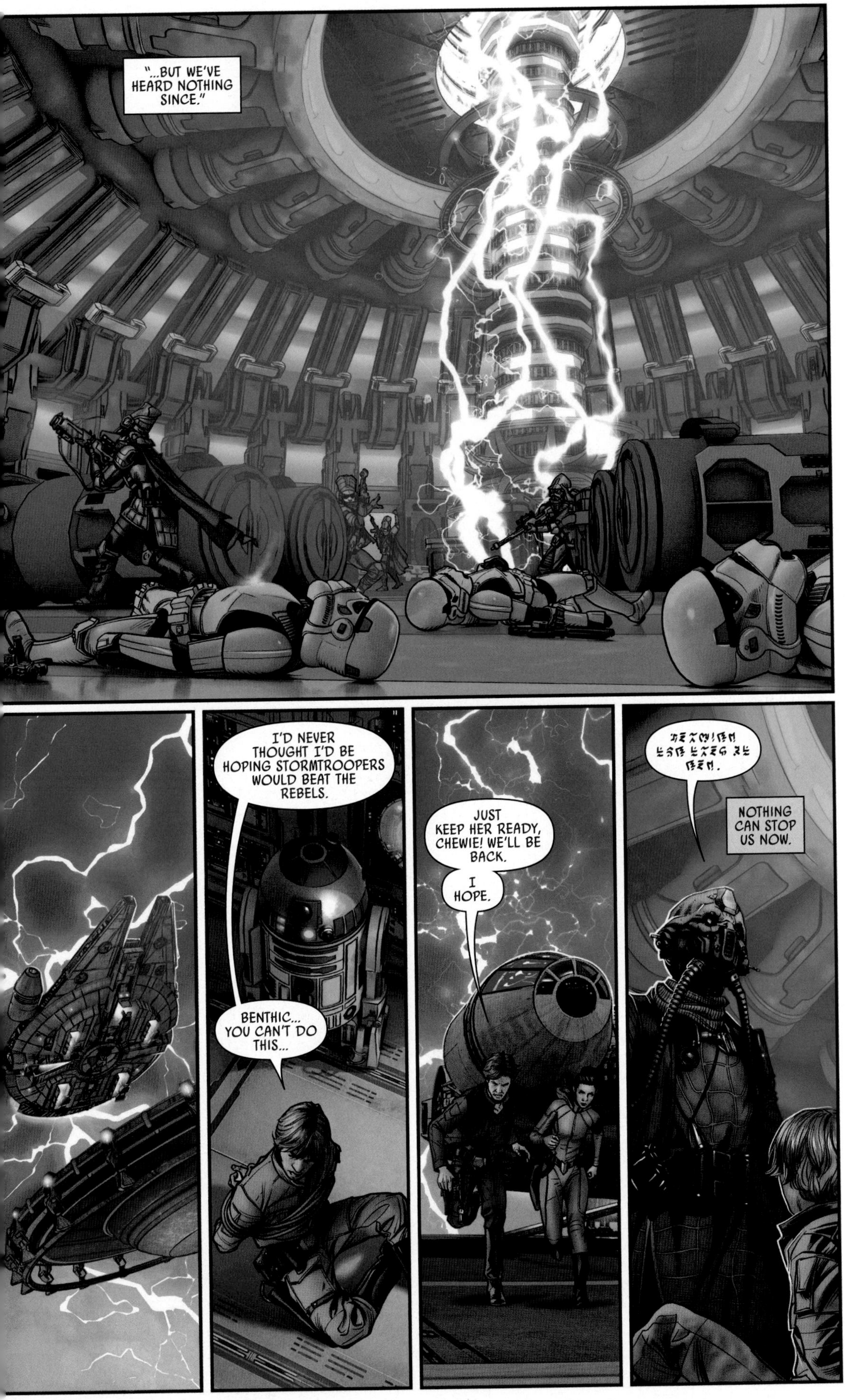
"...BUT WE'VE HEARD NOTHING SINCE."
I'D NEVER THOUGHT I'D BE HOPING STORMTROOPERS WOULD BEAT THE REBELS.
BENTHIC... YOU CAN'T DO THIS...
JUST KEEP HER READY, CHEWIE! WE'LL BE BACK.
I HOPE.
NOTHING CAN STOP US NOW.

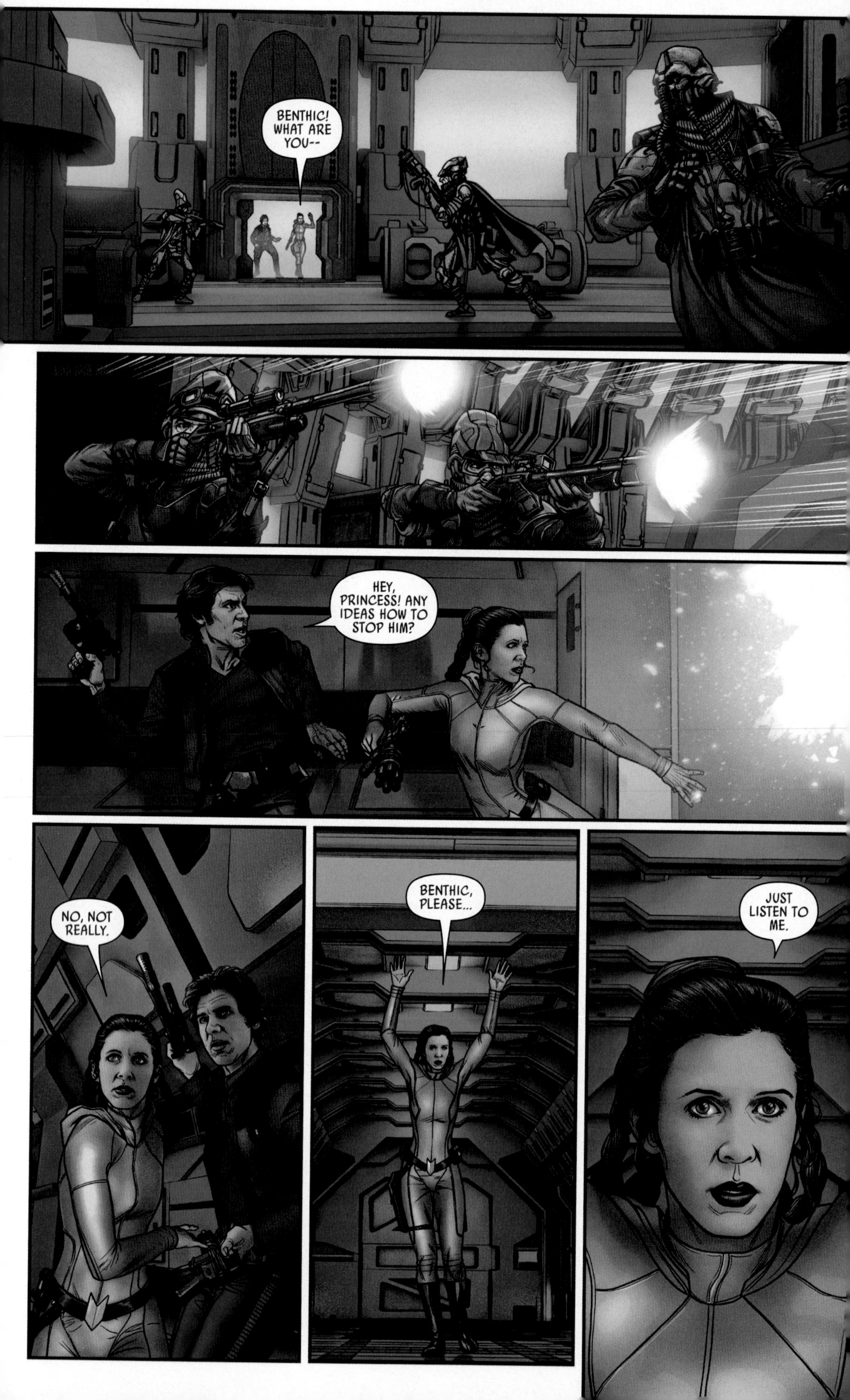

BENTHIC! WHAT ARE YOU--
HEY, PRINCESS! ANY IDEAS HOW TO STOP HIM?
NO, NOT REALLY.
BENTHIC, PLEASE...
JUST LISTEN TO ME.

CIBEALL. FOWIE IE AEWIESA.
TAGGRE GER AAGOG. GIEAGE
EGAIE. FOA GGARAGAER GOA
GAA EEAGAWEIAG.

FOAIG
TAGTA WIAA
AGGE EAWAGE
AGGT WIAA GAGGAE
TE AGAA IG AGAA
GEAAEA AGA
GAGIGAAGE
GGTA.

PRINCESS.
THIS IS LOGICAL.
ALDERAAN AND
JEDHA. SISTERS
IN PAIN. THE
SHU-TORUN ARE
ALL COMPLICIT.

THEIR DEATH WILL WARN
OTHERS WHAT WILL HAPPEN
TO THEM IF THEY FOLLOW
THE EMPIRE'S PATH.

I'VE HEARD
THAT PLAN BEFORE.
PLANETARY ANNIHILATION
TO KEEP DISSENTERS
IN LINE.

TARKIN
AND HIS DEATH
STAR.

FOA EGAAA
EG EGAGAWGEAIEA
AGAA. FGAAGOA AGAAG
AGAGAAAGIEA
GGEA AE.

THE DREAM OF
OVERTHROWING
THEM. THEY'VE TAKEN
EVERYTHING FROM
US.

THEY HAVEN'T. IF YOU DO THIS,
THEN *THEY* TAKE EVERYTHING.

IF YOU DO
THIS, EVEN IF WE WIN,
THEY WIN.

BECAUSE
WE'RE THEM.

YES,
SHU-TORUN
DIES IF YOU
DO THIS...

...BUT YOUR
DREAM DIES
TOO.

ᔐᑎᕁᑫᓀ ᕁᕐ ᔑᕐᔐᕁ
ᔕᑫᕁ᙮ᕐᕐ᙭ᔕᑫᔐᑫ ᕁᓀᔐᕁᕐ᙮
ᔐᕐᔐᔕᔕᕐᕁ ᔑᕐᔐᕁ
ᔕᑫᕁ᙭ᕐᔐᕁᕁᔕᕐ᙮᙮᙮

RETURN TO THE PRINCESS' PLAN.
RELEASE THE PRISONERS...

"...ᔕᑫᕐᑫᔑ ᕁᕐ ᔑᕐᔕᔕᑫᕐ ᑫ᙭ᕐᑫᕐ᙭ᑫᔕᕐ᙭
ᕁᑫ ᔕᑫᑫᑫᕐᑫᕐ ᑫᔐ᙭ᕐ᙭ᕐᕁ᙮"

"...LET US LEAVE THIS PLACE
OF ERRORS BEHIND."

AH, YES. DESTRUCTION! THE
VISIONS OF ISOPTER ARE
TRUE!

SUCH
BEAUTY! IT WILL
BE RECORDED IN
THE CULT
RECORDS.

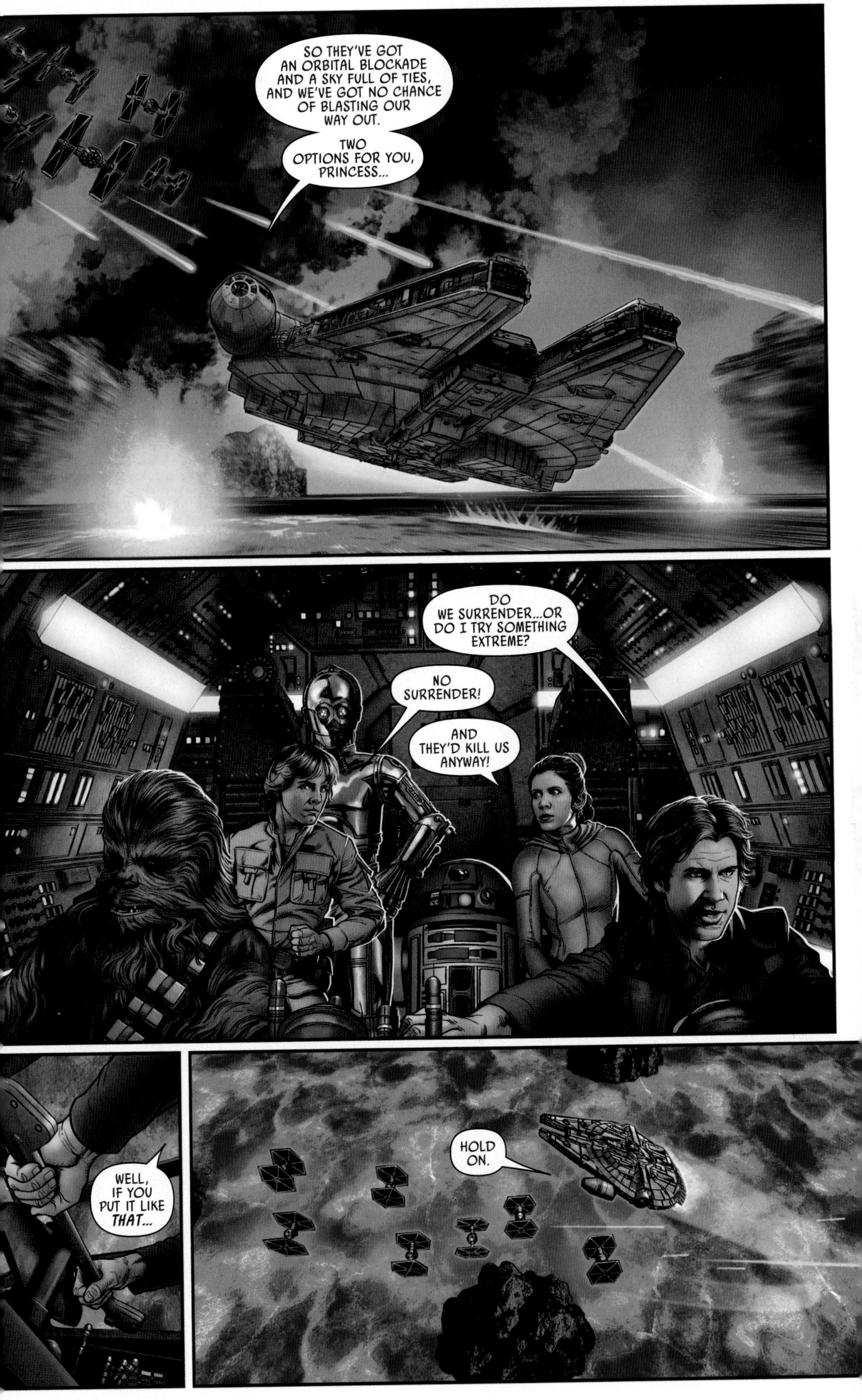
SO THEY'VE GOT AN ORBITAL BLOCKADE AND A SKY FULL OF TIES, AND WE'VE GOT NO CHANCE OF BLASTING OUR WAY OUT.
TWO OPTIONS FOR YOU, PRINCESS...
DO WE SURRENDER...OR DO I TRY SOMETHING EXTREME?
NO SURRENDER!
AND THEY'D KILL US ANYWAY!
WELL, IF YOU PUT IT LIKE *THAT*...
HOLD ON.

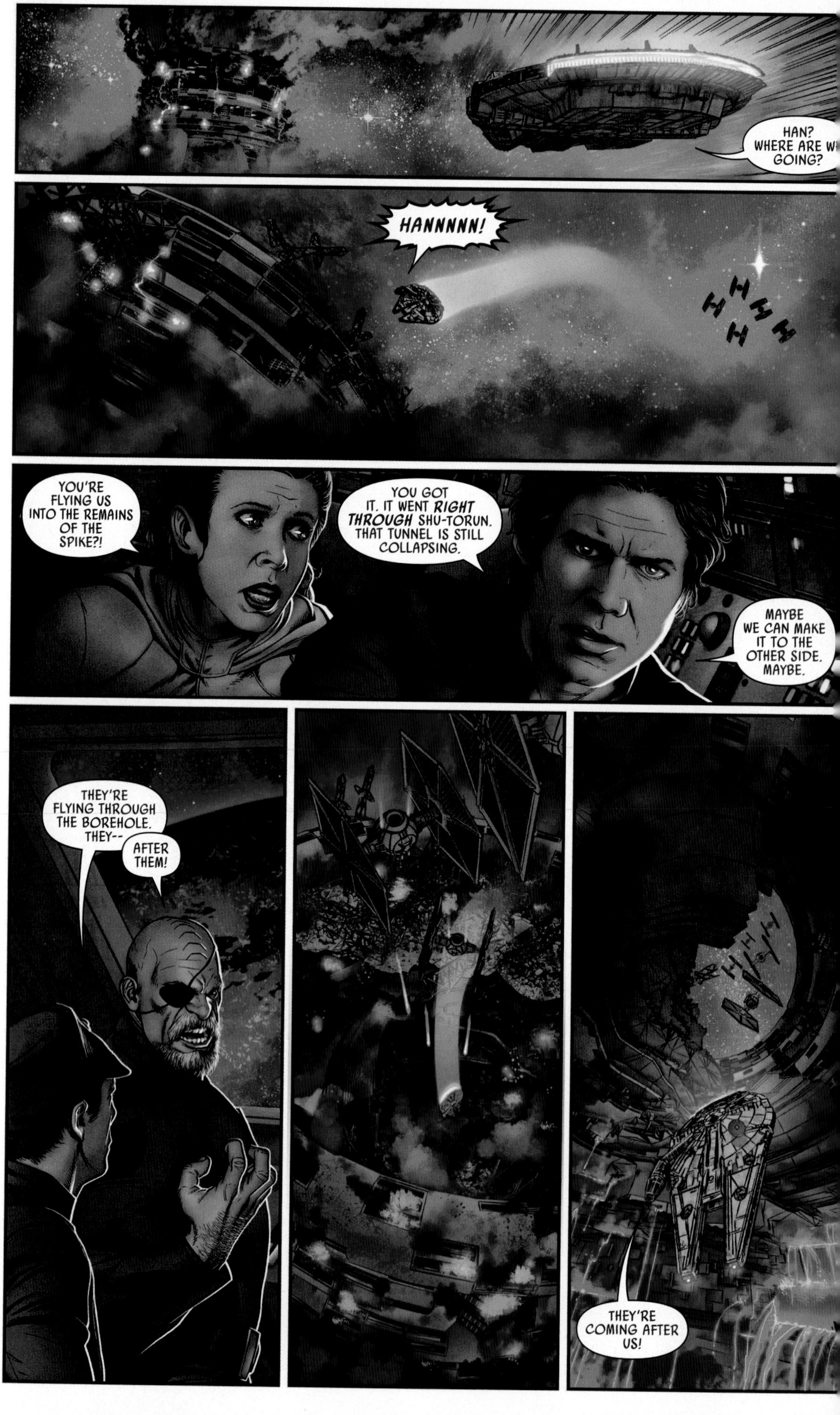
HAN? WHERE ARE WE GOING?
HANNNNN!
YOU'RE FLYING US INTO THE REMAINS OF THE SPIKE?!
YOU GOT IT. IT WENT RIGHT THROUGH SHU-TORUN. THAT TUNNEL IS STILL COLLAPSING.
MAYBE WE CAN MAKE IT TO THE OTHER SIDE. MAYBE.
THEY'RE FLYING THROUGH THE BOREHOLE. THEY--
AFTER THEM!
THEY'RE COMING AFTER US!

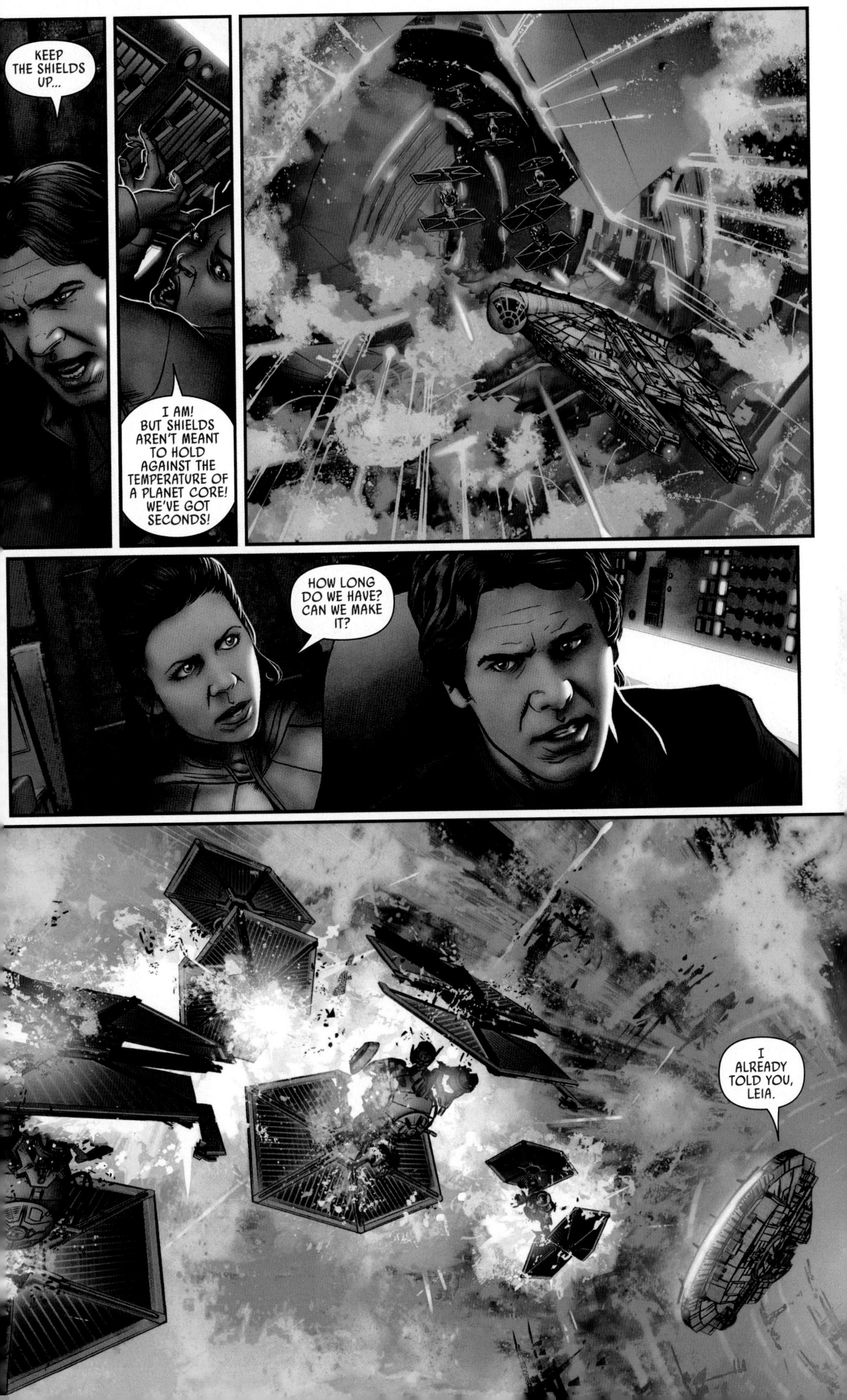
KEEP THE SHIELDS UP...
I AM! BUT SHIELDS AREN'T MEANT TO HOLD AGAINST THE TEMPERATURE OF A PLANET CORE! WE'VE GOT SECONDS!
HOW LONG DO WE HAVE? CAN WE MAKE IT?
I ALREADY TOLD YOU, LEIA.

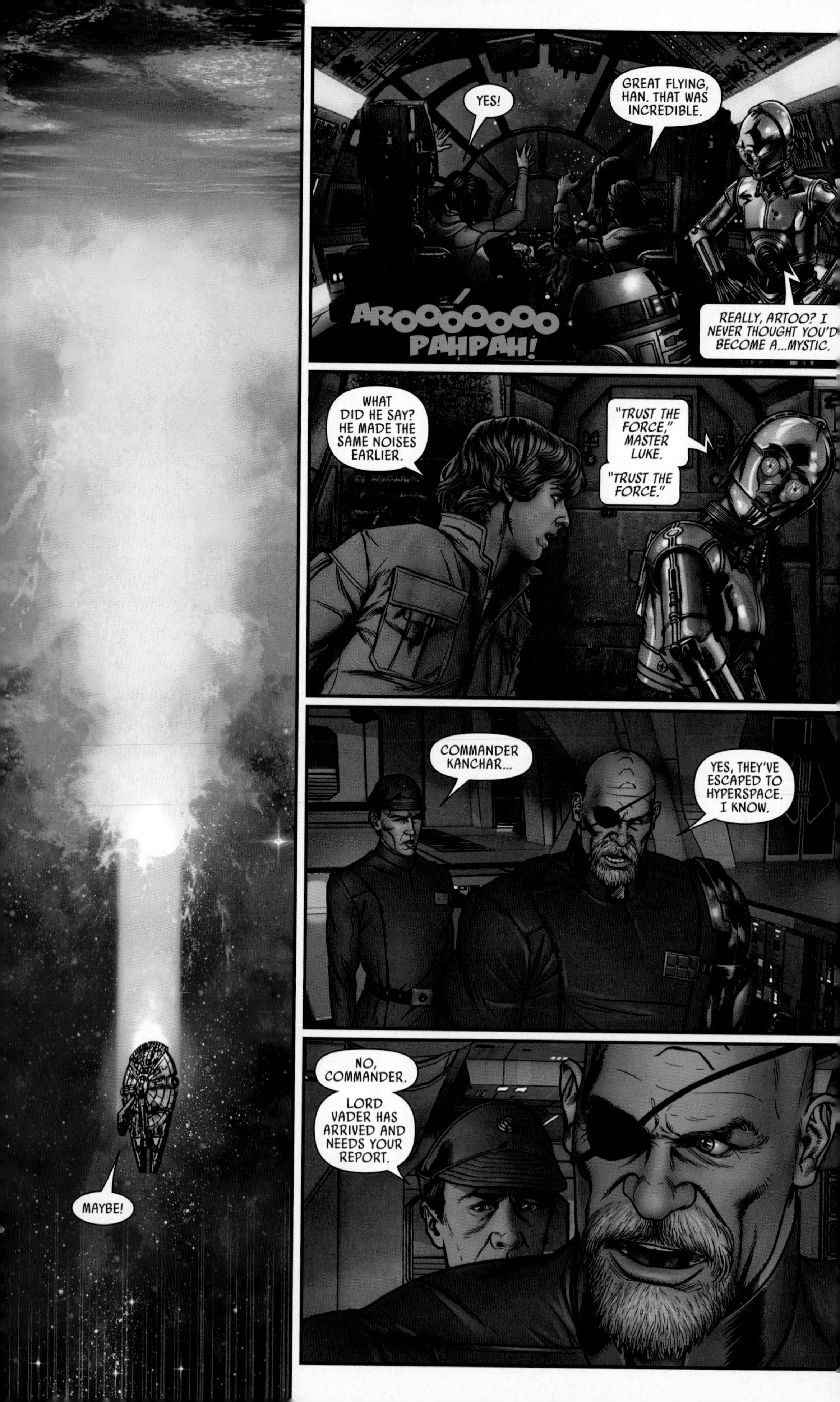
MAYBE!
YES!
GREAT FLYING, HAN. THAT WAS INCREDIBLE.
AROOOOOOOO PAHPAH!
REALLY, ARTOO? I NEVER THOUGHT YOU'D BECOME A...MYSTIC.
WHAT DID HE SAY? HE MADE THE SAME NOISES EARLIER.
"TRUST THE FORCE," MASTER LUKE.
"TRUST THE FORCE."
COMMANDER KANCHAR...
YES, THEY'VE ESCAPED TO HYPERSPACE. I KNOW.
NO, COMMANDER.
LORD VADER HAS ARRIVED AND NEEDS YOUR REPORT.

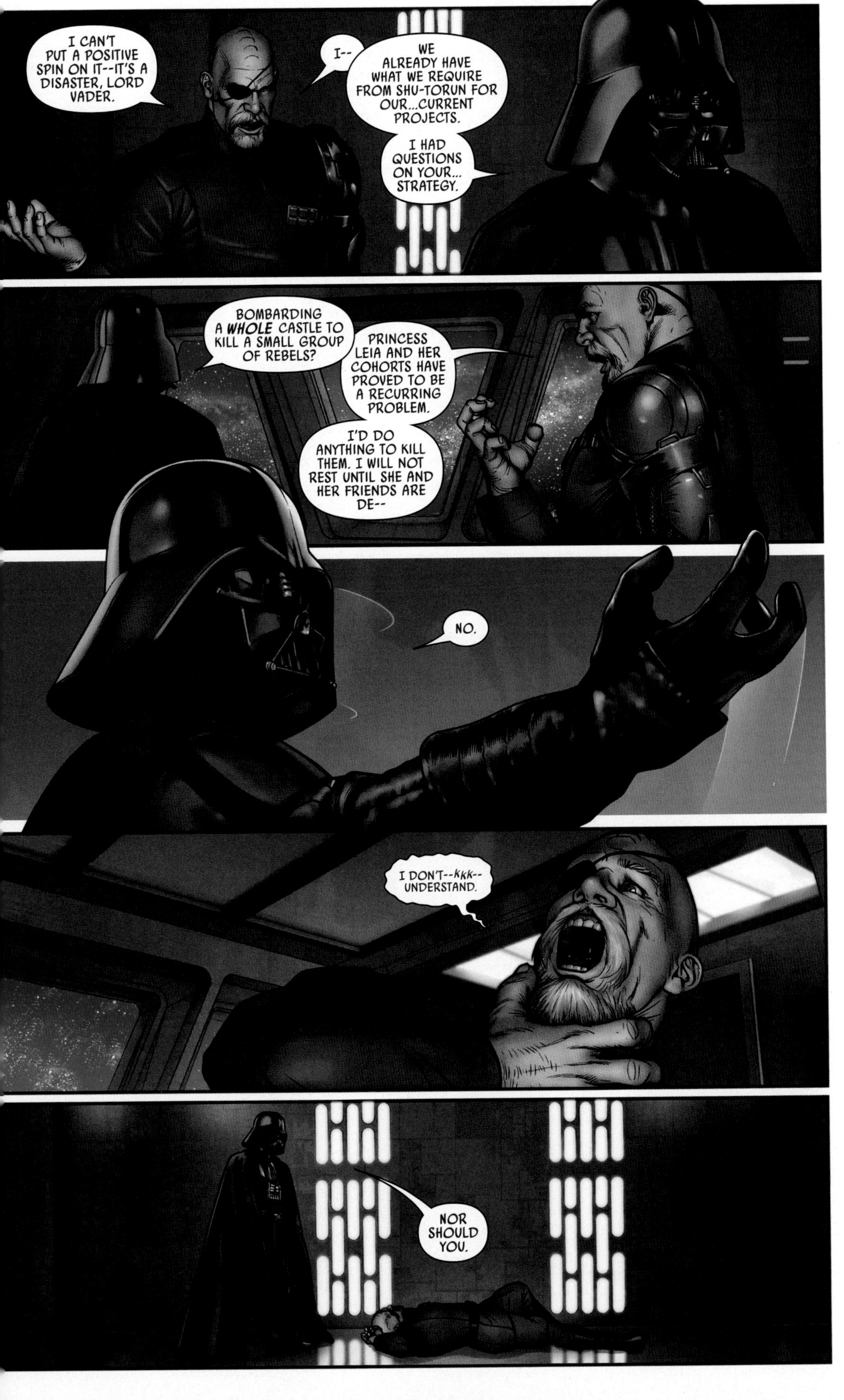
I CAN'T PUT A POSITIVE SPIN ON IT--IT'S A DISASTER, LORD VADER.
I--
WE ALREADY HAVE WHAT WE REQUIRE FROM SHU-TORUN FOR OUR...CURRENT PROJECTS.
I HAD QUESTIONS ON YOUR... STRATEGY.
BOMBARDING A *WHOLE* CASTLE TO KILL A SMALL GROUP OF REBELS?
PRINCESS LEIA AND HER COHORTS HAVE PROVED TO BE A RECURRING PROBLEM.
I'D DO ANYTHING TO KILL THEM. I WILL NOT REST UNTIL SHE AND HER FRIENDS ARE DE--
NO.
I DON'T--*KKK*-- UNDERSTAND.
NOR SHOULD YOU.

SO... IF WE'RE CLEAR OF ALL PURSUERS...

...WHAT DO WE DO WITH THIS SHIP FULL OF TRAITORS?

ᛁᛘᛉ ᛖᛋᛟᛉᛟᛉᛁᛘᛟ ᛟᛖᛩ. ᛒᛉᛉ ᛖᛩᛁᛘᛘ ᛉᛉᛉᛖᛉᛒᛟᛉᛟ ᛘᛖᛉ.

BE CAREFUL, BOY. WE STILL OUTNUMBER YOU.

WE DROP THEM OFF. BENTHIC AND HIS TROOPS GO BACK TO THEIR FIGHT, WHATEVER THAT MEANS NOW...

AND WE ALL LEARN FROM THIS.

WHERE YOU GOING? BACK TO JEDHA?

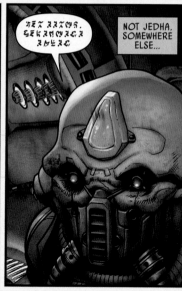

ᛉᛁᛉ ᛉᛉᛉᛟᛉ. ᛟᛩᛩᛉᛉᛟᛉᛉᛉ ᛉᛘᛉᛉᛟ.

NOT JEDHA, SOMEWHERE ELSE...

"ᛘᛟᛩᛩᛩᛉᛉᛉᛖᛁᛩᛘ ᛉᛘᛉᛉ ᛟᛩᛟ ᛉᛟᛉ ᛉᛉᛟᛉᛁᛩᛘᛩᛩᛩ."

"...SOMETHING ELSE FOR THE PARTISANS."

HEY, TWO TUBES. BEFORE YOU GO HEADING OFF TO GET BACK TO WHATEVER ENDLESS WAR YOU'VE GOT PLANNED, I WAS THINKING...

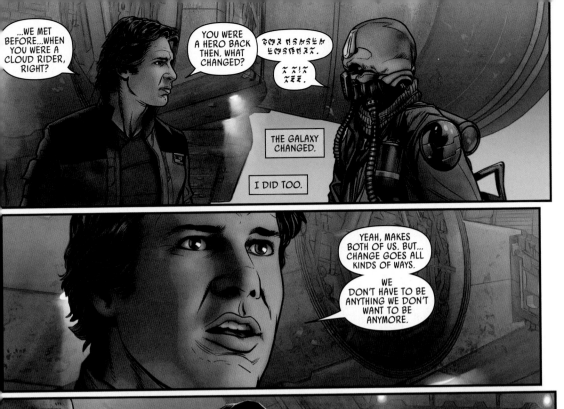

...WE MET BEFORE...WHEN YOU WERE A CLOUD RIDER, RIGHT?

YOU WERE A HERO BACK THEN. WHAT CHANGED?

ᚾᚱᚾ ᚾᚦᚾᚦᚾᚾ ᚾᚦᚾᚦᚾᚱᚾᛉ.

ᚾ ᚾᛉᚾ ᚾᚾᚾ.

THE GALAXY CHANGED.

I DID TOO.

YEAH, MAKES BOTH OF US. BUT... CHANGE GOES ALL KINDS OF WAYS.

WE DON'T HAVE TO BE ANYTHING WE DON'T WANT TO BE ANYMORE.

WOULD YOU STOP YAPPING AND HURRY UP?

WE NEED TO MEET UP WITH *HOME ONE* BEFORE IT CHANGES POSITION!

ESPECIALLY WHEN YOU GET THE RIGHT MOTIVATION.

ᚾ ᚾᚾᚾᚾ ᚾᚾᚾᚾᚾ ᚾᚾ ᚾᚾ. ᚾᚾᚾᚾᚾᚾ ᚾᚾᚾᚾᚾ ᚾᚾᚾᚾᚾ.

ᚾᚾᚾ ᚾᚾ ᚾᚾᚾ ᚾᚾᚾᚾ ᚾᚾᚾᚾᚾᚾᚾ ᚾᚾᚾᚾᚾ ᚾᚾ.

I WILL THINK ON IT. TRAVEL WELL, REBEL.

LET US SEE WHAT CHANGE BRINGS US.

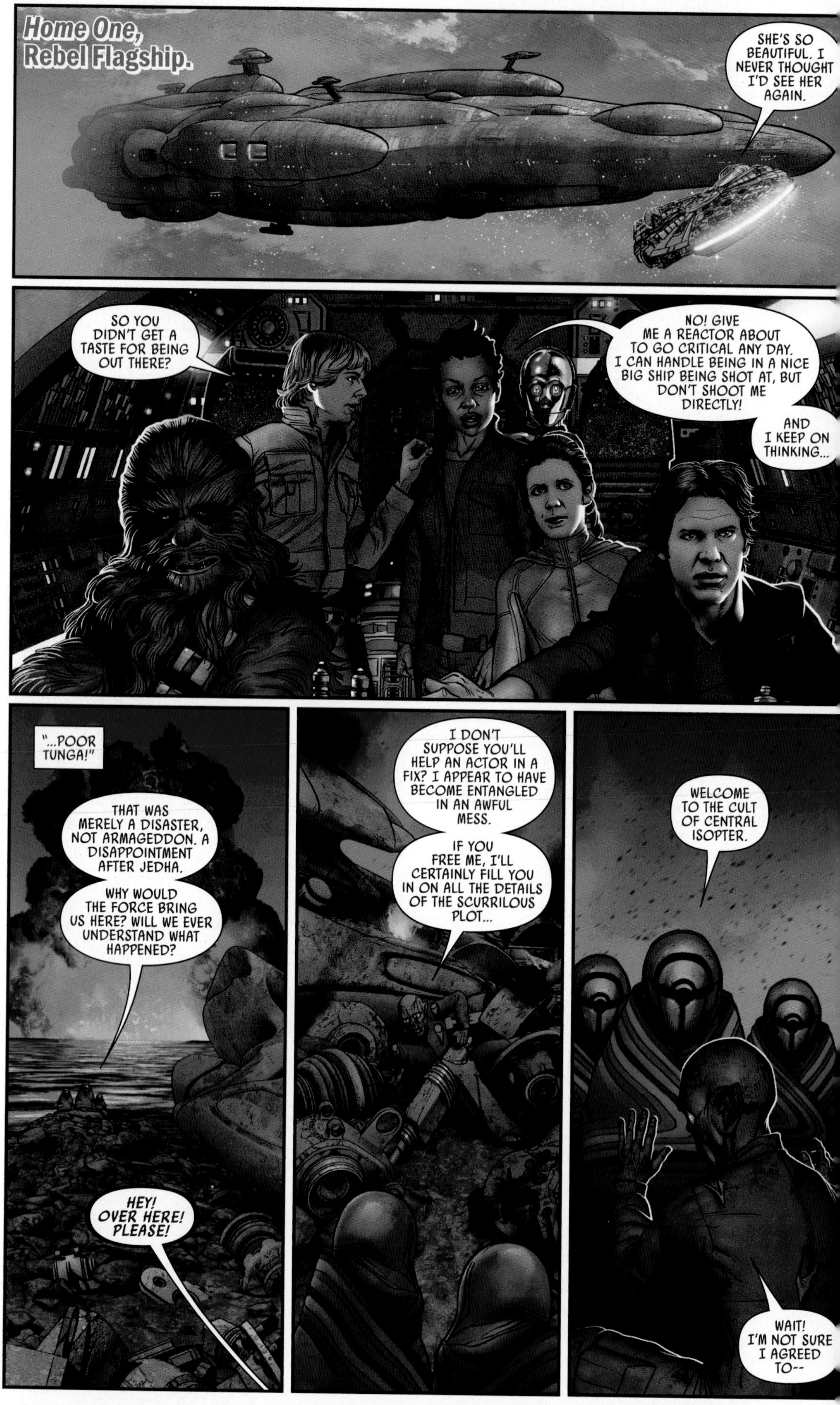

Home One, Rebel Flagship.
SHE'S SO BEAUTIFUL. I NEVER THOUGHT I'D SEE HER AGAIN.
SO YOU DIDN'T GET A TASTE FOR BEING OUT THERE?
NO! GIVE ME A REACTOR ABOUT TO GO CRITICAL ANY DAY. I CAN HANDLE BEING IN A NICE BIG SHIP BEING SHOT AT, BUT DON'T SHOOT ME DIRECTLY!
AND I KEEP ON THINKING...
"...POOR TUNGA!"
THAT WAS MERELY A DISASTER, NOT ARMAGEDDON. A DISAPPOINTMENT AFTER JEDHA.
WHY WOULD THE FORCE BRING US HERE? WILL WE EVER UNDERSTAND WHAT HAPPENED?
HEY! OVER HERE! PLEASE!
I DON'T SUPPOSE YOU'LL HELP AN ACTOR IN A FIX? I APPEAR TO HAVE BECOME ENTANGLED IN AN AWFUL MESS.
IF YOU FREE ME, I'LL CERTAINLY FILL YOU IN ON ALL THE DETAILS OF THE SCURRILOUS PLOT...
WELCOME TO THE CULT OF CENTRAL ISOPTER.
WAIT! I'M NOT SURE I AGREED TO--

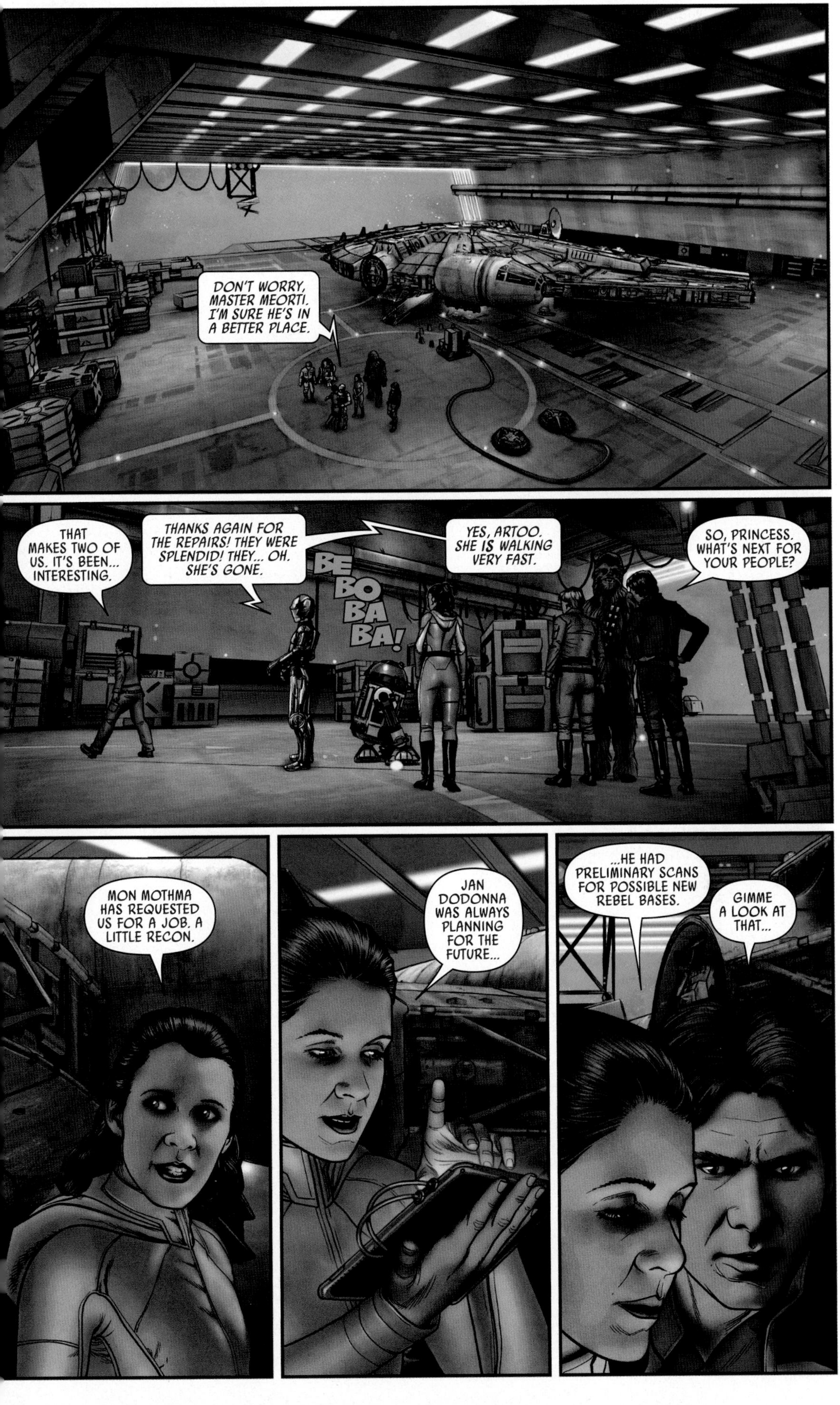
DON'T WORRY, MASTER MEORTI. I'M SURE HE'S IN A BETTER PLACE.
THAT MAKES TWO OF US. IT'S BEEN... INTERESTING.
THANKS AGAIN FOR THE REPAIRS! THEY WERE SPLENDID! THEY... OH. SHE'S GONE.
BE BO BA BA!
YES, ARTOO. SHE IS WALKING VERY FAST.
SO, PRINCESS. WHAT'S NEXT FOR YOUR PEOPLE?
MON MOTHMA HAS REQUESTED US FOR A JOB. A LITTLE RECON.
JAN DODONNA WAS ALWAYS PLANNING FOR THE FUTURE...
...HE HAD PRELIMINARY SCANS FOR POSSIBLE NEW REBEL BASES.
GIMME A LOOK AT THAT...

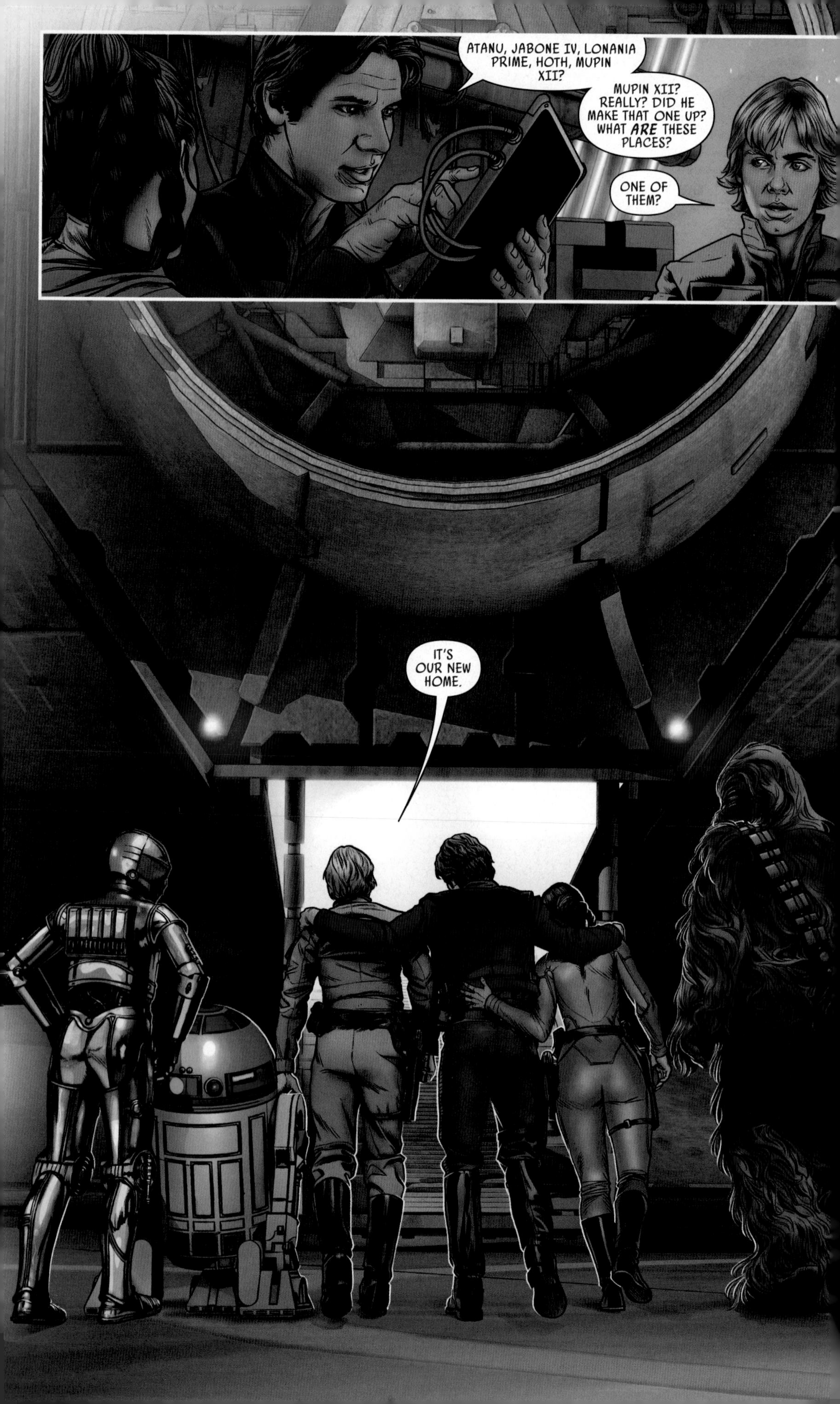
ATANU, JABONE IV, LONANIA PRIME, HOTH, MUPIN XII?
MUPIN XII? REALLY? DID HE MAKE THAT ONE UP? WHAT ARE THESE PLACES?
ONE OF THEM?
IT'S OUR NEW HOME.

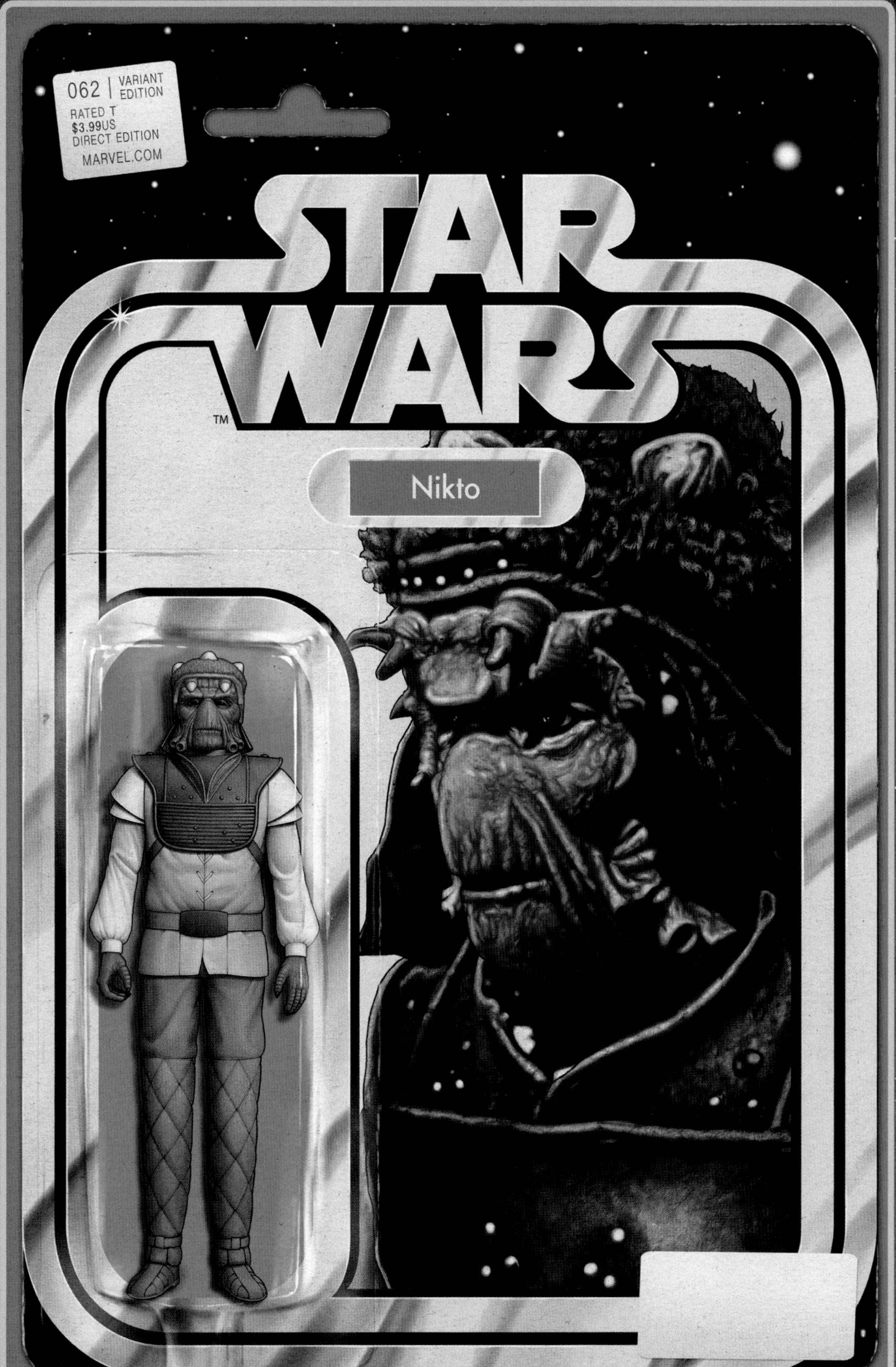

062 | VARIANT EDITION
RATED T
$3.99US
DIRECT EDITION
MARVEL.COM
STAR WARS
™
Nikto

***STAR WARS* 62 Action Figure Variant by**
JOHN TYLER CHRISTOPHER

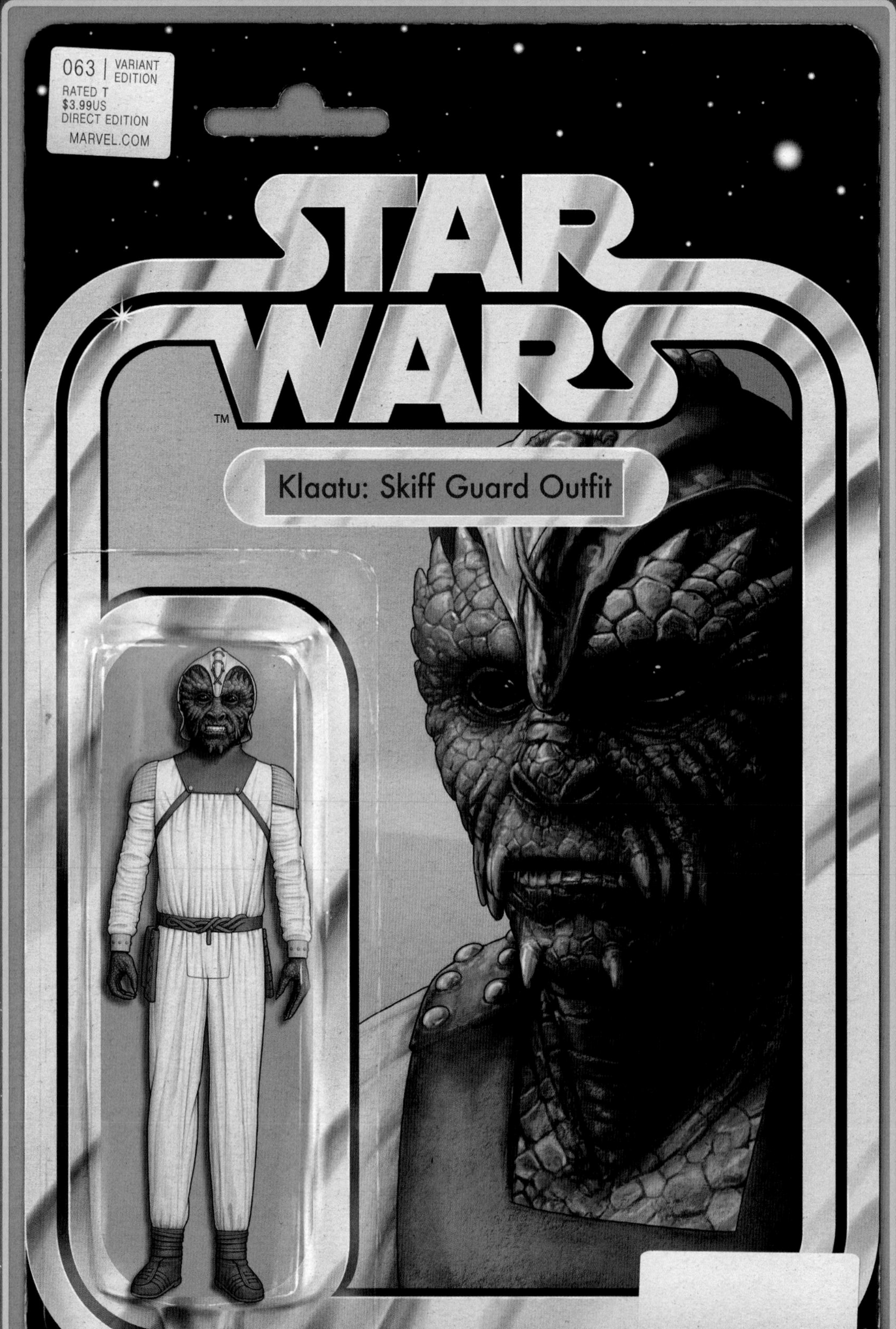
063 | VARIANT EDITION
RATED T
$3.99US
DIRECT EDITION
MARVEL.COM
STAR WARS
TM
Klaatu: Skiff Guard Outfit

STAR WARS **63 Action Figure Variant by**
JOHN TYLER CHRISTOPHER

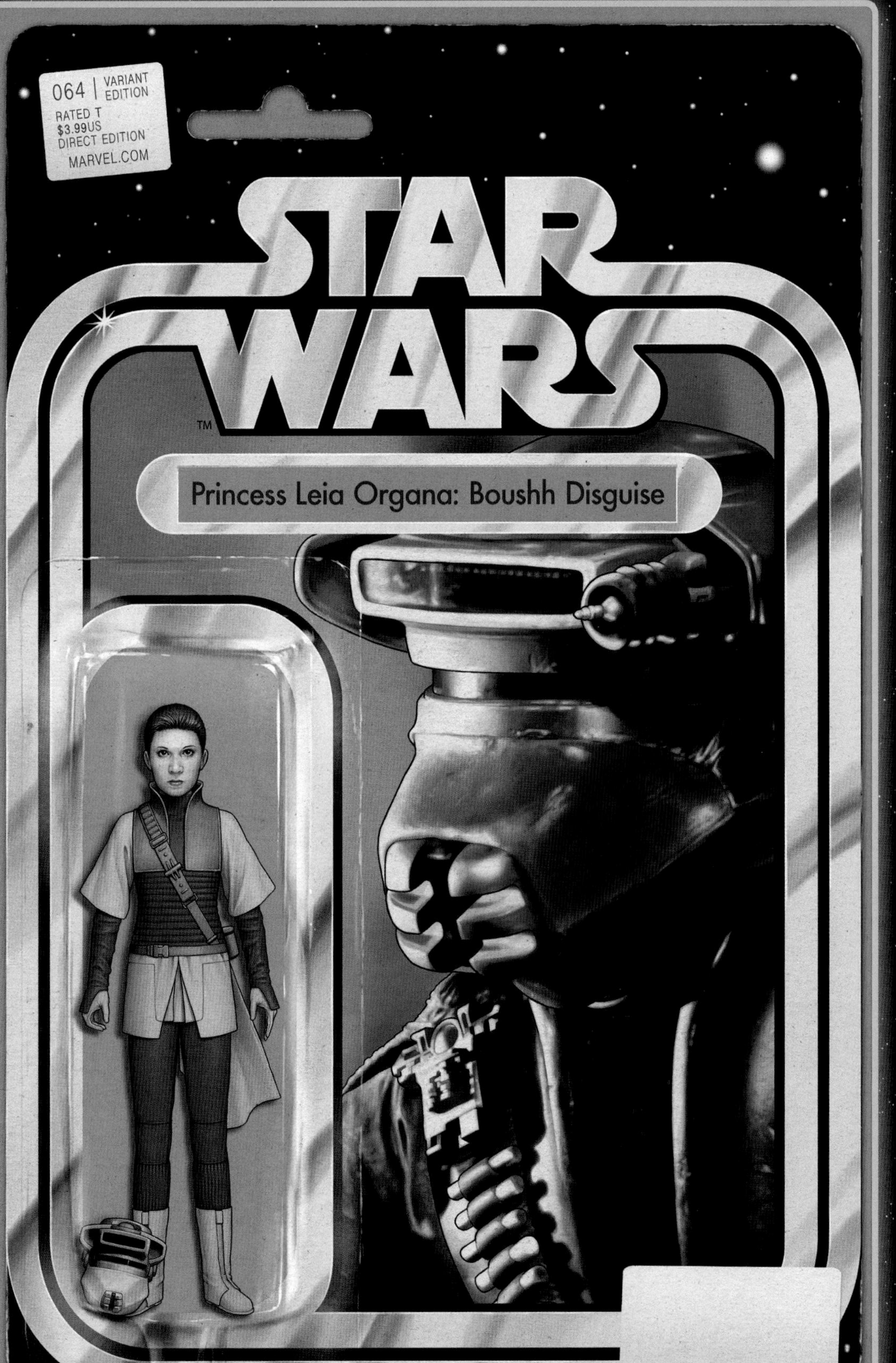
064 | VARIANT EDITION
RATED T
$3.99US
DIRECT EDITION
MARVEL.COM
STAR WARS
TM
Princess Leia Organa: Boushh Disguise

***STAR WARS* 64 Action Figure Variant by**
JOHN TYLER CHRISTOPHER

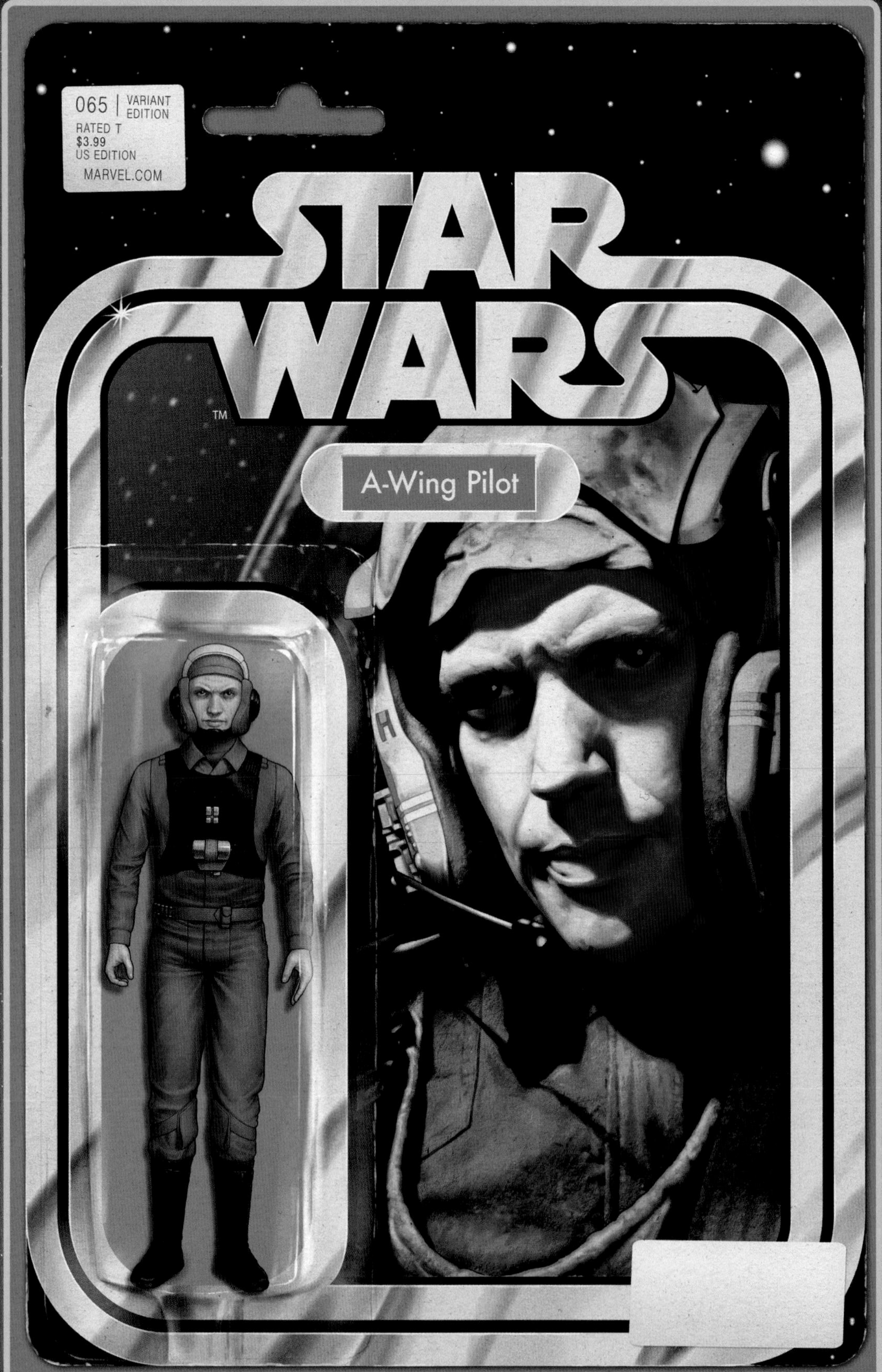
065 | VARIANT EDITION
RATED T
$3.99
US EDITION
MARVEL.COM
STAR WARS
TM
A-Wing Pilot

***STAR WARS* 65 Action Figure Variant by**
JOHN TYLER CHRISTOPHER

STAR WARS 66 Action Figure Variant by
JOHN TYLER CHRISTOPHER

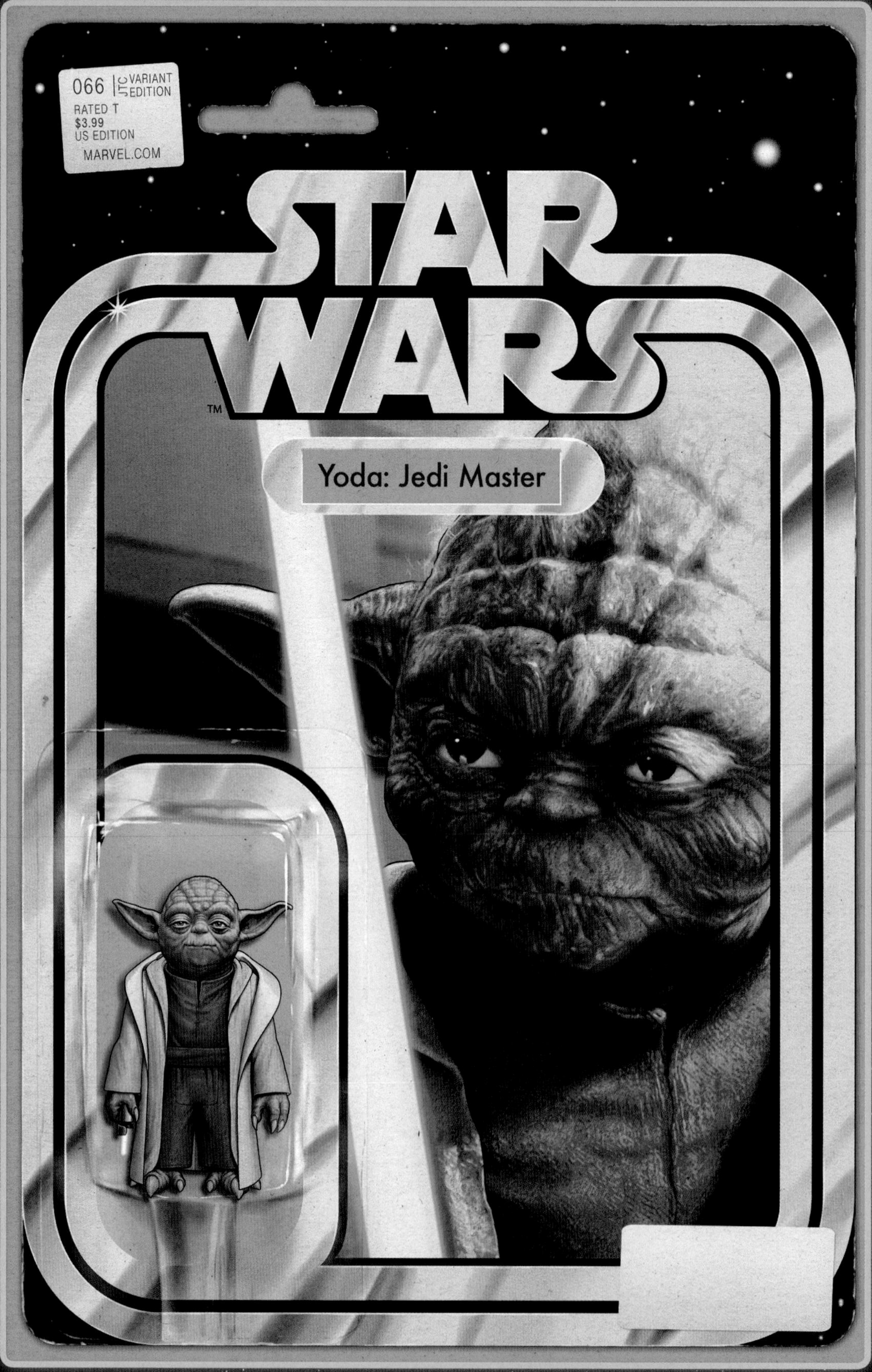
066 JTC VARIANT EDITION
RATED T
$3.99
US EDITION
MARVEL.COM
STAR WARS
Yoda: Jedi Master

***STAR WARS* 66 Action Figure Variant by**
JOHN TYLER CHRISTOPHER

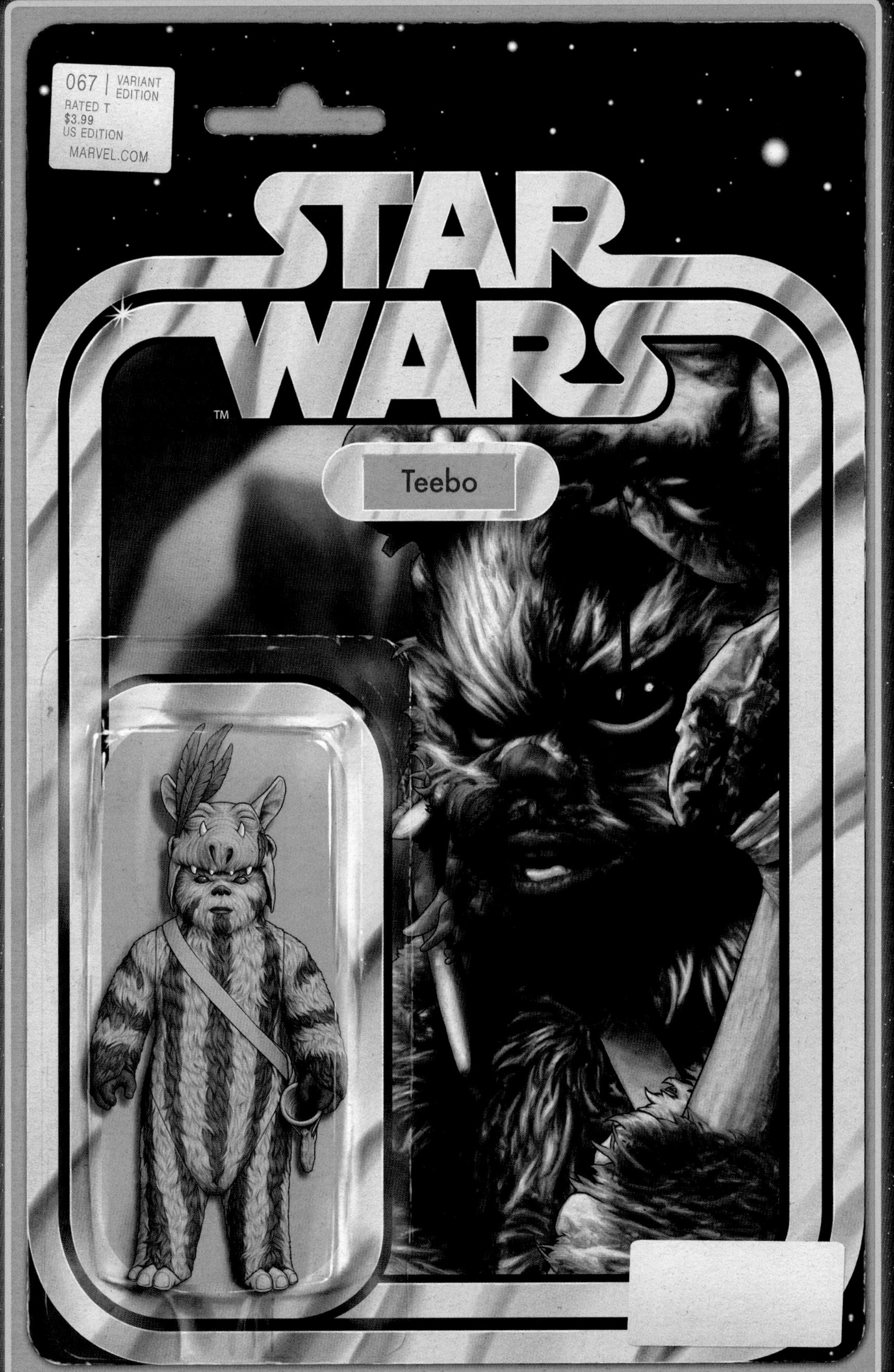
067 | VARIANT EDITION
RATED T
$3.99
US EDITION
MARVEL.COM
STAR WARS
TM
Teebo

STAR WARS 67 Action Figure Variant by
JOHN TYLER CHRISTOPHER

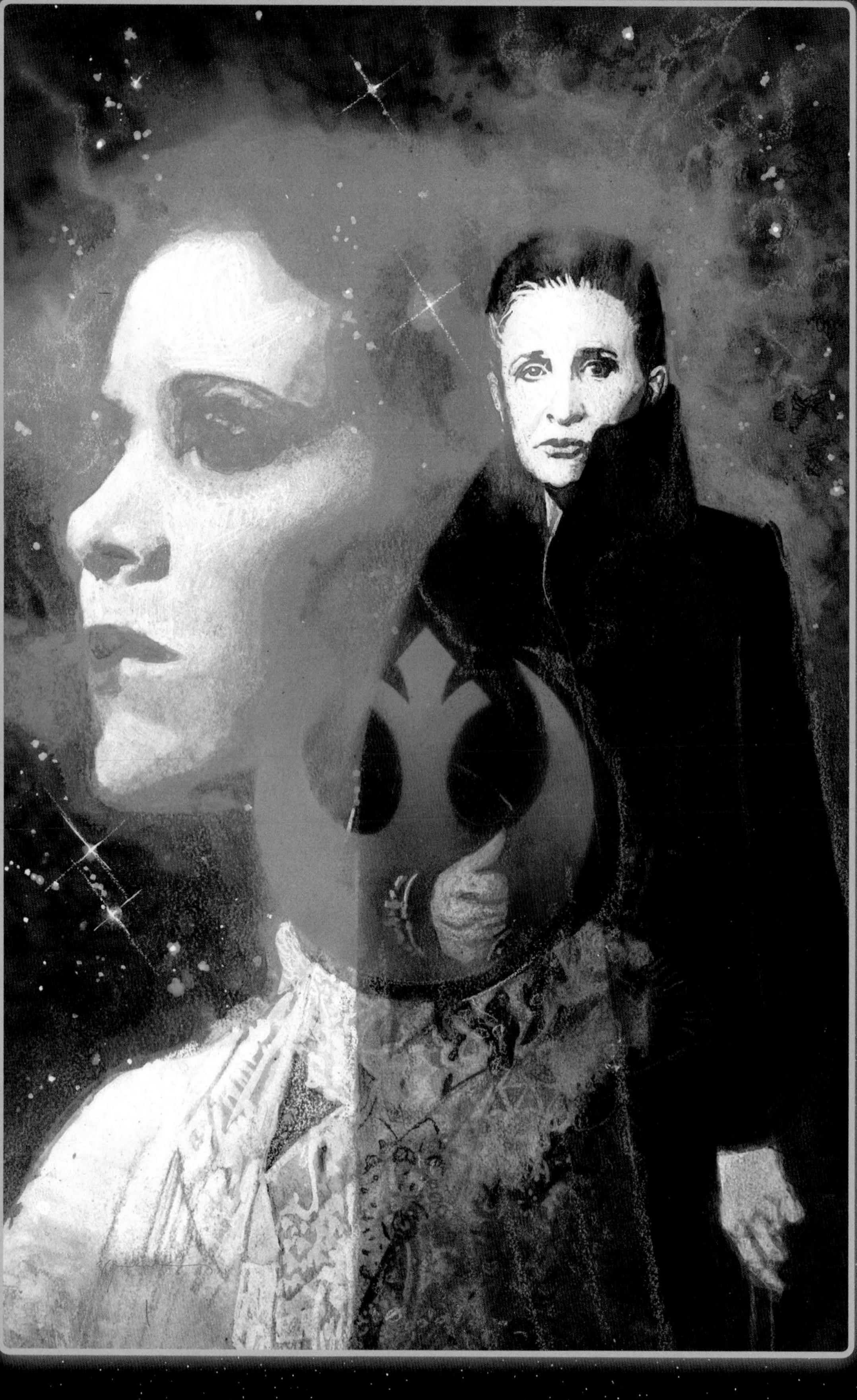

***STAR WARS* 67 Variant by**
BILL SIENKIEWICZ

AFTER BARELY ESCAPING DARTH VADER WITH HER LIFE, DOCTOR APHRA SETS OFF IN SEARCH OF RARE AND DEADLY ARTIFACTS!

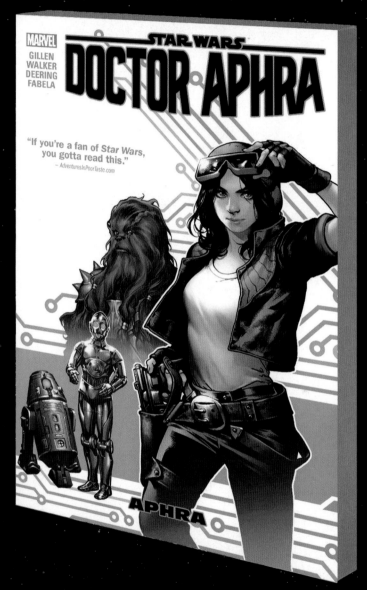

MARVEL

GILLEN
WALKER
DEERING
FABELA

STAR WARS
DOCTOR APHRA

"If you're a fan of *Star Wars*,
you gotta read this."
– AdventuresInPoorTaste.com

APHRA

MASTER WINDU LEADS A JEDI STRIKE FORCE ON A DEADLY CLONE WARS MISSION!

STAR WARS: JEDI OF THE REPUBLIC — MACE WINDU TPB
978-1302909413

ON SALE NOW
AVAILABLE IN PRINT AND DIGITAL WHEREVER BOOKS ARE SOLD

TO FIND A COMIC SHOP NEAR YOU, VISIT COMICSHOPLOCATOR.COM

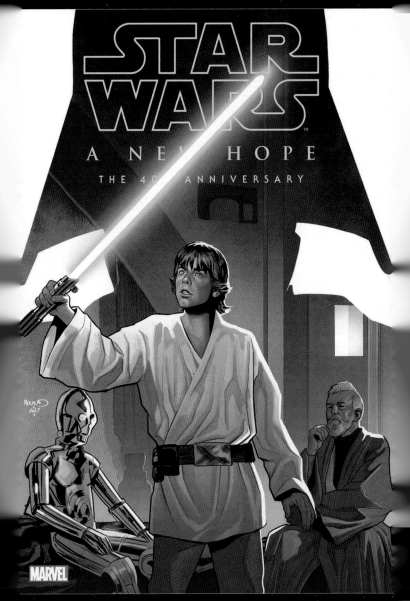

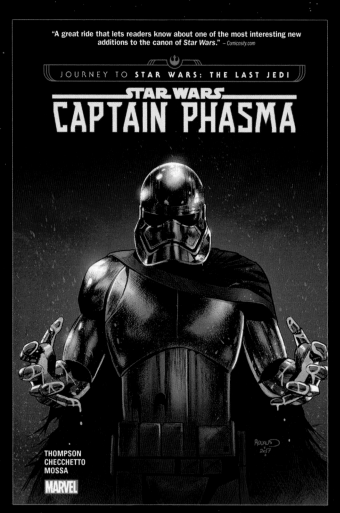

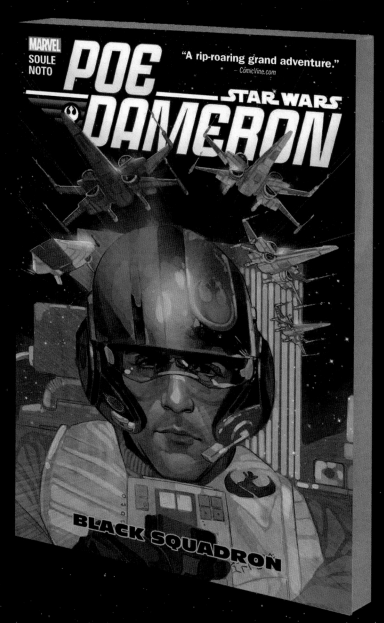

REBELLIONS ARE BUILT ON HOPE

FEATURES MATERIAL NOT SEEN ON THE BIG SCREEN!
noto
ROGUE ONE
A STAR WARS STORY

***STAR WARS: ROGUE ONE* ADAPTATION TPB**
978-0785194576

ON SALE NOW

AVAILABLE IN PRINT AND DIGITAL WHEREVER BOOKS ARE SOLD

TO FIND A COMIC SHOP NEAR YOU, VISIT COMICSHOPLOCATOR.COM

MARVEL Disney LUCASFILM

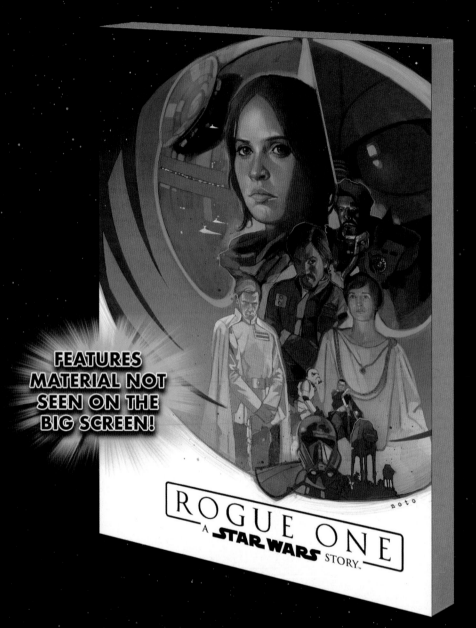